BETRAYAL
In Vietnam

"Epitaph for Vietnam"
—*Richmond Times-Dispatch*

BETRAYAL In Vietnam

Louis A. Fanning

ARLINGTON HOUSE·PUBLISHERS
NEW ROCHELLE, NEW YORK

Manufactured in the United States of America

Library of Congress Cataloging in Publication Data

Fanning, Louis A.
  Betrayal in Vietnam.

  Bibliography: pp. 248-252
  Includes index.
  1. Vietnamese Conflict, 1961-1975—United States.
2. United States—Politics and government—1969-1974.
3. Nixon, Richard Milhous, 1913- I. Title.
DS558.F36   959.704′3373   76-24841
ISBN 0-87000-341-0

To Kenneth W. Colegrove

An American Patriot

BETRAYAL: to fail or desert esp. in time of need
—*Webster's Third New International Dictionary*

Contents

Maps and Illustrations

Abbreviations

ARVN —Army of the Republic of (South) Vietnam

CA　　—Cambodian Army

CPUSA—Communist Party of the United States of America

DMZ　—Demilitarized Zone

NLF　—National Liberation Front

NVA　—North Vietnamese Army

PRG　—Provisional Revolutionary Government of the Republic of
　　　　South Vietnam

SVN　—South Vietnam

VC　　—Vietcong

Preface

In the spring of 1975 Americans were treated to the spectacle of a dying nation. Tuning in channel after channel on their television sets, they saw the death of the Republic of Vietnam portrayed in living color. As the cameras played over the human tragedy, certain scenes seemed to tell a story of their own. Among the more memorable episodes projected were those showing thousands of Vietnamese fleeing in terror before their Communist "liberators." In these presentations, frantic refugees were seen grasping at the undercarriages of helicopters or storming the American Embassy seeking any means to flee their embattled country. Perhaps the most tragic scenes of all were those that portrayed the men, women, and children of South Vietnam attempting to escape in overloaded boats under a hail of Communist rocket fire.

How did all this happen? Where was the vaunted army and air force of the Vietnamese Republic? Why did the greater percentage of over one million armed men simply lay down their arms and refuse to fight? Most of all, why was America, in the face of this debacle, frozen into a position of "masterful inaction"? What had happened to the most powerful nation in the world that caused the United States of America to allow a pygmy country of twenty million inhabitants to defeat it in battle? Why was the American President limited to ordering the removal of a few orphans and a pitiful number of those Vietnamese on the Communist blood-debt list?

The answer to these questions does not lie in the corruption of yet another Asiatic despotism, nor may it be found in the unquestioned ability of a dedicated North Vietnamese leadership. The major thesis of this study is that it was not the Hanoi Communists who won the war, but rather the American Congress that lost it. This thesis is supported by overwhelming evidence available to the serious researcher. Hidden in a bewildering maze of foreign aid bills, supplemental appropriations, Defense Department legislation, and Foreign Service allocations lies the singular fact that a Democratic caucus of the Congress of the United States, aided and abetted by a few liberal Republicans, cast the South Vietnamese people into Communist slavery.

Louis A. Fanning

March 1976
Farmingdale, New York

I / The War Before

In 1969 John P. Roche, a former national chairman of the Americans for Democratic Action, uttered these prophetic words:

> If the American people ever get it through their heads that liberal Democrats are rooting for an American defeat in Southeast Asia, we will be through politically for the rest of the century.[1]

The following story is a documentation of the role played by the liberal Democrats in the American defeat in Southeast Asia.

The Inheritance

On January 20, 1969, Richard M. Nixon was inaugurated as the thirty-seventh President of the United States. To his critics Nixon's reappearance on the national scene was a calamity of the first order. To his friends the President's reemergence in the political arena came as no surprise. To the general public the California Republican's election to the nation's highest office seemed incredible. Their amazement at this turn of events was primarily based on the negative manner in which the media had presented Nixon's loss of the California gubernatorial race in 1962.

The new President's inheritance from previous administrations was an unenviable one, to say the least. Taxes were skyrocketing, inflation was rampant, criminals ruled the streets, and the nation was divided over the "no-win" war in Vietnam. Nixon's legacy from the Vietnam War alone provided a challenge of considerable proportions.

[1] *Congressional Record,* December 18, 1969.

When the new Chief Executive was sworn into office in 1969, there were approximately 550,000 American troops in Vietnam, war casualties amounted to 300 men per day, and the draft totaled 34,000 inductees a month.

Roosevelt and Truman

American participation in Indochinese affairs, including the war, had been going on for more than a quarter of a century. The original American involvement in Vietnam took place in the administration of President Franklin D. Roosevelt during World War II. Roosevelt's intervention in Vietnamese matters was based on the President's virulent dislike of Western colonialism. From 1943 to the end of the war, Roosevelt used all the powers available to the American presidency to deny the French return to Indochina. He opposed the inclusion of French troops in Allied units scheduled to be deployed to the Far East and ordered his field commanders to refuse assistance to French military forces fighting the Japanese in Indochina. He joked with Stalin about his denial of General de Gaulle's request to provide ships for the French army's return to Indochina. And in the end, Roosevelt ordered the nation's secret intelligence organization, the Office of Special Services (OSS), to collaborate with the Communist-dominated Vietminh.[2]

An even deeper entanglement in the Vietnamese quagmire followed during the presidency of Harry S. Truman. Unfortunately for the Chinese people, in the fall of 1949 mainland China fell to the Maoists. After the fall of China, accusations were made that the Truman administration was "soft on Communism" and that the State Department harbored an excessive number of subversive personalities. In response to these charges, the President in the spring of 1950 extended direct military aid to France and the associated states of Indochina (Vietnam, Laos, and Cambodia).

Eisenhower Calls for Collective Defense

Following the signing of the Korean armistice in the summer of 1953, the Communists were able to devote their full attention to Indochina. A mistake in strategy placed a sizeable body of French troops in the isolated outpost of Dien Bien Phu. While the garrison of

[2] For a detailed discussion of OSS assistance to the Vietminh, see the appendix to Hearings Before The Senate Committee on Foreign Relations, "Causes, Origins and Lessons of the Vietnam War," May 9–12, 1972.

the fortress fought for their lives, President Dwight Eisenhower decided that without some form of collective support American military forces would not intervene in the Indochina War.

In accordance with the President's wishes, Secretary of State John Foster Dulles pursued the formation of the Asian defensive alliance. His efforts were rewarded in September 1954 with the signing of the Southeast Asia Collective Defense Treaty (SEATO). The treaty was signed in Manila by Thailand, the Philippines, the United States, the United Kingdom, France, Australia, New Zealand, and Pakistan. Article IV of the accord provided for joint action to meet aggression. An appendix to the agreement extended the provisions of Article IV to Cambodia, Laos, and Vietnam.[3]

In 1955, when the treaty was brought before the Senate for approval, Senator Mike Mansfield (D., Mont.), who had been a member of the American delegation in Manila, said:

The Southeast Asian Treaty is another part in the total pattern of strength which we have been trying to create throughout the free world. . . . The treaty ends with a declaration that the armed aggression which is referred to and which the United States declares would be dangerous to its own peace and security would be Communist aggression. [*Congressional Record*, February 1, 1955]

Following Mansfield's speech, the Senate ratified the SEATO Treaty on February 1, 1955, by a vote of 82–1.

As a result of the Geneva Conference held in the summer of 1954, Vietnam was divided into a Communist state in the north and a free state in the south. The future of South Vietnam was placed in the hands of the ardent Vietnamese nationalist Ngo Dinh Diem. The decision to place the Southern Republic under the control of Diem was loudly applauded in the United States. Senator Mike Mansfield (D., Mont.) referred to the South Vietnamese leader as "the savior of all Southeast Asia" (*Congressional Record*, May 13, 1957). New York Republican Senator Jacob Javits called him "one of the real heroes of the free world" (*Congressional Record*, May 13, 1957). Even the Kennedy clan were said to have supported the diminutive South Vietnamese leader. *

[3] For the text of the SEATO agreement, see U.S. Department of State, *American Foreign Policy: 1950–1955 Documents,* Vol. I, pp. 912–916.

* John S. Knight, head of Knight newspapers, has written that Joseph P. Kennedy, father of Senator Edward M. Kennedy, employed "the Harold Oram public relations firm, at a fee of $3,000 a month, to represent Diem as the man who could save Vietnam."

Kennedy Sends the Advisers

For a number of years it appeared as if the Diem government would prove to be a successful undertaking. However, by the fall of 1963 a renewal of guerrilla warfare led John F. Kennedy to assign more than 20,000 American military personnel to the defense of South Vietnam. Among his many comments regarding America's commitment to Vietnam, President Kennedy said:

> The United States, like the Republic of Vietnam, remains devoted to the cause of peace, and our primary purpose is to help your people maintain their independence. If the Communist authorities in North Vietnam will stop their campaign to destroy the Republic of Vietnam, the measures we are taking to assist your defense efforts will no longer be necessary.[4]

After the assassination of President Diem in November 1963, the situation in South Vietnam worsened. The succession of barracks generals who followed Diem contributed even further to the growing feeling of helplessness that gripped the country. This rapid turnover of governments in Saigon significantly reduced the ability of the Southern Republic to resist a Communist takeover.

Mr. Johnson's War

Following the assassination of John Kennedy, President Lyndon B. Johnson extended even greater military assistance to the beleaguered nation. The increased American naval presence and the North Vietnamese navy collided in the Gulf of Tonkin in August 1964. As a result of two North Vietnamese torpedo boats attacking a like number of American destroyers, Johnson ordered United States aircraft to destroy naval installations along approximately one hundred miles of the coastline of North Vietnam. The obvious increase in military activities in Vietnam led the President to seek congressional approval for his actions. Accordingly, on August 7 the Congress approved a Southeast Asia Resolution giving overwhelming support to the President's actions by a vote of 88–2 in the Senate and 416–0 in the House. The Gulf of Tonkin Resolution gave the President a clear mandate from the Congress to take all "necessary" steps to repel aggression in Southeast Asia.[5]

[4] *Why Vietnam* (Washington: Government Printing Office, 1965), p. 3; former Republican National Chairman Rogers C.B. Morton believes that President Kennedy's escalation in Vietnam was strongly "supported" by his younger brother "Ted" (*Congressional Record,* October 13, 1969).

[5] Text of the resolution is in *Department of State Bulletin,* Vol. 51 (August 24, 1964), p. 268.

Among remarks made by congressional members in support of the Gulf of Tonkin Resolution were the following:

SENATOR WILLIAM FULBRIGHT (D., Ark.):
I recommend the prompt and overwhelming endorsement of the resolution now before the Senate. . . . The resolution further expresses the approval and support of the Congress for the determination of the President to take such action as may be necessary, now and in the future, to restrain or repel Communist aggression in Southeast Asia. [*Congressional Record,* August 6, 1964]

SENATOR JACOB JAVITS (R., N.Y.):
I shall support the resolution, because I think we must defend freedom in that area, or else see the balance of a large segment of the world tipped against freedom. The degree of our resistance under the action that may be taken in Southeast Asia, under the resolution, will determine not only future events in Vietnam, but also the freedom of Malaysia, India, Pakistan, and Indonesia, and perhaps even Australia and New Zealand. [*Congressional Record,* August 6, 1964]

SENATOR MIKE MANSFIELD (D., Mont.):
The President has acted against repeated Communist provocations in the Tonkin Gulf. . . . He has counseled with the congressional leadership, the relevant committee chairmen. . . . He asks for and will have, in this endeavor, the support of the Congress and the people of the United States. [*Congressional Record,* August 6, 1964]

The resolution did not impress the Vietcong greatly, and they stepped up their military activities in South Vietnam. By the spring of 1965 it was apparent to astute observers that South Vietnam was about to be engulfed by the "Red Tide." This conclusion led the Johnson administration to send two marine battalions into active combat in Vietnam in March 1965. For the next three years, the rice-paddy war mushroomed until America had committed almost a half-million men to defend the Vietnamese Republic. During this period, congressional support for the war was widespread.

Among remarks made by members of Congress over these years were:

SENATOR BIRCH BAYH (D., Ind.):
There can be little question that if we are to turn tail and run, the entire Southeast Asia area . . . would come under Communist domination. . . . We are dealing with Communist conspirators who frankly make no bones about the fact that they desire to conquer the world. [*Congressional Record,* March 16, 1965]

SENATOR FRANK CHURCH (D., Idaho):
I think that the United States has an interest in doing all it can to discourage the spread of Communism in the underdeveloped world. [In-

terview on American Broadcasting System Program "From the Capital," February 7, 1966]

SENATOR FRED HARRIS (D., Okla.):
It is not a civil war. The security of the free world is involved here. The security of the United States is in jeopardy there. If we do not live up to our commitment to South Vietnam to help them keep their country free, we shall have to draw the line elsewhere, in Thailand, or Malaysia, or Hawaii, or Seattle and San Francisco. The line must be drawn somewhere. . . . It has been said that we should dishonor commitments made by three presidents of the United States and withdraw from South Vietnam and abandon the people of South Vietnam, who have been struggling for national security and independence. There is no question that this is not the proper course for this country. [*Congressional Record,* April 13, 1965]

SENATOR EDWARD M. KENNEDY (D., Mass.):
The fundamental moral question facing the United States is, Are we going to say to the seventeen million people of South Vietnam that because you have not been able to establish a national identity that you are going to be taken over by a strong aggressive force? Because you are still struggling, are we going to let you go down the drain, so to speak? Are we concerned at all about people in a far and distant land? Do we want to defend freedom? We do, because this is our commitment, our heritage, our destiny. [Speech to Lowell Technological Institute students, November 1965]

SENATOR EUGENE MCCARTHY (D., Minn.):
We must stand firm against any compromise that would mean accepting other than an honorable peace and would not establish the condition that would permit South Vietnam to choose its own government and determine its own policy. [*Congressional Record,* March 8, 1966]

SENATOR GEORGE MCGOVERN (D., S. Dak.):
Since we have become steadily more involved in the Vietnamese struggle for the past eleven years, mistaken or not, we cannot now abruptly withdraw and leave our South Vietnamese ally at the mercy of guerrilla forces. [Letter to his constituents, February 1965]
Actually, North Vietnam cannot benefit any more than South Vietnam from a prolonged conflict. I would hope that we would be prepared to wage such a conflict rather than surrender the area to Communism. [*Congressional Record,* January 15, 1965]

SENATOR EDMUND MUSKIE (D., Maine):
It is not our objective to conquer any country or to destroy any regime. It is to stop aggression in South Vietnam. Why? . . . we believe freedom is at stake. We believe that containment of expansionist Communism regrettably involves direct confrontation from time to time, and that to

retreat from it is to undermine the prospects for stability and peace. [*Congressional Record*, March 1, 1966]

On January 30, 1968, during a religious holiday known as Tet, the vastly underrated Communists mounted a general offensive throughout South Vietnam. The go-for-broke decision on the part of the Hanoi leadership proved to be a military disaster for the Vietcong (VC) units. It has been estimated that after Tet the VC had to use troop fillers from North Vietnam in seventy percent of their unit spaces.

While it may have been a military setback for the Communists, faulty reporting in the United States distorted the attack out of all proportion. The American people, lulled to sleep by government reports of successes in Vietnam, were not prepared for an assault on their forces in the magnitude reported. Their surprise turned to displeasure, and when Senator Eugene McCarthy (D., Minn.) ran as a "stalking horse" against Lyndon Johnson in a New Hampshire primary race, the Minnesota senator gained considerable support. There is a good probability that with their understanding of the general instability in democracies during election periods, the Hanoi leadership had timed the Tet offensive to the American primary races. Their analysis of the political processes in America turned out to be correct, and within two weeks after the New Hampshire primary, President Johnson threw in the towel. On March 31, 1968, the President announced that he had ordered a halt to the bombing of most of North Vietnam, that he would not be a candidate in the next elections, and that he hoped to enter into negotiations with the enemy in the near future.

Three days later the Hanoi leadership accepted Johnson's proposal, and on May 3 negotiations began in Paris. The speed with which the Communists had accepted the President's offer was due to the simple fact that the North Vietnamese leaders had already decided to seek a negotiated end to the war. The determination to take the conflict to the bargaining table had been made in early 1967. It was based on the politburo's conclusion that "as a small country fighting the big and rich United States," North Vietnam could not hope for victory on the battlefield. The decision was not, however, an admission of defeat. The party leaders merely felt that they could win more at the negotiating table than in the field. During the year, their intentions had been carried to Moscow by Premier Pham Van Dong and to Peking by Le Duan, first secretary of the Vietnam Workers Party. The Soviets had responded favorably, but the Maoists had opposed negotiations, even as a contingency. Instead, the Chinese proposed that the North

19

Vietnamese continue the war until China could intervene more decisively. Le Duan is reported to have reserved the final decision to the North Vietnamese leadership, as they were carrying the burden of the fighting.

At this point, it appears that North Vietnam's leaders were on the horns of a dilemma. If they proceeded with their plans to negotiate an end to the war, their actions would alienate the Chinese. On the other hand, if they continued to fight, their losses would grow unbearable. The predicament was solved when President Johnson simultaneously offered the inducement of seeking a diplomatic end to the war and also agreed to halt the bombing.[6]

The American delegation to the peace talks was led by W. Averell Harriman, ex-governor of New York State and the Democratic party's perennial negotiator with the Communist world. The North Vietnamese were represented by Minister of State Xuan Thuy, a secretary of the Central Committee of the Vietnam Workers Party. When the two spokesmen met and after the preliminaries were over, both sides presented their basic positions. Xuan Thuy demanded that the United States cease all "acts of war on the whole territory of the Democratic Republic of Vietnam" (the euphemism the Hanoi leadership used to describe North and South Vietnam). Harriman declared that the United States was in Vietnam "to preserve the right of the South Vietnamese people to determine their own future without outside interference or coercion." As the stated goals of the antagonists appeared to be irreconcilable, the talks entered into a long impasse.

While the negotiators were meeting, the Communists launched an offensive against Saigon. Their actions should have surprised no one, as the Hanoi leadership has a long history of successfully coordinating their efforts between the battlefield and the negotiating table. A primary example of this skilled manipulation on the part of the North Vietnamese was exhibited in November 1953. At that time Ho Chi Minh, in his famous interview with editor Nycop of the Swedish newspaper *Stockholm Afternooner Expressen,* indicated that he was seeking peace with the French and wanted to negotiate an end to the war. Naturally the Hanoi leader's pursuit of peace was widely acclaimed by the news media. What the reporters were not allowed to see, however, were Ho Chi Minh's secret orders to surround Dien Bien Phu, which had been issued on the same day as the offer to negotiate.

On the last day of October 1968, Lyndon Johnson ordered a complete halt to the bombing of North Vietnam. The President's orders

[6] Interrogation of Le Ngoc La, deputy chief of the Vietcong Intellectual Propaganda Section in Saigon, captured in South Vietnam in May 1967.

were based on a series of compromises reached with the North Vietnamese in Paris. These "understandings" were apparently a one-sided affair. The American negotiators reportedly agreed to halt the bombing of North Vietnam in exchange for certain Communist considerations. These concessions included the right to send unarmed reconnaissance flights over North Vietnam and an agreement not to use the demilitarized zone between North and South Vietnam as a major infiltration route. After the bombing had been stopped, North Vietnamese leaders claimed that the reconnaissance flights violated their sovereignty. When questioned about what appeared to be Communist faithlessness, the American negotiators responded that "the other side" had not openly agreed to anything but seemed to acquiesce by their silence when the points of agreement were raised.

When the air assault of North Vietnam was suspended, the South Vietnamese Communist leadership found it hard to believe. A few months after the bombing was stopped, Lieutenant Colonel Le Xuan Chuyen, a captured Vietcong division commander, said: "When I first heard of the complete bombing halt I thought it must be a joke, and I laughed. But when I realized the United States was serious, I was dumbfounded by the stupidity."[7]

[7] *Los Angeles Times,* February 19, 1969.

II / The Return of Richard Nixon

In the fall of 1969 Senator Frank Church (D., Idaho) said:

> After all, Democrats in the White House led this country into Vietnam. If President Nixon fails to lead us out, it may become his war, but it is not Nixon's war yet. For eight years we Democrats bore the responsibility. Now we must wear the hair shirt longer than eight months. [*Congressional Record*, September 29, 1969]

The senator's protestations of guilt and his refusal to cast aspersions on President Nixon make good reading. Church's deeds failed to match his words, however, and he became a key spinner of the foreign-policy web around the executive branch of the government.

The National Commitments Resolution

On November 5, 1968, the American people went to the polls and elected Richard M. Nixon as their President. Sixteen days after the new Chief Executive was inaugurated, the opposition party fired the opening gun in its battle with the new President and the office he represented. The fact that the conflict would lead to the total defeat of America in Vietnam and the betrayal of the South Vietnamese people seemed only incidental to the men in power on Capitol Hill.

On February 5, 1969, Senator William Fulbright (D., Ark.) introduced legislation on the floor of the Senate known as the "National

Commitments Resolution" (S.Res. 85). The resolution provided that a national commitment for the use of armed forces or financial resources of the United States was invalid unless it was in the form of a treaty, statute, or concurrent resolution approved by both chambers of Congress.[1] It is worth noting that the National Commitments Resolution was remarkably similar to legislation previously introduced to the Foreign Relations Committee by Senator Fulbright in 1967. The Committee had approved the 1967 resolution, with minor revisions, but had not sent it to the floor "since Democrats feared it would be a rebuke to the Johnson administration's Vietnam policy."

Debate on the new measure lasted only five days, with a majority of the Senate speaking in favor of its passage. On June 19, 1969, when the resolution was introduced, Fulbright warned that America was already overcommitted to "unilateral military action in much of the world," and a continuation or expansion of this trend would lead to the "militarization" of American life. His solution, not surprisingly, was to increase the power of the Congress over the "deployment of armed forces." He did not explain, however, how the congressmen were going to position their troops, or who would be the congressional commander in chief.

The major opposition to the resolution was offered by Senator Everett M. Dirksen. Criticizing the measure, the Illinois Republican stated his belief that other nations would assume that the Congress had handcuffed the President in foreign-policy matters. The legislation was nonetheless approved on June 25 by a roll-call vote of 70–16. The significance of this formal expression of opinion by the Senate escaped many astute political observers at the time. The reason for their oversight was that as a "sense of the Senate" resolution it did not have the effect of law, and consequently the President was not bound to obey its restrictions. This neglect has now been corrected, and careful viewers of the national scene agree that the National Commitments Resolution was an important link in the fence of foreign-policy restrictions constructed around the presidency.

More Negotiations

Five days after the first of the year, President-elect Nixon appointed Henry Cabot Lodge as the new American representative to the Paris peace negotiations. The appointment of Lodge brought to an end the tenure of Ambassador Averell Harriman. As a final gift to the incoming delegations, the negotiators had arrived at a decision re-

---

[1] Text and background in *Congressional Quarterly Almanac*, 1969, p. 177.

garding the shape of the table.* According to their solution, the four delegations—the United States, the Democratic Republic of Vietnam, (North Vietnam), the Republic of Vietnam (South Vietnam), and the National Liberation Front (NLF)—were to sit at a circular table 13 feet 1½ inches in diameter. There were to be no name plates, flags, or markings. They also agreed to the placement of two rectangular tables (5½ by 3 feet) eighteen inches from either side for the secretarial staff of the delegations.

At his first full meeting on January 25, the new American representative proposed that the neutrality of the demilitarized zone (DMZ) between South and North Vietnam be renewed. The North Vietnamese negotiator, Xuan Thuy, rejected Lodge's request and demanded that the United States halt its war of aggression against Vietnam. Thuy ended his tirade with the significant comment that "only on a political basis can we settle military problems." At this point the conference appears to have degenerated into a contest of wills between unyielding adversaries. The Communist side continued to stress a preference for the consideration of political matters. At the same time the Americans and their Vietnamese allies claimed that the immediate cessation of the killing in South Vietnam was the most important item for the conference to consider. Following the development of this deadlock in the negotiations, Le Duc Tho, the political leader of the North Vietnamese delegation, emplaned for Hanoi. The South Vietnamese vice-president, Nguyen Cao Ky, also returned to Vietnam.

Thirteen days after Tho returned to Hanoi, the North Vietnamese Army (NVA) and their Vietcong allies opened a spring offensive. Major cities throughout South Vietnam were subjected to extensive mortar and rocket bombardment. In launching these attacks, the Hanoi leadership was following a practice advocated by North Vietnamese General Nguyen Van Hinh, who had previously stated:

> We will take advantage of the opportunity offered by the negotiations to step up further our military attacks. In fighting while negotiating, the side which fights more strongly will compel the adversary to accept its conditions.

The American and South Vietnamese forces reacted to the Communist attacks and opened offensives of their own in the Ashau Valley and around the city of Saigon.

* A prominent critic of the governor has stated: "For ten months he was America's chief negotiator at the Paris peace talks—a period in which the United States swapped some of the greatest military concessions in the history of warfare for an agreement on the shape of a bargaining table."

Vietnamization Begins

On March 19, 1969, at the peak of the Communist offensive, Melvin R. Laird, secretary of defense, appeared before the Senate Armed Services Committee and proposed a revised version of an old idea for turning over the war to the South Vietnamese. The secretary, in presenting the new concept, was in fact refurbishing a practice developed during the Johnson administration, with a significant difference. Laird's basic proposal was to replace American ground force units with troops of the Army of the Republic of Vietnam (ARVN). This procedure had been part of the overall strategy of General William C. Westmoreland as far back as 1967.

The major difference between his plans and the previous administration's intentions was that Laird envisioned returning a "substantial" number of the replaced American soldiers to the United States. The entire program of replacing U.S. forces with ARVN units, and subsequently withdrawing the Americans has become known as "Vietnamization." In order to expedite the whole process, Laird requested that an additional $156 million be added to the defense budget.

A week after Secretary Laird had proposed the Vietnamization process, congressional critics condemned the President's war policies in the halls of Congress. On March 21, sixteen representatives rose in the House and indicated their dissatisfaction with the way the Nixon administration was handling the war. The majority of the dissenters were New York City Democrats. Among those taking part in the condemnation were Benjamin Rosenthal, Lester L. Wolff, Allard Lowenstein, William Ryan, and Edward Koch (*Congressional Record,* March 21, 1969).

Lowenstein urged "an orderly retreat" of American forces from Vietnam. Rosenthal called for a phased withdrawal of U.S. troops as a means of forcing the Vietnamese government to face up to its problems. Wolff spoke out for free elections and the elimination of war profiteering. While the approach of the representatives was varied, their conclusion was the same. They all agreed to oppose the passage of any future Defense appropriations bills which contained monies for expenditure in Vietnam.

The next day Secretary of State William P. Rogers went before the Senate Committee on Foreign Relations and presented his views on Vietnam. In a formal statement to the Committee, the secretary repeated President Nixon's desire to achieve an honorable peace in Vietnam. He stated that the administration did not seek a military victory in Vietnam, nor did it want military escalation. Rogers also listed the mutual withdrawal of North Vietnamese and American forces from Vietnam as a basic issue under contention. He reserved the settlement of the political structure in Vietnam for the Vietnamese themselves and offered to respect whatever choice they made.

On April 30, 1969, in Paris, the NLF representative stated that if the plan that he had previously submitted were adopted, the talks would proceed harmoniously. In response to this demand, President Nixon countered with a proposal of his own. In a nationwide television address on May 14, the American Chief Executive presented a new approach for ending the war. The President's unexpected offer included the concept of mutual troop withdrawal and, with the approval of President Nguyen Van Thieu, the holding of internationally supervised elections in South Vietnam. The NLF received some unexpected assistance in gaining support for their program when Leonid Brezhnev, secretary general of the Communist party of the Soviet Union, announced support of the latest Vietcong peace bid.[2]

While Secretary Brezhnev proclaimed his support for the NLF in Moscow, Presidents Nixon and Thieu met on Midway Island. At the conclusion of a five-hour meeting on June 8, the two national leaders announced that a reduction of 25,000 U.S. combat forces in Vietnam would be made by the end of August. In their joint communiqué, they also spoke favorably of the rapid progress made by ARVN in preparing to assume additional combat responsibilities.

During Thieu's absence from Vietnam, the NLF and other Communist groupings in South Vietnam founded the Provisional Revolutionary Government of the Republic of South Vietnam (PRG). The Vietnam Workers party in Hanoi has stated that the reason for the formation of the PRG was to perfect "the system of revolutionary administration in South Vietnam."[3] From the greater amount of information available, it appears that the party had merely formed another front organization that would be more amenable to its direction. The formation of innumerable front organizations by the Vietnam Workers party is a standard procedure in the forty-year history of the organized Communist movement in Vietnam. In forming and reforming organizations, the party will often use the same people in different positions, with power distributed according to its needs. The creation of a multiplicity of front groups serves a variety of purposes for the party. It convinces their enemies that a large and growing number of organizations are favorable to the Communist point of view and involves an ever-expanding number of people in pursuing a common

---

[2] *Pravda*, June 8, 1969.

[3] *An Outline History of the Viet Nam Workers Party: 1930–1970* (Hanoi: Foreign Languages Publishing House, 1970), p. 90.

goal. But foremost among its reasons for founding new groupings is the party's fear that "power tends to create power." The acceptance of this concept forces party leadership to reconstitute and purge organizations on a constant basis, lest a subordinate power center develop a political following of its own.

Near the end of June 1969 Representative Benjamin Rosenthal (D., N.Y.) became irritated with what he said was a movie that "glorified" the Vietnam War. The motion picture, *The Green Berets,* had been produced by John Wayne's Batjac Productions. The movie, which featured John Wayne as a special forces colonel, combined combat action with dialogue that supported American fighting men in Vietnam. The accusations were made at a news conference for which Rosenthal had arranged the screening of excerpts from the movie. Following the projection of the film, the New York politician accused Wayne of making a propaganda movie. He also criticized the Defense Department for providing assistance to Wayne for which it failed to recover the full cost of services rendered. It is worth noting that there is no record of Representative Rosenthal's having called a news conference in 1975 to protest the filming of the award-winning pro-Vietcong propaganda movie *Hearts and Minds.*

The Nixon Doctrine Outlined

Near the end of July 1969, President Nixon left Washington on a global tour. On his trip he visited various European and Asian countries. While on the Far Eastern leg of his journey, the President stopped on the island of Guam where he outlined a new Asian policy. The program, later known as the Nixon Doctrine, was presented as a background briefing at an informal news conference. It was not intended for direct quotation. The Chief Executive began his comments with a description of the importance of face-to-face conversations between leaders of the countries of the world. When Nixon came to the substance of his remarks, he posed a question as to the role of America in Asia after the end of the war in Vietnam. The President then proceeded to answer his own question. He said that, like it or not, the United States is a Pacific power, that America's involvement in her last three wars had begun in Asia, and that potentially the greatest threat to future peace would arise in the Pacific.

Nixon's solution to these problems was threefold: (1) the United States would keep its current treaty commitments, (2) America would provide a nuclear umbrella over its allies, and (3) Asian nations would have to carry the responsibility for their own defense. In his presentation, the President was very specific regarding the fact that

America's future policies in Asia would reject the possibility of being dragged into "conflicts such as the one we have in Vietnam."[4]

During the informal session that followed the speech, the reporters questioned the President about the effect of American withdrawal in the Pacific on Asian security. In his response Nixon emphasized that United States policy in Asia would not be one of removal, but more a practice of non-intervention. The President extended his answers to this question and explained how troop departures were affecting the war in Vietnam. He reported that General Earle G. Wheeler, chairman of the Joint Chiefs of Staff, had found that the "Thieu government" and the South Vietnamese military leadership were responding very effectively in meeting their own requirements.

Still More Negotiations

During the summer months of 1969, the negotiations in Paris and the fighting in Vietnam entered into what appeared a passive stage. There was a brief flurry of activity when the Communists denounced President Thieu's offer of July 11 to allow NLF participation in South Vietnamese elections as "trickery." The obvious intransigence of the North Vietnamese was condemned at the end of the month by President Nixon in Saigon, when he said: "We have gone as far as we can or should go in opening the door to peace, and now is the time for the other side to respond."

Realizing that the war was at a standstill, the Communists unlimbered their propaganda artillery and fired several rounds at the Nixon-Thieu negotiating position. To the North Vietnamese Communist, wars are fought by successfully orchestrating all segments of life in a massive assault against the enemy. To Truong Chinh, the Hanoi ideologist, "newspapers, photographs and exhibitions" form a part of the orchestra, and world opinion is the audience.[5]

In furthering the public opinion portions of their assault against Washington and Saigon, the Hanoi strategists inaugurated a series of lavish "social receptions" in Paris. The gatherings usually numbered around 2,000 guests, which included some 400 television and newspaper reporters. One of these "receptions" was held near the end of July 1969 in a mammoth ballroom of the expensive Hotel George V. The host for the occasion was the new Provisional Revolutionary Government. The announced purpose of the occasion was to bid farewell

---

[4] *Public Papers of the Presidents of the United States: Richard Nixon, 1970*, pp. 543–547.

[5] Truong Chinh, "The Resistance Will Win," *Primer for Revolt* (New York: Frederick A. Praeger, 1963), p. 209.

to a member of the PRG's negotiating team in Paris and to welcome his replacement, Mme Nguyen Thi Binh.*

After the Western news reporters arrived and the champagne was flowing freely, the North Vietnamese officials, accompanied by French-English interpreters, stationed themselves in various locations around the ballroom. As the media representatives struggled to accurately transcribe every word uttered by Le Duc Tho or Xuan Thuy, the interviews turned into a political victory for the North Vietnamese. When the reporters left the ballroom, they were somehow discussing the significance of the establishment of the PRG and comparing its founding in importance to the birth of the North Vietnamese Republic.

The summer lull in the fighting was broken in the first week of August by a series of mortar, infantry, and rocket assaults against the major cities of South Vietnam. The possibility exists that the Hanoi leadership may have ordered these attacks to coincide with the opening of secret negotiations in Paris. On August 4, 1969, President Nixon sent his special assistant, Henry Kissinger, to the French capital for the purpose of meeting clandestinely with Le Duc Tho. During their first meeting, Kissinger informed Tho that America wanted a "just settlement." The presidential assistant also stated that he recognized the North Vietnamese would be in Vietnam long after "we have left, and therefore it is in our interest that we make a settlement that you will want to keep."

Near the end of August, the Citizens Committee for Peace with Freedom in Vietnam issued a special nine-member report on Vietnam. The committee, which had been founded in 1967 by Presidents Eisenhower and Truman, had sent a special delegation to Vietnam, Laos, Thailand, and Paris to study and report on the war. Members of the commission included Dr. Edmund Gullion, dean of the Fletcher School of Law and Diplomacy, Tufts University, and Mrs. Oswald B. Lord, former U.S. Representative on the United Nations Human Rights Commission.

Among their findings, the advisory group reported that the North Vietnamese retained a kind of initiative through the use of sanctuaries in Laos, Cambodia, and north of the DMZ. They warned that during short periods of time, striking from their sanctuaries, the enemy could double American casualties. The commission noted that Vietnamization appeared to be working, and the Vietnamese were perhaps "over eager for the transfer." In conclusion the report listed

* The NLF took great pride in representing Mme Binh as being of humble peasant background. In actuality, she is the daughter of a former colonial official in the French Administration of the 1930s; see *Réalities Cambodiennes,* November 20, 1970.

nine recommendations, mostly dealing with Vietnamization. While the majority of the suggestions had been submitted by previous groups, a single item on the list told a story of its own. The recommendation was listed as Number Four and read, "That American editors and correspondents . . . give much more coverage to ARVN sacrifices and progress."

On September 3, 1969, North Vietnamese leader Ho Chi Minh died. His funeral was held in Hanoi's Ba Dinh garden before a crowd of over 100,000 people. In his eulogy to the founder of the North Vietnamese Republic Le Duan, party first secretary, read from Ho's will and urged the Vietnamese people to continue fighting against the United States until final victory. The eighty-one-year-old Ton Duc Thang, a longtime friend of Russia, was elected to replace Ho Chi Minh as president of the Northern Republic.

Five days after the committee had submitted their report, Premier Pham Van Dong, speaking in Hanoi, sharply attacked Vietnamization. The occasion was the twenty-fourth anniversary of the founding of the Democratic Republic of Vietnam. In his address the premier said: "Vietnamization . . . is nothing but hackneyed juggling. To use Vietnamese to fight Vietnamese is indeed an attractive policy for the United States."

The Demonstrations

The battlefield failures, the stalled negotiations, and the threat of a successful "Vietnamization" of the war posed a real challenge to the North Vietnamese politburo. In order to find an answer to this predicament, the Hanoi leadership followed their standard method of solving difficulties. This process consists of conducting a searching examination of all aspects of the current problem. After the critical analysis, a review of past solutions in similar situations is undertaken. If it is discovered that any of these practices could be successfully applied to the current situation, that procedure is usually adopted.

In the case of the 1969 impasse, the party leaders could not help but recognize a similarity to the summer of 1953. For at that time the battlefield was also contested, negotiations were not proceeding rapidly, and the French were conducting their own brand of "Vietnamization."

Proceeding from this conclusion, the party ordered a special fall offensive. The assault was to be composed of three prongs: the first thrust on the battlefield, the second push at the negotiating table, and the final effort on the enemy's home front. Only this time, while other factors remained the same, the American homeland was substituted for metropolitan France.

To coordinate these efforts on a worldwide basis, the party arranged for a liason meeting of their international associates in Stockholm, Sweden. The initial consultations were held May 16–18, 1969, at the Emergency Action Conference of the Stockholm Conference on Vietnam. Mme Nguyen Thi Binh headed the NLF delegation and Nguyen Minh Vy represented North Vietnam. The American representatives included Dr. Carleton Goodlett, a leading official in the World Peace Council and a leader of the National Mobilization Committee to End the War in Vietnam (MOBE). Goodlett was accompanied by Professor William C. Davidon and John Wilson of the Student National Coordinating Committee (SNCC). Subsequent planning was conducted when the World Peace Assembly met in Communist East Berlin on June 21–24, 1969. American delegates to the East Berlin conference included Dr. Goodlett and Irving Sarnoff, a member of the Communist Party of the United States of America (CPUSA).

The assembly received formal greetings from Leonid Brezhnev, general secretary of the Communist Party of the Soviet Union, and Alexei Kosygin, chairman of the Council of Ministers of the USSR. In their prepared text the Soviet leaders called for "mass actions of peace supporters and participants of various antiwar movements."

Sarnoff, who addressed the assembly, demonstrated his fear of the successful "Vietnamization" of the war and stated that "the heroic Vietnamese people . . . will not be fooled as the neocolonialists now try to force Vietnamese to fight Vietnamese." His intentions for America were clearly indicated when he said: "The honeymoon is now over and the struggle to end the war and bring the GIs home will . . . be renewed." In closing, Sarnoff described how the Communists would organize the antiwar effort in America when he commented:

> Our task is to broaden the base and understanding of our movement to include the many organized groups who are in motion around specific issues—wages, welfare, prices, taxes, racism, repression, housing—and to make them understand that there can be no improvement until the war in Vietnam is ended and the national priorities are reordered.[6]

After the assembly adjourned, various American antiwar groups were summoned to a meeting in Cleveland, Ohio, during the weekend of the Fourth of July. The conference included delegates from

[6] Staff Study by the Committee on Internal Security, House of Representatives, 91st Congress, 2nd Session, "Subversive Involvement in the Origin, Leadership and Activities of the New Mobilization Committee to End the War in Vietnam and its Predecessor Organizations," 1970, p. 33.

CPUSA, the Trotskyist Socialist Workers Party (SWP), the Young Socialist Alliance (YSA), and the Student Mobilization Committee to End the War in Vietnam (SMC). The extended sessions were attended by Sarnoff and Wilson, and as a result of their daily meetings, the conferees formed the New Mobilization Committee to End the War in Vietnam, which became known as the New Mobe.

Following a July 4 meeting, New Mobe leaders announced that an intensive campaign against the war in Vietnam would be organized across the United States. While they approved the scheduling of varied antiwar activities throughout the summer, it was clear that their ultimate goal was the launching of a two-part fall offensive. According to instruction leaflets distributed to their followers, a nationwide moratorium would be held on October 15. A march on Washington was scheduled for November 15, along with a simultaneous action on the West Coast.

At the end of July 1969, during a meeting of the project directors of New Mobe, it was decided to include a "March of the Dead" in the Washington demonstration. This dramatic activity envisioned parade participants being issued placards with the name of a serviceman killed in Vietnam. The marchers would then move past the White House in a single file and on to the Capitol building where the street drama would end.

In the middle of September, New Mobe held a press conference in New York City for the purpose of publicizing the fall offensive. Following release of the details of the moratorium and the Washington march, Senator Fred Harris of Oklahoma, the Democratic National Chairman, called a secret caucus on Capitol Hill. The meeting on September 26 was attended by twenty-four liberal Democrats. Among those present were Senators Edmund S. Muskie, Edward M. Kennedy, George S. McGovern, Walter F. Mondale, Birch Bayh, Claiborne Pell, and Mike Gravel. The House was represented by Allard K. Lowenstein, Brock Adams, Edward P. Boland, John Conyers, Jr., and Robert Kastenmeier. During the caucus, these influential congressional leaders agreed to support the nationwide moratorium and to develop a set of resolutions calling for the withdrawal of all American troops from Vietnam. They also discussed the possibility of forcing the Senate to shut down on October 15 by simply failing to attend. As he left the Vandenberg room, where the caucus had met, Harris declared: "It's time to take off the gloves on Vietnam."[7]

The demonstrators received other support for their efforts from various foreign sources. On October 6 Tran Buu Kiem, chairman of the South Vietnam Liberation Students' Union, sent a message to "Ameri-

[7] *New York Times*, September 27, 1969.

can students and youth on the occasion of the 1969 fall struggle movement." In his letter he wished the students great success and wrote, "The heroic struggle of the friends in New York, Washington, Oakland, and Berkeley has been much appreciated by the South Vietnamese youth and students."

A few days before the moratorium was scheduled to begin Representative Wayne L. Hays (D., Ohio), a former history teacher, discovered that he would have to attend a meeting of the North Atlantic assembly in Brussels. In remarks made before the House regarding his absence, he said:

> I am debating whether I should go or whether I should stay here and single-handedly break up the design of a few self-appointed emissaries of Hanoi to make it appear the House of Representatives is on their side.

Representative Abner J. Mikva (D., Ill.) responded:

> I happen to be one of the people who expect to take part in the special orders tomorrow. Is the gentleman suggesting that I am an emissary of Hanoi?

Hays answered:

> No, I would not suggest that. I think you are just an unwitting tool in an effort which is to their advantage, because the only people who can get any benefit out of this kind of performance, trying to make it appear that the majority of the House supports that position, are the North Vietnamese, because it is certainly doing something that Hanoi wants done.

The next day, the militants received important recognition of their activities. On October 14, 1969, a message was relayed via Paris to the United States from Pham Van Dong, the premier of the North Vietnamese government. In his telegram, the politburo leader encouraged "U.S. progressive people," praised the fall offensive, and wrote: "Our people's patriotic struggle is precisely the struggle for peace and justice that you are carrying out" (*Congressional Record*, October 14, 1969).

In the early afternoon of the day Dong's communication was received in the United States, Representative Sam Steiger (R., Ariz.) gave his impression of the motives of certain individuals for supporting moratorium activities when he said:

> What really concerns me is that it has been embraced by politicians who apparently are willing to put their own temporary political profit above country at a time when it was never more critical. [*Congressional Record*, October 14, 1969]

That same evening, twenty-three Democrats and one Republican attempted to force an all-night session in the House of Representatives. Each speaker had previously been granted unanimous consent to address the House for one hour. The first of the antiwar advocates, Andrew Jacobs, Jr., rose to speak at 7:30 P.M. Reading from a prepared text, Jacobs claimed that he believed Nixon was sincere in his views about the Vietnam War, but disagreed with the President's methods and urged the ending of hostilities. The Indiana Democrat was followed by Ogden Reid (R., N.Y.), who related the Vietnam War to the fact that "our air and water have become more polluted." Abner J. Mikva (D., Ill.), who spoke later, claimed that the Vietnam War had "diverted" the United States from the urgent social and economic problems we face here at home and urged the application of war dollars to eliminate "hunger."

Representative Benjamin Rosenthal recommended an immediate "massive withdrawal" of American troops and advocated the establishment of a coalition government in South Vietnam. His advice was immediately opposed by Edward J. Derwinski (R., Ill.), who called the New York Democrat's attention to the failure of coalition governments in China, Rumania, Hungary, and other countries. Rosenthal answered Derwinski's comparisons with a claim that the mixed grouping in Laos was actually working.*

Representative William F. Ryan (D., N.Y.) attacked American participation in the war and stated that "in Vietnam the United States intervened in what was essentially a civil war." Ryan later charged that America's ambassador to South Vietnam, Ellsworth Bunker, was a champion of outdated policies. He also recommended that all funding for military activities in South Vietnam be halted and the NLF be allowed to participate in that country's government.

At 10:05 P.M. a point of order was made that a quorum was not present. The roll was called and only 210 Members responded, eight short of the number necessary to enact legislation. A parliamentary discussion was held, and it was conceded that there were two alternatives—either a motion to adjourn, or to "instruct the Sergeant at Arms to produce the missing members." Representative James H. Quillen (R., Tenn.) moved to adjourn, further parliamentary inquiry ensued, and finally the Members were polled on the question of ad-

---

* The extent to which the coalition government was "working" in Laos had been demonstrated by the assassination of Colonel Ketsana Vong Souvan, a senior neutralist leader. A further illustration of the success of the mixed administration was shown when Communist forces chased neutralist tank units from positions they had been guaranteed under the terms of the peace agreement.

journment. When the votes were counted, there were 113 yeas and 109 nays, the total of which, incidentally, equaled a quorum. The House adjourned at 11:15 P.M.

The next day the Vietnam moratorium unfolded across America. An estimated one million people participated in antiwar demonstrations or peace rallies. Many major universities and schools shut their doors for the day. Leaflets were distributed on college campuses calling for an end to the war and urging students to go to Washington, D.C., on November 15, 1969 "for a massive demonstration against the war machine."

At one of the rallies, Senator Eugene McCarthy addressed a large audience at Rutgers University in New Brunswick, N.J. In his speech the Minnesota Democrat said:

> I think history would see nothing wrong if Nixon does preside over the first military defeat of this country, but would regard it instead as a measure of statesmanship.[8]

In Boston Senator Edward M. Kennedy (D., Mass.), in an address to the World Affairs Council, urged that the United States make "an irrevocable decision" to withdraw ground combat forces from Vietnam by the end of 1972. The senator said that his decision to recommend withdrawal was arrived at only after a "hard compromise."

Senator Edmund S. Muskie was the main speaker at Bates College in Lewiston, Maine. The senator told the students that he regretted the President's failure to seize the day as an opportunity to "unite rather than divide the country." Among the Maine Democrat's solutions to the Vietnam War, the "withdrawal of our military forces in an orderly way" seemed to take top priority. He also suggested that the Saigon government widen its "political base."

Senator Barry Goldwater (R., Ariz.), in remarks to the California Federation of Republican Women, gave his impression of the moratorium and its supporters. In a hard-hitting address, the senator described President Nixon's Vietnam critics as desiring "to end the war in Vietnam—just so we can do it without winning." He described Washington as a

> wonderland where men who spent thirty years committing this nation to an extreme policy of internationalism, who ran up a foreign aid bill of $122 billion, and who loaded down the American taxpayer with every conceivable kind of boondoggle that might garner a few liberal votes are now talking about economy and cutting government expenditures. [*Congressional Record,* October 16, 1969]

[8] *New York Times,* October 16, 1969.

Goldwater ended his speech with a call for support of the President as the "Commander in Chief."

In the weeks following the moratorium activities, the antiwar groups seemed to tone down their protests, as if they were waiting for some momentous event. The President seized the occasion to announce an important change in the conduct of the war in Vietnam. While he had previously indicated that the demonstrations would not affect administration decisions regarding the war, his November 3 speech contained indications that he had heard the protests "loud and clear." Nixon began his address with a review of how the situation in Vietnam appeared when he was inaugurated. The Chief Executive discussed the wide range of options American negotiators had offered to the North Vietnamese. He said that all of the peace proposals had been rejected by the Hanoi leadership, who had demanded the "unconditional acceptance of their terms" which included the immediate withdrawal of all American forces and the overthrow of the South Vietnamese government "as we leave."

The President also described an unproductive exchange of letters he had conducted with Ho Chi Minh. The most significant part of Nixon's speech went:

> We have adopted a plan which we have worked out in cooperation with the South Vietnamese for the complete withdrawal of all U.S. combat forces and their replacement by South Vietnamese forces on an orderly scheduled timetable.[9]

This statement represented at least a recognition of the political power of the supporters of the moratorium. There is every reason to believe that prior to the Communist-planned fall offensive, American military strategy included the maintenance of a residual force of more than 200,000 men in Vietnam for a considerable period of time. These troops were to be stationed along the coastline and, thanks to American naval supremacy, could be supplied and defended with comparative ease. They would be used to support the South Vietnamese army, which would carry the burden of engaging the Communist enemy on a daily basis.

On the other hand, the President's decision may merely have been a recognition of reality and the granting of a meaningless concession to the protesters. There is a considerable amount of support for assuming that Nixon's announcement of total Vietnamization was merely a political maneuver. The correctness of this assumption is shown by the continued retention of a large number of American troops in South Vietnam into the 1970s. Congressional response to the Chief

---

[9] *Congressional Quarterly Almanac,* 1969, p. 90A.

Executive's speech was mixed; however, several congressmen commented that "Nixon was on the right track." National reaction was generally favorable and supporters rallied to the President's cause by organizing "unity" rallies in various towns and cities.

As the November 13–15 antiwar activities in Washington approached, congressional support for the protests seemed to weaken. By this time, several congressmen who had previously supported the demonstrations became aware of the radical nature of the antiwar leadership and removed themselves from active participation in the peace movement. This dissociation may have been helped by the extended attack launched on their position in the halls of Congress. Almost every day after the October 15 moratorium, Republican and conservative Democratic congressmen had read into the record the gruesome activities of the Vietcong. They had also related Hanoi's support for the moratorium activities or presented the thinking of North Vietnamese ideologists. Typical examples of the attack on the Vietcong and their friends may be found in the *Congressional Record* for November 8, 1969. Entries for that day include, among other things, the congratulatory messages to the American demonstrators from Mme Nguyen Thi Binh and Xuan Thuy. A few hours after the complimentary telegrams were laid before the Senate, Senator Carl T. Curtis (R., Neb.) read to his colleagues a newspaper editorial that had appeared in the *Omaha World-Herald* on October 30. The editorial, entitled "Counterpoint," included quotations from American peace groups or politicians, followed by stories of events in Vietnam. Among the quotes and comments were the following:

> The names of Vietnamese villages destroyed by the United States will be called out.
>> —November demonstration plan, Clergy and Laymen
>> Concerned About Vietnam

> Two VC battalions struck in the earliest hours . . . when every building was ablaze, the Communists took their flamethrowers to the mouth of each trench. . . . The bodies of 252 people, mostly mothers and children, lay blistered, charred, burned to the bone. . . . The massacre at Dak Son was a warning . . . to cooperate.
>> —John G. Hubbell, *Reader's Digest*

> Both reality and reason impel us to declare our support for the formation of a coalition government that will include the significant participation of the National Liberation Front.
>> —Senator Vance Hartke (D., Ind.)

> For a newborn revolutionary power to be lenient with counterrevolutionaries is tantamount to committing suicide.
>> —Truong Chinh, Communist official
>> [*Congressional Record,* October 13, 1969]

On November 13 President Nixon paid a surprise visit to the House of Representatives. In his prepared remarks the Chief Executive expressed sincere "appreciation" to the 300 members of the House who had supported a resolution urging a "just" peace in Vietnam. Following a short speech to the representatives, the President moved to the floor of the Senate. In his address to the senators, he supported the desirability of consultation between the executive and legislative branches of the government in foreign policy matters. The President also thanked the sixty senators who had written to Ambassador Lodge urging a just peace in Vietnam.

As Nixon addressed the Congress, thousands of war protesters began to gather in Washington. The demonstrators were encouraged when Senator Claiborne Pell (D., R.I.) announced his support for their efforts in the Senate. In his comments regarding the events of the coming weekend, the Rhode Island politician said, "I supported the goals of the October moratorium, and I support now the goals of the moratorium activities planned for today and tomorrow."

However, the senator also voiced considerable concern over the possibility of violence. He claimed that the young Trotskyites or the radical faction of the Students for Democratic Society (SDS) were known troublemakers. Pell ended his remarks by indicating sympathy for the South Vietnamese people and said that he was in favor of "international efforts to provide asylum for South Vietnamese citizens whose lives might be placed in jeopardy by withdrawal of our troops" (*Congressional Record,* October 13, 1969).

At 6:00 P.M. November 13, 1969, the "March Against Death" began at the entrance to Arlington National Cemetery. The placard-carrying demonstrators marched past the White House and proceeded to the Capitol where they placed their posters in one of forty coffins. Some 45,000 protesters participated in a march that lasted forty hours.

On the evening of the next day, militant radicals began to gather in Du Pont Circle. The rally, for which a permit had been issued, was sponsored by the "Revolutionary Contingent," a coalition of the Weathermen, Revolutionary Youth Movement II, the Mad Dog Caucus, and Youth Against War and Fascism. At 8:30 P.M., after some 2,500 persons had arrived in the circle, the crowd began to move toward the South Vietnamese Embassy. Their previously avowed purpose was to serve an "eviction notice" on the South Vietnamese government. The militants indicated they would not seek violence, but would "be prepared to defend ourselves." The marchers chanted, "Ho, Ho, Ho Chi Minh, the NLF is gonna win" and carried unfurled Vietcong flags.

As the crowd crossed Twenty-second Street, the police moved to arrest its leaders. The demonstrators reacted by throwing rocks, bricks, and bottles at the officers. The police responded by loosing the first of many gas barrages. At this point the mob broke into several smaller groups and proceeded to march up and down Connecticut, Massachusetts, and New Hampshire Avenues in window-breaking forays. In the ensuing disorder a civilian automobile and a police vehicle were overturned and set afire. The riot continued until 1:00 A.M., when the police managed to restore order.

By Saturday morning some 250,000 war protesters had gathered in Washington. The march against the war began at 10:15 near the Capitol building and moved down Pennsylvania Avenue. Following the parade, the marchers and their supporters gathered near the Washington Monument for a giant rally.

The main speakers of the day were Democratic Senators George McGovern, Eugene McCarthy, and Charles Goodell (R., N.Y.). Goodell, a former political moderate, had been appointed by Governor Nelson Rockefeller to complete the unexpired term of the assassinated Robert Kennedy.*

David Dellinger, self-professed Communist and cochairman of New Mobe, was also on the speaker's platform. Entertainment for the day was provided by Pete Seeger, Arlo Guthrie, and Peter, Paul, and Mary.

A little before 4:30 P.M., groups of radicals left the main rally and marched to the Justice Department. The militants were carrying Vietcong flags and shouting the usual "Ho, Ho, Ho Chi Minh." This time two new slogans, "Free Bobby Seale" and "Stop the Trial," were added to the din. These chants referred to the current trials of Bobby Seale, the Black Panther leader, and the Chicago conspirators.

The mob, which by now numbered about 6,000, began banging on the gates leading into the buildings that housed the government agency. A Vietcong flag was raised on a nearby flagpole, and a red-paint bomb was exploded on an adjacent wall. The police, who had exhibited extended patience, fired a canister of tear gas at the rioters. The crowd broke and ran along Constitution Avenue in another window-breaking spree. The disorders continued into the evening until about 8:00 P.M., when they were brought under control.

An allied West Coast demonstration held in San Francisco drew an

---

* The new senator's conservative outlook had been a vital ingredient in Rockefeller's choice to balance the New York senatorial representation. Goodell, who was up for reelection in 1970, surprisingly veered sharply to the left after he was sworn into office. During 1969, in a matter of a few months, he attacked (among other things) the Greek junta, the defense budget, biological warfare, the government's public housing policies, and the war in Vietnam.

estimated 100,000 participants. The speakers included ex-Senator Wayne Morse, Black Panther leader David Hilliard, and Chicago conspiracy defendant Rennie Davis. The crowd was generally peaceful; however, their enthusiasm was dampened by torrential rains.

The Cooper-Mansfield-Church Amendment

The Senate having voted favorably on the National Commitments Resolution at the end of June 1969, it was not until the middle of August that another real threat to the President's war powers was disclosed. The challenge was presented by John Sherman Cooper, a senior Republican senator from Kentucky, who offered a restrictive amendment to the defense procurement bill. The proviso would in effect have prohibited the introduction of United States combat forces into Thailand or Laos. After a lengthy discussion with Senator Gordon Allott (R., Colo.) regarding the correct wording of the legislation, Cooper withdrew his proposal.

The following month the Kentucky politician resubmitted his amendment, which the Senate approved on September 19. But the provision was later removed in a House-Senate conference. In spite of the fact that the Cooper amendment had been deleted, the defense procurement bill continued to contain restrictive clauses. For the first time, a ceiling was set on the financial support that could be granted certain Southeast Asian military forces:

> . . . not to exceed $2,500,000,000 of the funds authorized for appropriation for the use of the United States under this or any other Act are authorized to be made available for their stated purpose to support: (1) Vietnamese and other Free World Forces in Vietnam, (2) local forces in Laos and Thailand; and for related costs, during the fiscal year 1970, on such terms and conditions as the Secretary of Defense may determine.[10]

During the year, other attempts had been made in both chambers of Congress to reduce or eliminate funds for the Vietnam War. House Democrats had strongly attacked the supplemental appropriations bill, which contained additional funds for various government programs. When this measure appeared on the floor of the House, Bob Eckhardt of Texas proposed that the $640.1 million intended for the army be eliminated, and William F. Ryan of New York tried unsuccessfully to delete the Vietnam appropriations altogether.

It was not until the close of the year that legislation was enacted that promised to interfere seriously with the Commander in Chief's conduct of the Vietnam War. Senator Cooper had not relaxed his

[10] Public Law 91-121, November 19, 1969.

efforts to incorporate legislation limiting United States military activities in Laos and Thailand. After the rejection of his amendment to the procurement bill, the senator found another opportunity to offer his antiwar proposal when the Senate considered the 1970 defense appropriations bill. Unfortunately for the Kentucky Republican, he was unable, due to a family illness, to be in attendance when the bill was considered. His inability to attend the December 15, 1969 session, however, when defense appropriations were considered, did not prevent the submission of the restrictive amendment. In his absence Majority Leader Mike Mansfield introduced the Cooper proposal to exclude United States combat forces from Laos and Thailand.

Following presentation of the measure, the Senate engaged in a lengthy discussion of the war then raging in Laos. Senator Fulbright, chairman of the Foreign Relations Committee, questioned the cloak of secrecy the administration had placed around America's contribution to the Laotian War. He said it was his opinion that if the Senate was expected to vote intelligently on what would be done with the monies in the program, it would have to be better informed. Mansfield suggested a closed-door session of the Senate "to better educate" senators about the situation.

Shortly before the doors of the Senate were closed, Senator Fulbright observed that American planes were "flying tactical missions in support of the Laotian army in the civil war now taking place in northern Laos." Mansfield answered this issue directly and stated:

> "Civil war" is a term you have to use with discretion. If it were a struggle between the Pathet Lao and the Royal Laotian forces, it would be a civil war; but when 50,000 North Vietnamese are backing up and supporting the Pathet Lao, then you have to recognize that a foreign government has intervened in what had become up to that time a civil war, but what, with this intervention, became other than a civil war. [*Congressional Record,* December 15, 1969]

From the well-censored transcript of the secret session it appears that during the confidential debate a group of senators strongly challenged administration policies in Laos. The critics were led by Senators Fulbright, Mansfield, and Church. In the course of the discussions it was revealed that the United States military establishment in Laos was very extensive and that American planes had been used to bomb the Ho Chi Minh Trail. Administration critics did not appear to be especially concerned with the bombing. Their opposition to the Pentagon's activities in Laos and Thailand seems to have centered on the commitment of American ground combat troops to those countries.

Once the Senate doors were opened, a misunderstanding arose regarding the intent of the Cooper-Mansfield portion of the legislation. Senator Church reworded the amendment, and in its final version the restrictive section of the bill read:

> In line with the expressed intention of the President of the United States, none of the funds appropriated by this Act shall be used to finance the introduction of American ground combat troops into Laos or Thailand.[11]

The introductory clause, which was in accord with statements the President had made, was added to make the amendment more acceptable to administration supporters. The Senate approved the Church substitute 73–13, and on December 15, 1969, the Cooper-Mansfield amendment was adopted by a roll-call vote with 80 in favor of the measure and 9 opposed.

In spite of the conciliatory language, the press reported the congressional action as restrictive in nature. In its December 16 commentary on the previous day's congressional activities, the *Washington Post* article covering the Laotian debate was headed: HILL ACTS TO CURB ASIA ROLE—SENATE VOTES $69.3 BILLION IN DEFENSE FUNDS.

This time the press reported the realities of the occasion, and another restriction on the President's conduct of the Indochina War had been enacted. By the end of 1969 the National Commitments Resolution had been passed by the Senate. A ceiling had been put on the Indochina War budget, and the Commander in Chief was precluded from using American ground combat forces in Laos and Thailand.

[11] Public Law 91-171, December 29, 1969.

III / The Assault Mounts

In 1970, during a debate in the Senate, Senator Robert P. Griffin (R., Mich.) remarked, on the possible passage of the McGovern-Hatfield end-the-war amendment:

> Up to now we have not been losing the war in Southeast Asia. But, unfortunately, and to the delight of the enemy, there is some danger that we could lose in the United States a war that the enemy has been unable to win on the battlefield in Southeast Asia. [*Congressional Record*, May 5, 1970]

The senator's observations would prove to be timely, for 1970 was the year that congressional liberals added Cambodia to their forbidden zone.

State of the Union

On January 22, 1970, Richard M. Nixon delivered his annual State of the Union message to the Congress. Sensing the growth of forces opposed to his policies in Vietnam, the Chief Executive issued an appeal for patience and firmness in the face of enemy intransigence. He stated that America must always regard peace in the world as its first priority. The President described his goal in Vietnam as bringing a "just" peace to that war-torn part of the world. He added that it should be the kind of peace that the next generation would be able to keep.

Eight days later Nixon held his first televised news conference of the year. After the questioning had begun, Helen Thomas of United Press International raised the issue of a new enemy offensive in Vietnam. The President responded by indicating that he was reviewing reports that the North Vietnamese had increased their infiltration rate into the Southern Republic. He warned that the United States was prepared to deal "strongly" with the increase in infiltration. In the course of the questioning, one of the reporters mentioned the subject of Vietnamization. The President addressed this issue and explained that in his eyes Vietnamization meant the promise to withdraw all American combat forces from Vietnam and replace them with Vietnamese. Nixon then restated the criteria on which the withdrawal of the American troops would be based. These basic points, which had been enumerated on previous occasions, were: (1) the level of enemy activity, (2) the progress in the Paris peace talks, and (3) the ability of the South Vietnamese to absorb the necessary amount of training. The newsmen seemed to accept the President's comments favorably, and the conference closed in a friendly fashion.

The Vietnamization program appears to have met with approval throughout America, and the vocal criticism of Nixon's policies in Vietnam generally subsided. The quiet did not last long, though, as the Democrats again called in their heavy artillery and fired a major salvo at the administration.

Vietnam Policy Proposals

For some time, the Senate Foreign Relations Committee had been a focal point of opposition to the President's conduct of the war in Vietnam. In the first days of February 1970 this antagonism was channeled into a series of hearings on recent proposals submitted to Congress regarding the war. Senate committee investigations are usually held to consider the ramifications of various bills that have been submitted to that legislative body. Hearings are often important sessions at which committee members honestly seek the advice they need. On the other hand, some inquiries are carefully staged proceedings where the information extracted is prejudicial in nature and reinforces the opinions of the dominant committee members.

Unfortunately for the better interests of the United States, Senate Foreign Relations Committee investigations under the leadership of Senator Fulbright fell into the latter category. Indeed, when the Committee held open sessions on issues pertaining to Indochina, the meetings were commonly referred to as a "hoax." The major reason for this generally accepted view of the Committee proceedings was not hard to find. Senator Fulbright's open opposition to the war in Vietnam was well known and had been the subject of numerous lead articles in prominent Eastern newspapers.

For the careful analyst, a close reading of the transcript of the 1970 hearings, entitled "Vietnam Policy Proposals," fully demonstrates the senator's prejudices regarding the Vietnam War. There are innumerable occasions where Fulbright put words in a person's mouth and drew conclusions the witness did not intend.

Among the witnesses to appear before the February 1970 inquiry was Senator Charles Goodell (R., N.Y.), who testified in behalf of his bill entitled the "Vietnam Disengagement Act of 1969." As a part of his statement favoring the passage of this legislation, the senator claimed: "No 'blood bath' of Catholics or other anti-Communists was reported following the Communist assumption of power in 1954." Goodell's comment about the absence of a calculated massacre in North Vietnam simply does not match the greater amount of evidence available.[1]

Following the New York politician's appearance before the Committee, Senator Harold E. Hughes (D., Iowa) explained a resolution he and Senator Thomas F. Eagleton (D., Mo.) had submitted concerning the lack of political liberties in South Vietnam. In his testimony the Iowa Democrat carefully spelled out the commitment of the United States government to South Vietnam, saying:

> My opinion is that the commitment to the present government of South Vietnam is to support their forces with American combat troops, armaments and supplies, Navy and Air Force tactical fire power until some distant point in the future when there can be reached some sort of political solution, under which the South Vietnamese people themselves can make a self-determination as to their own government.[2]

On the second day of the hearings, Chairman Fulbright questioned Senator Hugh Scott (R., Pa.). The Pennsylvania senator had appeared before the Committee in order to present a resolution supporting "the President's efforts to negotiate a just peace in Vietnam." During the chairman's interrogation of the witness, the following exchange took place regarding President Nixon's statements about the "irreversibility" of Vietnamization:

> SENATOR SCOTT: In my judgment if, in the course of the progressive withdrawal of American forces, and therefore a de-escalation of the war, this process and the process of Vietnamization were endangered by un-

---

[1] According to Bernard Fall, the total loss of life in North Vietnam due to the activities of Viet Minh executioners in 1954 was 50,000 killed and 100,000 imprisoned. Hoang Van Chi, a prominent Vietnamese nationalist, has estimated the toll at over 500,000. Even the North Vietnamese Communist Party newspaper admitted the extent of the pogrom and at a later date announced the "return of some of the confiscated churches and imprisoned priests"; see *Nhan Dan,* August 24, 1956.

[2] Hearings Before the Senate Committee on Foreign Relations, "Vietnam Policy Proposals," 1970.

wanted and marked increase in the aggressiveness of the other side, the President, not for the purpose of reversing the trend, but for the purpose of protecting the entire process, would, as Commander in Chief, unquestionably take such actions as might seem proper to him at that time, and he has indicated that he might resort to the use of such American power as is necessary to protect the withdrawal process and the Vietnamization of the war.

THE CHAIRMAN: If I understand you correctly, when you say irreversible, you contemplate withdrawal of all forces, provided that the other side does not take advantage of this withdrawal and do things which would provoke some retaliation or would, I assume, cast some doubt upon the stability of the South Vietnamese government as it now exists. To put it another way, if the North Vietnamese and the Vietcong are quite content to accept Mr. Thieu and Mr. Ky and to be nice and not cause any trouble, then we will withdraw. Is that an accurate way to describe it? If not, I wish you would correct it and state it more accurately.

SENATOR SCOTT: Mr. Chairman, those are not my words.[3]

Later in the day, Senator George McGovern (D., S.Dak.) appeared before the Committee in defense of a resolution urging the immediate withdrawal from Vietnam of all United States forces. The Dakota Democrat described his measure and then launched into a tirade against American participation in what he referred to as "an essentially local struggle involving various groups of Vietnamese."

If this statement represents the best thinking of Senator McGovern, then to say the least, South Dakota is represented by a man whose impression of the world could improve with the addition of a little knowledge. Demonstrable evidence that North Vietnam is very much indebted to the USSR and the People's Republic of China for its industrial system, ideology, and weaponry is easily obtainable.[4]

While attacks on the President's policies were being waged in the Senate Foreign Relations Committee, the Democrats opened a new front. On February 9, 1970, the Democratic Policy Council adopted a resolution urging that all American troops be withdrawn from Vietnam within eighteen months. The measure had been drafted by ex-

---

[3] Ibid., pp. 72–73.

[4] The extent of Soviet assistance to the North Vietnamese in the industrial area alone has been well described by a Russian visitor to that country. The traveler had driven an automobile through most of North Vietnam in the late 1950s. He reported that everywhere he went he met "engineers from Uralmash," Leningrad power engineers and Moscow tool builders; see B. Vaily'yev, "Anxieties of Captain Dong," *Nedya,* Russian (Moscow: No. 18, April 1967), p. 12. Even the North Vietnamese National Planning Board was established with Soviet and Chinese Communist assistance, as freely admitted by Le Duan in his work *The Vietnamese Revolution.*

governor Averell Harriman, the former United States delegate to the Paris peace talks. The resolution urged an escalation of the negotiations toward a "peaceful political settlement." It encouraged the appointment of a high-level negotiator to replace acting Chief Delegate Philip Habib, who had remained in Paris after the resignation of Ambassador Lodge in December. The policy statement also insisted that the Thieu government broaden its base of power and include persons "who represent wider public opinion desiring a peaceful solution and who are prepared to negotiate such a statement."

The Nixon Doctrine Elaborated

Nine days later President Nixon issued a report to the Congress and the nation entitled, "United States Foreign Policy for the 1970s: A New Strategy for Peace." In his message the Chief Executive indicated a definite shift in American foreign policy. The change was based primarily on what the President believed to be a "shattered" unity in the international Communist movement and the growth of an adversary relationship between Soviet Russia and Communist China. Henceforth, he said, the United States would deal with all nations of the world as if they were operating in their own self interest and not as if they formed a part of some monolithic bloc.

Projecting his thoughts on foreign policy, the President uttered a series of comments that described the Nixon Doctrine in a very concise manner. He agreed that the United States would help its friends, but that "America cannot—and will not—design all the programs, execute all the decisions, and undertake all the defense of the free nations of the world."

When discussing Vietnam, Nixon reviewed his trip through the Far East in 1969 and stated that he had not met a single Asian leader who wanted the United States to execute a hasty withdrawal from Vietnam. He added that his program for South Vietnam entailed negotiations coupled with Vietnamization. While the President believed that the Paris deliberations were stalled, he said that there had been "tangible progress" in strengthening the South Vietnamese armed forces and pacification was "succeeding."

The lack of movement in the peace talks appeared to bother Nixon greatly. He did not seem to understand why the Hanoi leadership had failed to come to terms. His irritation was apparent when he said, "We stopped the bombing ... we began the withdrawal of United States forces from Vietnam, and we agreed to negotiate with the National Liberation Front," and still the enemy did not respond. What the President apparently did not comprehend was that the

"BUTCHERS!"

North Vietnamese were realizing all their major objectives by merely remaining intransigent. Until some move was made by the American side that compelled Hanoi to resume the negotiations, the peace talks would remain at a standstill.

Near the end of his report, the President made what appeared to be strong overtures to Communist China. After reflecting upon Europe's many past injustices to the Middle Kingdom, Nixon extended the olive branch to the People's Republic:

> But it is certainly in our interest, and in the interest of peace and stability in Asia and the world, that we take what steps we can toward improved practical relations with Peking.

He also referred to the resumption of meetings between United States and Chinese representatives in Warsaw and indicated an interest in seeing China "reenter the international community."[5]

The following month, on March 14, 1970, the Democrats issued an acidic critique of the President's "State of the World" report. The statement was released by Averell Harriman. The criticism extended to all parts of Nixon's message and contained comments like "pious preachments, singularly empty phrases," and "simplistic sermonizing." Harriman saved his strongest condemnation until he came to the President's remarks on Vietnam. At this point the ex-Governor charged the administration with failing to provide leadership in the war effort and placing America at the whim of the Thieu regime.

Anniversary of the Hue Massacre

On March 2, 1970, Vietnamese in the city of Hue held a prayer service to honor the memory of the victims of an earlier Communist massacre. The bloodletting had occurred during the 1968 Tet offensive, when a combined North Vietnamese and Vietcong military force had captured the ancient city. The liquidation lists included civil servants, school teachers, university professors, men, women, children—in fact, anyone who could be remotely classified as an anti-Communist.

As the NVA/VC forces entered the city, the intended victims were herded into groups of ten and bound together with rattan ropes. The columns of prisoners were then marched off to freshly dug graves where their skulls were crushed with a short hard stick, and in many cases the victims were buried alive. Villagers who lived next to the execution sites reported that agonizing screams were heard throughout several successive nights.

[5] *Public Papers of the Presidents, Richard Nixon, 1970,* pp. 116–190.

After the allied forces had recaptured the city, the remaining residents rushed out to conduct a frantic search for their missing relatives. What they found instead was a series of mass graves. There were fourteen burial places in Gia Hoi, twelve at Tang Quang Pagoda, three at Bai Dau, twenty at Kings Tu Duc and Dong Khanh Tombs. By mid-1970 some 4,000 individual burial sites had been uncovered.[6]

Land Reform in South Vietnam

On March 26, 1970, the Saigon authorities launched a land-reform plan that proved to be very successful. The undertaking was an extremely ambitious enterprise known as the "Land to the Tillers" program.[7] The master design for the new project envisioned nothing less than providing ownership rights to thousands of landless peasants. In order to achieve this objective, the government expropriated fallow acreage from wealthy property owners and distributed the land to the small farmers. Priority in the distribution of the property was given to the "present tiller," parents and children of the dead, and discharged veterans. As originally envisioned, the new program involved the redistribution of over 2,250,000 acres of fertile farmland with fair compensation to the former landlords.

The Battlefield

During the final months of 1969, when North Vietnamese General Vo Nguyen Giap prepared his plans for the coming year, the outlook for 1970 was precarious. As the Hanoi general viewed his opponent, the enemy commander in chief was a wily individual, given to acting in an unpredictable manner. Though Richard Nixon had renounced a military victory, he had not indicated a willingness to accept defeat. If the Americans were to succeed in their policy of Vietnamizing the war, General Giap's forces would also be denied military success. To the hero of Dien Bien Phu, the acceptance of anything less than victory was unthinkable. This conclusion led him to plan an active and vigorous campaign for the coming year. In developing his strategy for 1970, Giap viewed the war from an international perspective. Admittedly, the focal point of the active fighting was Vietnam,

[6] Probably the best assessment of the use of terror as an instrument of war by the Vietnamese Communists is a 125-page monograph published in 1970 by Douglas Pike for the United States Mission in Saigon, entitled, "The Viet Cong Strategy of Terror."

[7] Law No. 003/70 of March 26, 1970, governing the Land-to-the-Tiller Policy in the Republic of Vietnam.

but to the Hanoi general the world was the battlefield. An inventory of his forces revealed that some of North Vietnam's most effective allies were in the United States. American Communist party members, ambitious politicians, and manipulable college students composed a large and active part of the forces Hanoi had at its disposal.

Giap calculated that on the fighting front itself, American military strength was still too powerful to overcome. A series of coordinated attacks during the first few months of the year, however, could yield significant returns at the stalled negotiations and improve Hanoi's military position. After completing his strategic appraisal, the general prepared to launch a series of attacks on enemy positions throughout the world. As a part of his overall intentions, Giap planned to drive the Royal Laotian forces away from the Ho Chi Minh Trail and to expand the size of the Cambodian sanctuary. Once these goals had been reached, a more determined attack on United States and South Vietnamese forces could be undertaken. The whole tableau, however, must be carefully coordinated with the American antiwar effort to obtain maximum effect.

In developing the North Vietnamese campaign in America, Giap had to rely heavily on the efforts of antiwar groups located in the United States. His work was made easier, though, when Louis Schneider of the American Friends Service Committee and James Forest of the World Peace Council appeared in Hanoi in December 1969.[8] The Americans were in North Vietnam as a part of a six-man peace group that was arranging an international antiwar conference to be held at Stockholm in January. During a meeting with North Vietnamese Premier Pham Van Dong and Vietcong representative Trung Cong Dong, the delegation coordinated its plans with those of General Giap for the coming American campaign. The Hanoi leaders and the American delegates decided that the spring 1970 antiwar program in the United States would operate under the slogan of "Vietnam Appeal." Four major areas of concentration were chosen: special emphasis was to be given to demands for the withdrawal of United States and allied troops from Vietnam, the formation of a new international conference on the war would be urged, United States war crimes were to receive constant exposure, and support for the efforts of the Provisional Revolutionary Government was to be maximized.

Having wound up their meetings with the Hanoi leadership, the peace delegation traveled to Stockholm for a secret conference. When they arrived in Sweden, the American part of the antiwar group was increased by the addition of Dr. Carlton Goodlett and John McAuliff of New Mobe.

[8] *Congressional Record,* April 16, 1970.

At the January conference, the international delegates accepted the four-point program previously developed in Hanoi. The American representatives adopted the same plan after making minor variations to suit the United States. New Mobe organizer McAuliff described their strategy as calling for "an immediate and unconditional" removal of United States troops from Vietnam. He stated that the calls for withdrawal were to be focused on three particular issues: (1) "repression," (2) the draft, and (3) the economy. The projected 1970 timetable included:

(1) January 15—day of discussion against United States "genocide";
(2) Month of February—protests against the Chicago Conspiracy trial;
(3) March 14–15—civil disobedience at draftboards;
(4) April 14–15—protests against the "war tax";
(5) Last two weeks in April—the second phase of the "Who pays—Who profits" campaign at stockholders meetings of large corporations, including Honeywell, General Electric and Gulf Oil;
(6) Month of May—demonstrations at United States military bases.

Five days after the Stockholm conference ended, 15,000 NVA/Pathet Lao troops massed near the Plain of Jars in central Laos. The large assault force had been assembled by infiltrating 13,000 North Vietnamese soldiers into Laos during the early days of January. The addition of these troops brought Hanoi's military forces in Laos to over 67,000 men. Their Laotian opposition was unworthy of consideration, except for the courageous Meo tribesmen commanded by Vang Pao, an anti-Communist general.

After a month of hard fighting, the NVA/Pathet Lao forces captured the strategic plain. The Communist victory was not without losses, however, as they had come under severe aerial bombardment by American B-52s stationed in Thailand. Once the Hanoi forces had expanded their bridgehead in Laos, they began moving massive supply convoys down the Ho Chi Minh Trail in the direction of their Cambodian sanctuaries.

The rising level of warfare in Indochina caused Senate doves to increase their opposition to American participation in the actual fighting. Senator Stuart Symington (D., Mo.) raised the issue of the increased United States military activities in Laos and stated that it was not solely confined to the Plain of Jars. Senator Albert Gore (D., Tenn.) questioned the administration's failure to release testimony regarding Laos taken in a previous closed session of the Senate Foreign Relations Committee. The Tennessee Democrat claimed that the

Committee transcript would show the depth of American involvement in the small Southeast Asian country.

The continuing criticism prompted President Nixon to release a detailed 3,000-word account of American participation in the Laotian war. In the written statement, issued on March 6, 1970, at Key Biscayne, Nixon reviewed America's growing participation in the war in Laos. In his opening comments the Chief Executive revealed that he had sent letters to British Prime Minister Harold Wilson and Soviet Premier Alexei Kosygin asking their help in restoring the 1962 Geneva Agreements for Laos. The President believed that as cochairmen of the conference, the British and Russian leaders had "particular responsibilities" for seeing that the 1962 accords remained in force.

In the report Nixon observed that after the 1962 neutralization agreements had been concluded, the United States withdrew its 666 personnel who had been assisting the Laotian government. On the other side, he stated that only a "token forty men" passed through International Control Commission check points, which left "6,000 troops in the country." According to the President, the number of North Vietnamese soldiers in Laos had increased to "33,000 in mid-1967, 46,000 in mid-1968, and 55,000 in mid-1969." In response to this obvious invasion, the Chief Executive said that the United States had answered the requests of Prime Minister Souvanna Phouma and provided assistance to the beleaguered Laotian government. However, Nixon added, American assistance had not included "ground combat troops," nor were there any plans for introducing these type of soldiers into Laos in the foreseeable future.

The President also said that one of the major reasons for American bombing in Laos was that the North Vietnamese were continuing to pour supplies down the trail. He ended his statement with the remark that America desired nothing more in Laos than a return to the Geneva Agreements "and the withdrawal of North Vietnamese troops, leaving the Lao people to settle their own differences in a peaceful manner."[9]

Senator Fulbright continued to press the President on the extent of the United States role in Laos. On March 16, at the reconvened hearing on "Vietnam Policy Proposals," the Arkansas Democrat revealed testimony that Secretary of State Rogers had previously given to a closed session of Fulbright's Foreign Relations Committee. The senator quoted Rogers as saying that the United States had no plans to commit ground combat troops to Laos even though it was "overrun" by the Communists. Fulbright's remarks were made during the ques-

[9] Department of State Publication 8524, "The Scope of U.S. Involvement in Laos: A Statement by President Nixon," released May 1970.

tioning of Under Secretary of State Elliot L. Richardson, who told the Committee that ground troops would not be sent to Laos without congressional approval. However, he indicated that the approval might only consist of discussions with congressional leaders. One additional comment of the under secretary, regarding presidential authority to use American air forces in the Laotian War, aroused considerable interest among Committee members. In Richardson's opinion, the President did not need additional congressional authority to engage in air warfare over Laos, as this type of combat support had begun under the Johnson administration. He also asserted that the executive branch of the government did not need the 1964 Gulf of Tonkin Resolution to support its activities in Laos. Instead, Richardson claimed, the President based American assistance to the Laotian government on his powers as Commander in Chief under Article II of the Constitution.[10]

The next month, the administration released the long-awaited transcript of the secret hearings on United States involvement in Laos. Chaired by former Air Force Secretary Stuart Symington, a subcommittee of the Senate Foreign Relations Committee had held the hearings in October 1969. The release of the transcript had been delayed because of a previous government policy of secrecy regarding United States participation in the Laotian war.

During the inquiry, the main administration representative had been William H. Sullivan, deputy assistant secretary of state for east Asian and Pacific affairs. Other government witnesses included Daniel Oleksiw of the United States Information Agency (USIA) and Loring A. Waggoner, community development area adviser for the Agency for International Development (AID) in the North Nam Ngum area of Laos.

In his testimony before the committee, Sullivan had stated that the basic "obligation" of the United States to Laos was contained in Article IV of the SEATO Treaty. He described the article and said that when the powers signatory to the agreement believed that the treaty was being violated they were to consult jointly with the Laotian government "in order to consider means which might prove to be necessary to ensure the observance of these principles."

As the questioning progressed, Sullivan described the existence of a sizeable Soviet military force in Laos back in 1961. The exchange revealing the extent of the Russian commitment follows.

MR. SULLIVAN: Soviet military forces were then in Laos at that time; yes, sir.

[10] Hearings Before the Senate Foreign Relations Committee, "Vietnam Policy Proposals," 1970.

SENATOR MANSFIELD: There were?

MR. SULLIVAN: Yes, sir.

SENATOR MANSFIELD: How large was the force?

MR. SULLIVAN: We never knew exactly, but there were at least 500, according to our estimates. They were there flying aircraft and providing logistics support and a military advisory mission.[11]

The alarming part of Secretary Sullivan's testimony was that Soviet fliers had recently been reported carrying troops and supplies on the Laotian front.

The most heavily censored part of the transcript dealt with American military involvement in Laos. Administration forces scored a minor victory when a September 1962 letter from Laotian Prime Minister Souvanna Phouma requesting "weapons" and "ammunition" from the United States government was produced. In the end, the most significant result of the hearings was that they revealed the extent to which the American military role had expanded in Southeast Asia. The hearings had lost a considerable amount of their anticipated impact thanks to the previous release of much of the information. Some of the controversial issues had been explored extensively in various newspapers and magazines before the administration released the transcript. Among the commentaries was an article written by Senator Alan Cranston (D., Calif.) and published in the *Nation* on March 30, 1970. In his analysis the California Democrat discussed "civilian" pilots employed by the CIA, "mercenaries" hired by AID, and the increased American bombing of targets in Laos. Cranston also addressed a gratuitous insult to the American fighting men when he said: "I submit that to the Vietnamese girl who is raped, it makes little difference whether Americans or South Vietnamese assault her." The senator's greatest fear seemed to be that the "Nixon administration still seeks victory in Vietnam" (*Congressional Record,* April 14, 1970).

After the conquest of the strategic Laotian plain and the arrival of additional convoys in Cambodia, the Communists began improving their sanctuary areas. These sanctuaries extended in a wide arc running from the southern part of Laos through the eastern provinces of Cambodia. They included some thirteen military bases in Cambodia alone. These support areas formed the backbone of the Communist supply system for their war effort in South Vietnam. It has been estimated that in early 1970 a monthly average of 4,000 tons of war equipment and supplies arrived in these bases from North Vietnam.

[11] Hearings Before the Subcommittee on United States Security Agreements and Commitments Abroad of the Committee on Foreign Relations, United States Senate, "United States Security Agreements and Commitments Abroad: Kingdom of Laos," 1970, p. 419.

This total was increased by the addition of another 3,000 tons which passed through the port of Sihanoukville.

The Cambodian sanctuaries had formed an integral part of the Communist war effort since 1964, when they were allowed to establish minor supply transshipment areas with the approval of Norodom Sihanouk, the mercurial Cambodian leader. Sihanouk's rationale for granting the establishment of these bases on Cambodian soil was probably based on his concluding that Hanoi was going to win the war in Vietnam. The Cambodian prince has long been a barometer of military successes and failures in the Indochinese battles. It is worthy of note that at some point in 1967 he was known to have expressed his unhappiness with the Communist presence on Cambodian soil.

The extensive series of North Vietnamese bases in Cambodia had been the subject of an earlier investigation by a subcommittee of the House Armed Services Committee. In the summer of 1968 members of the subcommittee had traveled to Vietnam and conducted a personal investigation of the existence of Communist strongholds in Cambodia. After a series of explorations, the House members concluded that, indeed, the North Vietnamese and Vietcong were using the eastern provinces of Cambodia as troop-concentration areas, training centers, and supply headquarters. The advisory body also observed that "following the battles at Loc Ninh and Dak To in 1967" the enemy had retreated to privileged sanctuaries in Cambodia. In its August 1968 report, the subcommittee recommended that "certainly the commander of United States Forces in Vietnam should be given the discretionary authority to direct hot pursuit when the military situation demands it."[12]

The continuing buildup of Communist forces inside Cambodia alarmed Sihanouk greatly. In the spring of 1970 the prince's fears caused him to travel to Paris, Moscow, and Peking, where he hoped to obtain assistance in reducing the size of the Communist forces in his country. During Sihanouk's absence, Cambodians began demonstrating against the presence of Hanoi's forces in the eastern provinces. The protest marches began in the Parrot's Beak area, which is about thirty-three miles from Saigon, and spread to Phnom Penh, the nation's capital. Sihanouk, who had landed in Moscow on March 13, 1970, announced that he was going to return to Cambodia. At the same time, the caretaker government ordered Hanoi's troops to leave the eastern provinces immediately. The following day Lon Nol, the prime minister, appealed to all the nations of the world for military

---

[12] Report of the Special Subcommittee on National Defense Posture of the Committee on Armed Services, United States House of Representatives, "Review of the Vietnam Conflict and its Impact on U.S. Military Commitments Abroad," 1968, p. 17.

and political assistance in removing the Vietnamese Communists from his country.

By this time Cambodia was in the throes of a national reaction to anything Vietnamese. The situation was so volatile that Sihanouk delayed his return to Phnom Penh. The prince's decision may have been due to information he had received of the turmoil then in progress in Cambodia. On March 18 the political activity culminated in the ouster of Sihonouk as head of state. On that day, acting under the constitution, both houses of the Cambodian legislature unanimously deposed their national leader. The new government was appointed immediately and consisted of Cheng Heng as head of state, Lon Nol as prime minister, and Sirik Matak as deputy prime minister. With the exception of changing Cheng Heng's title from acting head of state to head of state, the new appointees merely retained the positions to which they had previously been appointed to by the absentee prince. On the day that he was removed as Cambodia's leader, Sihanouk flew to Peking, which became the headquarters of his government-in-exile.

Upon Sihanouk's removal, Lon Nol called in the Vietcong and Hanoi ambassadors in Phnom Penh and suggested that their military forces leave his country. He also ordered the closing of the Port of Sihanoukville to the entry of Communist military supplies.

The Hanoi leadership appears to have been just as surprised as were other governments at the overthrow of the Cambodian prince. Their initial reaction was of a defensive nature, and they took what measures they could to protect their bases in Cambodia. After considering various courses of action, the North Vietnamese politburo ordered a two-pronged attack on Cambodia and Vietnam. The Vietnamese part of the assault, however, was meant to serve as a feint, which would occupy the United States/Saigon forces in their own defense. At the same time, the men from Hanoi would move out of their Cambodian sanctuaries and launch a general offensive against the forces of the Lon Nol government.

On March 29, 1970, North Vietnamese troops began moving westward in the direction of Phnom Penh from their sanctuary bases. A few hours later the Communists shelled the major cities of Vietnam and launched fierce ground attacks against Cambodian strong points. Within a matter of days the stronger Hanoi forces had pushed Lon Nol's soldiers out of the Parrot's Beak area, which was abandoned to North Vietnamese control on April 10.

Five days later the American part of General Giap's spring offensive unfolded across the United States. Demonstrations against the war and war-related taxes were held in cities, on college campuses, and in front of Internal Revenue Service offices. In the majority of cases the protests were peaceful, but in an alarming number of rallies, violence-prone radicals seized control of the proceedings. College students again seemed to form the backbone of the protest groups. The use of manipulable persons seems to be axiomatic to revolutionary practice. It appears to be easy for the Communists and other political leaders to whip up desire for change among young people who have not been long exposed to the abstract social and economic ideas abroad in the world—particularly when their rebellion is organized by professional revolutionaries, encouraged by radicalized faculty, and supported by ambitious politicians. Additional reinforcement of the revolutionary attitudes of these young people is also increased when craven university and college administrators bow to the student demands.

The most serious riots occurred at Harvard University, where demonstrators threw rocks, bottles, and bricks at the police. Columbia University also came in for its share of damage when rampaging students broke windows and spattered paint on campus buildings. The dictatorial implications of these events did not escape the attention of Gardiner Ackley, former chairman of the Council of Economic Advisers under Presidents Kennedy and Johnson. Ackley, who had returned to the University of Michigan as a professor of economics, wrote about the activities on his campus that day. In a long discourse published in the *Detroit News* on April 15, 1970, he described a meeting of his department in response to student demands that all classes "in our building be shut down, or else." According to the former presidential adviser:

> We discussed this while the entrances to the building were sealed, and while the halls outside the room in which we were meeting were patrolled by men carrying pipes and clubs.
>
> We sought guidance from the college and were told: "Do what you think best; you will have no protection." And so we cravenly capitulated, in fear—if not of our own safety—for that of our students and our employees.
>
> That day, the truth lay in those clubs. [*Congressional Record,* April 20, 1970]

One of the larger peace rallies was held in New York City's Bryant Park, where 25,000 demonstrators gathered. The first speaker of the day was William Kunstler, the defense lawyer for the Black Panthers. In his speech the radical attorney blistered John Lindsay, mayor of New York City, for not speaking in defense of the Panther movement. He ended his address with a call for unity among antiwar groups. Earlier in that day, at a demonstration outside the Internal Revenue Service office in the city, Pete Seeger had issued a call for radical action, and said: "Most of us are tired of words, words, words."

The tax protests proved to be fairly successful, and demonstrations were held at a number of Internal Revenue Service offices across the nation. The rallies focused "on the relationship of the war in Vietnam to the economic crisis facing the nation." The antitax gatherings were supported by twenty-five senators and congressmen. They were:

> Congressman Jonathan Bingham (D., N.Y.)
> Congressman George Brown (D., Calif.)
> Senator Frank Church (D., Idaho)
> Congressman John Conyers (D., Mich.)
> Congressman Don Edwards (D., Calif.)
> Congressman Donald A. Fraser (D., Minn.)
> Senator Charles Goodell (R., N.Y.)
> Senator Fred Harris (D., Okla.)
> Senator Mark Hatfield (R., Ore.)
> Senator Harold Hughes (D., Iowa)
> Congressman Andrew Jacobs (D., Ind.)
> Congressman Edward Koch (D., N.Y.)
> Congressman Allard K. Lowenstein (D., N.Y.)
> Senator Eugene McCarthy (D., Minn.)
> Congressman Richard McCarthy (D., N.Y.)
> Senator George McGovern (D., S.Dak.)
> Congressman Abner Mikva (D., Ill.)
> Senator Walter Mondale (D., Minn.)
> Congressman Richard Ottinger (D., N.Y.)
> Congressman Donald Riegle (R., Mich.)
> Congressman Benjamin Rosenthal (D., N.Y.)
> Congressman William Ryan (D., N.Y.)
> Congressman Louis Stokes (D., Ohio)
> Congressman John Tunney (D., Calif.)
> Congressman Charles Vanik (D., Ohio)
> [*Congressional Record,* April 16, 1970]

While the protests at the tax offices had met with some support on a national scale, the April 15 moratorium did not seem to generate as much enthusiasm as had previous organized dissent.*

The Communist assault in Vietnam sparked an energetic response by units of the South Vietnamese army. Since some of the NVA/VC units had conducted their attacks from Cambodian sanctuar-

* On April 20 the Vietnam moratorium committee announced it was disbanding. The moratorium leaders stated that their reasons for dismantling the committee was their disappointment with the "poor turnout" for the April 10 rallies and the feeling the public was "tired of protests."

ies, Saigon units crossed over the border with the permission of the Lon Nol government and destroyed a North Vietnamese base camp.

The increasing tempo of the war led Senator Stephen M. Young (D., Ohio) to deliver a speech in the Senate against corruption in South Vietnam and the repression of the Thieu-Ky regime. In his diatribe the Ohio Democrat conducted an historical review of earlier events. According to the senator, there should have been an election held in all of Vietnam in 1956. It was his opinion that had such an election been held, Ho Chi Minh would have vanquished any competition. For authority, Senator Young quoted a much-abused passage issued in 1963 by former President Dwight D. Eisenhower. The senator said:

> This election was called off by President Diem who was installed as President in Saigon by our Central Intelligence Agency. It was evident that Ho Chi Minh had the backing and support of eighty percent of all the people of both South and North Vietnam. President Eisenhower so stated in his memoirs. [*Congressional Record*, April 16, 1970]

What Eisenhower really said and what he meant is better revealed through a more complete quotation. Eisenhower had been discussing the poor electoral appeal of Bao Dai, the ex-Vietnamese emperor, when he added:

> I have never talked or corresponded with a person knowledgeable in Indochinese affairs who did not agree that had elections been held at the time of fighting, possibly eighty percent of the population would have voted for the Communist Ho Chi Minh as their leader rather than Chief of State Bao Dai.[13]

A portion of this quotation taken out of context surely would lead to the senator's conclusion. When the entire statement is presented, however, it is obvious that Eisenhower's comments are only valid when contrasting Ho Chi Minh's voter appeal with that Bao Dai. It has been estimated by knowledgeable wags that Shirley Temple could have won an election over Bao Dai in 1956.

Four days after Senator Young delivered his attack on the South Vietnamese government, President Nixon addressed the nation on television. The Chief Executive's speech was billed as a progress report on Vietnam. According to Nixon, the North Vietnamese had conducted "new offensives" in Laos, Cambodia was the victim of "overt aggression," and the enemy had "stepped up" his attacks in South Vietnam. On the other hand, he said, the training of the South Vietnamese army had "exceeded" expectations, and pacification was making "very significant advances." The President also revealed that ne-

---

[13] Dwight D. Eisenhower, *The White House Years: Mandate for Change, 1953–1956* (Garden City, New York: Doubleday and Company, Inc., 1963), p. 366.

gotiations in Paris showed no real progress. In spite of the increased enemy activity in Southeast Asia, however, he announced the withdrawal of 150,000 additional United States forces from Vietnam over the next twelve months. The removal of these troops would bring the total amount of soldiers withdrawn under the Nixon administration to 265,000, leaving 284,000 American military personnel in Vietnam. The President repeated a previous warning and said that if in his opinion increased enemy action endangered United States military forces, he would "not hesitate to take strong and effective measures to deal with that situation." Nixon again reviewed the main points of what he considered to be a just political settlement. These principles were: first, the settlement would reflect the will of the South Vietnamese people; second, withdrawal of all United States and NVA troops; third, apportionment of political representation as it actually exists; fourth, creation of machinery to fairly establish representative political power; and last, the United States agreed to abide by the outcome of the political process.

A few days after the President's speech, the Citizens Committee for Peace with Freedom in Vietnam released its second report. Members of the committee had conducted a fact-finding mission in Laos, Cambodia, and Vietnam. Based upon their extended investigations, they issued a commentary containing the important statement that disengagement was feasible, "provided the withdrawal of American forces is closely geared to demonstrated and continuing improvement in the capabilities of the South Vietnamese." The advisory group wrote that the Vietcong were so fearful of Vietnamization that Major Tran Do, their chief political commissar, had called it "a shrewd scheme . . . stubborn, cruel, and insidious." In their comments on Cambodia, the commission members discussed the downfall of Norodom Sihanouk and declared:

Cambodia suddenly became a loose ball on the field. One side—Hanoi—has moved quickly to cover a fumble which could have cost it the game.

Hanoi should be in deeper trouble with its troops far in enemy territory at the end of a long supply line, placed between two fires. But it is much more probable that against only a weak and solitary Cambodia, Hanoi can convert this break to strengthen its whole position from the Plain of Jars to the Gulf of Siam, and to put at peril not only Vietnamization but also the safety of American troops.[14]

The next day President Nixon, who had drawn the same conclusion, informed the nation that United States troops had entered Cambodia. He said that the sanctuary raid was not an invasion and added that

[14] "A report to the Citizens Committee for Peace with Freedom in Vietnam," April 29, 1970.

the areas in which the attacks were launched "are completely occupied and controlled by North Vietnamese forces."[15]

The President's actions sent congressional opponents of the war into a fever of excitement. There were accusations of duplicity and dictatorial behavior, and assertions that Cambodia's neutrality had been violated.* How it was possible to violate the neutrality of a nation which was partially occupied by enemy troops, the critics did not bother to explain. Further, charges were made that the Chief Executive had acted against the will of the Cambodian people. These claims were laid to rest on May 5, 1970, when the Lon Nol government issued a statement that expressed "gratitude" to President Nixon for his support of their small country.[16] The attack on the NVA/VC bases in Cambodia was made by a combined United States/ARVN assault force. However, American penetration was limited to twenty-one miles from the Vietnamese border. The President also said that the incursion would be of a "limited" duration.

In response to the Cambodian raid, Senator McGovern issued a clear call for nationwide violence when he said:

> Nor should we feel comfortable in telling our constituents who oppose the war that we are making common cause with them, or in cautioning them to keep the protests peaceful and within the law. [*Congressional Record,* April 30, 1970]

The senator was so upset by the possibility of an American victory in the offing that he falsely claimed that bodies seen floating down the Mekong from Cambodia had been killed "with armament supplied by us" (*Congressional Record,* May 11, 1970).† Clifford P. Hansen (R., Wyo.) challenged McGovern's comments and later disproved the claim that American weapons had been used to murder the Vietnamese. In a speech given in the Senate on May 12, Senator Hansen said that he had explored this matter with the White House and the State Department. He reported:

> It is clear that we have given no aid to Sihanouk since 1965. . . . Thus the bodies could not have been killed with weapons we or our allies gave to Cambodian forces. [*Congressional Record,* May 12, 1970]

[15] "The Cambodia Strike: Defensive Action for Peace, A Report to the Nation by Richard Nixon," April 30, 1970.

[16] *Department of State Bulletin,* June 22, 1970.

* Neutrality is defined by an international authority as "immunity from use by belligerents." It does appear from all the evidence available that Cambodia had not been immune from use by one of the belligerents (North Vietnam) since 1964. The irrationality of the congressional opposition is demonstrated by the simple fact that if their logic had prevailed in 1945, France would still be occupied by Nazi armies.

† On April 27, 1970, *Newsweek* magazine had published an article which described large numbers of Vietnamese bodies floating in the Mekong River near Neak Luong.

David Brinkley, a well-known opponent of the war, reported American activities in Cambodia for the National Broadcasting Company network in a manner that Senator Robert J. Dole (R., Kansas) described as "playing on emotions." In his news analysis concerning U.S. military movements in the sanctuary raid, the NBC reporter said, "There is something infinitely sad about a Sherman tank running over a see-saw." Dole responded to Brinkley's comments by saying:

> There is something infinitely sad, also, about the killing of American soldiers by an enemy who, until now, was allowed to kill with impunity from a protected sanctuary.
>
> And there is something infinitely twisted about Mr. Brinkley's effort to make the American people think that America's leaders and America's soldiers are in the business of fighting little children. [*Congressional Record,* May 7, 1970]

In the nation itself, some of the antiwar activists heard Senator McGovern's call for protests, and riots erupted on several college campuses. The most significant reaction to the senator's call for demonstrations "outside of the law" was exhibited at Kent State University, where four students were killed in a series of violent confrontations with National Guardsmen. While the majority of national gatherings opposed the presidential move in Cambodia, large numbers of Americans supported Nixon's actions as Commander in Chief. One of these groups, the New York City construction workers, led by their president Peter J. Brennan, demonstrated throughout the downtown area of the great metropolis. The workers, who composed the greater part of the construction tradesmen in the New York area, marched around City Hall and called for "love of country and love and respect for our country's flag."

At the end of June President Nixon reported to the American people on the success of the Cambodian raid. In his address he reassured the nation and said that United States ground forces had been completely withdrawn from Cambodia. The Chief Executive then itemized the significant number of enemy stores and personnel that had been destroyed and killed:

> According to the latest estimates from the field, we have captured: 22,892 individual weapons—enough to equip about 74 full-strength North Vietnamese infantry battalions; and 2,509 big crew-served weapons—enough to equip about 25 full-strength North Vietnamese infantry battalions; more than 15 million rounds of ammunition or about what the enemy has fired in South Vietnam during the past year; 14 million pounds of rice, enough to feed all the enemy combat battalions estimated to be in South Vietnam for about 4 months; 143,000 rockets, mortars, and recoilless rifle rounds, used against cities and bases. Based

on recent experience, the number of mortars, large rockets, and recoilless rifle rounds is about equivalent to what the enemy shoots in about 14 months in South Vietnam; over 199,552 antiaircraft rounds, 5,482 mines, 62,022 grenades, and 83,000 pounds of explosives, including 1,002 satchel charges; over 435 vehicles and destroyed over 11,688 bunkers and other military structures. And while our objective has been supplies rather than personnel, the enemy has also taken a heavy manpower loss—11,349 men killed and about 2,328 captured and detained.[17]

In the final section of his speech, the President emphasized that in the future there would be no American ground personnel in Cambodia except for the staff of the embassy in Phnom Penh. He also indicated that the Saigon forces would probably remain in Cambodia in order to halt the reestablishment of enemy strongholds along South Vietnam's border. The list of captured and destroyed enemy material was very extensive and supported the validity of the administration's decision to enter Cambodia. The overwhelming destruction of enemy instruments of war had proven that pundits such as Joseph Kraft, who advised against the sanctuary raid, were reporting their usual biases instead of the news.*

Additional confirmation of the success of the incursion was discovered when Nguyen Van Nang, the deputy commander of the Communist second subregion, which included Saigon, rallied to the government's side. In a deposition taken in early June the senior Communist official said:

> The second region had planned to launch a general offensive in May 1970, but failed to do so because of the overthrown Sihanouk government and the operation of the United States and Vietnamese Armed Forces in Kampuchea [Cambodia].[18]

The South Vietnamese were so impressed with the results of the campaign that their foreign minister, Tran Van Lam, included the topic in a speech delivered before a diplomatic conference in New Zealand. In his address Minister Lam stated that the closing of Sihanoukville had curtailed the supply of offensive weapons to enemy gunners. He added:

> It is not sheer coincidence that Communist attacks by rockets and mortars have been reduced to almost nil after the destruction of the Cambodian sanctuaries (in May the whole of the IV Corps not one single

---

[17] "Cambodia Concluded: Now It's Time to Negotiate, A Report to the Nation by Richard Nixon," June 30, 1970.

[18] *Vietnam Bulletin,* June 14–20, 1970.

* On May 7, 1970, Joseph Kraft, in an article in the *Washington Post* had claimed that the American troops who entered Cambodia ended up "burning a bunch of dusty native villages" (*Congressional Record,* May 7, 1970).

round of 122 mm rocket and only 2 rounds of 107 mm rockets as against [a previous] monthly average of 25 rounds of 122 mm and 100 rounds of 107 mm).[19]

Congressional Activity

The day after the American Chief Executive announced the successful completion of the sanctuary raid, the Senate adopted the long-debated Cooper-Church amendment. The measure, which would limit presidential action in Cambodia, was added to the foreign military sales bill. The debate in the Senate regarding Cooper-Church had lasted 34 days and involved some 288 speeches. The amendment had originally been cosponsored by Senator John Sherman Cooper, (R., Ky.) and Frank Church (D., Idaho). The text of the Cooper-Church amendment, as passed by the Senate, read:

Limitations on United States involvement in Cambodia.
In concert with the declared objectives of the President of the United States to avoid the involvement of the United States in Cambodia after July 1, 1970, and to expedite the withdrawal of American forces from Cambodia, it is hereby provided that unless specifically authorized by law hereafter enacted, no funds authorized or appropriated pursuant to this act or any other law may be expended after July 1, 1970, for the purposes of
(1) Returning United States forces in Cambodia;
(2) Paying the compensation or allowances of, or otherwise supporting, directly or indirectly, any United States personnel in Cambodia who furnish military instruction to Cambodian forces or engage in any combat activity in support of Cambodian forces;
(3) Entering into or carrying out any contract or agreement to provide any contract or agreement to provide military instruction in Cambodia, or to provide persons to engage in any combat activity in support of Cambodian forces; or
(4) Conducting any combat activity in the air above Cambodia in direct support of Cambodian forces. Nothing contained in this section shall be deemed to impugn the constitutional power of the President as Commander in Chief, including the exercise of that constitutional powers which may be necessary to protect the lives of United States armed forces whenever deployed. Nothing contained in this section shall be deemed to impugn the constitutional powers of Congress including the power to declare war and to make rules for the government and regulation of the armed forces of the United States.[20]

[19] Ibid., June 29 to July 5, 1970.
[20] *Congressional Quarterly Almanac*, 1970.

During the long debate, several attempts had been made to dilute the amendment. Administration supporters came closest to defeating an integral part of Cooper-Church on the day of passage. In the course of debate the previous day, Senator Robert P. Griffin (R., Mich.) had offered an amendment to subsection (3) of the amendment, which if adopted would have read:

> (3) entering into or carrying out any contract or agreement to provide military instruction in Cambodia by United States personnel or to provide United States personnel to engage in any combat activity in support of Cambodian forces. [*Congressional Record,* June 29, 1970]

What Griffin's proposal would have done was to allow the United States to pay the salaries of allied forces who desired to assist the Cambodians.*

During the ensuing discussion, the Michigan senator succeeded in gathering considerable support for the passage of his amendment. As a matter of record, on the first ballot the Griffin change to Cooper-Church was approved by a vote of 47–46 (*Congressional Record,* June 30, 1970). After a motion was made to reconsider the balloting, however, a new vote was taken, and this time the Griffin proposal was defeated by 47 nays to 46 yeas. The key change had been made by Senator Stuart Symington (D., Mo.), who reversed his position on the Griffin amendment. Subsequent balloting eroded the voting power of the anti–Cooper-Church forces, and the Griffin revision was defeated. In the final vote approving Cooper-Church, 42 Democrats and 16 Republicans voted in favor of the amendment. They were opposed by 11 Democrats and 26 Republicans.

After Senate passage of the Cooper-Church amendment, the measure was discussed again in the House. Congressman Donald W. Riegle (D., Mich.) informed his fellow representatives on July 9 that he favored instructing House conferees to accept the amendment as passed by the Senate. Riegle based his recommendation on the belief that the amendment was directly in line with President Nixon's "Cambodian policy objectives." Wayne Hays (D., Ohio) disagreed with Riegle's understanding of the President's desires and said that the Michigan congressman's "pipeline to the White House, if he ever had one, is pretty badly plugged up." When the Michigan Democrat's motion came to the floor, it was tabled by a vote of 237 to 153. After the failure of the House to instruct its conferees to accept the Cooper-

---

* It was rather widely known at the time that President Nixon had arranged for Thai military forces to go to the aid of the beleaguered Cambodians. Senate action on the measure caused the President to cancel his plans to send Thai advisers and troops to assist the Cambodians.

Church amendment, the joint conference remained deadlocked over the issue for six months.

The foreign military sales bill also included another limiting clause which repealed the 1964 Gulf of Tonkin Resolution. The story of the removal of this measure from the books is a little unusual, since it was actually revoked twice. For some time Senator Fulbright had been developing a resolution in his Foreign Relations Committee to repeal the Gulf of Tonkin legislation. On May 15, 1970, the committee had reported the Fulbright measure, which was known as S. Con. Res. 64.

The following month Senator Dole, apparently operating with the administration's approval, offered an amendment to the foreign military sales bill that would accomplish the repeal of the Gulf of Tonkin Resolution (*Congressional Record,* June 22, 1970). This unexpected move to eliminate one of the major war props of the previous Johnson administration surprised Senator Fulbright greatly. In fact, the Arkansas Democrat was so enraged by Senator Dole's actions that he urged the proposal be tabled. The Senate failed to support the motion to table and, two days later, voted in favor of repealing the Gulf of Tonkin Resolution. Senator Fulbright was still not satisfied with the appropriateness of the Dole amendment and on July 10, the Senate also passed S. Con. Res. 64.

On July 2 President Nixon announced the appointment of David K. E. Bruce as the American representative to the Paris peace talks. The retired diplomat's previous assignment had been as ambassador to Great Britain. He was viewed as a "giant" by his friends, who were probably referring to his analytical ability.* Nixon made the announcement of the new appointment at a one hour "conversation" with three news commentators. The television personalities were John Chancellor of the National Broadcasting Company, Eric Sevareid of the Columbia Broadcasting System, and Howard K. Smith of the American Broadcasting Company. In the course of the discussion the Chief Executive was asked, in view of the rescinding of the Gulf of Tonkin Resolution, "What legal justification do you have for continuing to fight a war that is undeclared in Vietnam?" Nixon responded:

Well, first, Mr. Smith, as you know, this war, while it was undeclared, was here when I became President of the United States. I do not say that critically; I'm simply stating the fact that there were 549,000 Americans in Vietnam under attack when I became President. The President of the United States has the constitutional right—not only the right but the

* Hanoi responded to the appointment of David Bruce by returning Xuan Thuy to the negotiations in Paris.

responsibility—to use his powers to protect American forces when they are engaged in military actions.[21]

Later in the month, further vindication of the President's decision to destroy the NVA/VC arms sanctuaries in Cambodia was received from that country. In an interview conducted in Phnom Penh, Siri Matak, Cambodia's deputy premier, declared that "if the United States had not intervened we would be in a very desperate position now." He continued: "Events have not been well understood in America," and added, "When President Nixon decided to intervene, opinion in the United States thought it was aggression." The deputy premier observed that it was unfortunate the matter was so little understood in America, and said, "The true aggression was by the North Vietnamese and Vietcong." Matak declared his gratefulness for United States assistance and acknowledged that the friendly troops from South Vietnam, with his approval, were "staying with us for a while."[22]

Near the end of August, student protestors committed an act of violence from which the antiwar movement never fully recovered. In the early morning hours of August 24, 1970, a bomb ripped through the Army Mathematics Center on the University of Wisconsin campus. The physical destruction was severe enough, but the explosion had killed a graduate student and injured four others. The dead man was Robert Fassnacht, thirty-three years old, a research assistant in physics who had been working late in the laboratory. A native of South Bend, Indiana, Fassnacht was married and the father of three small children. The ironic part of the tragic event was that according to Fassnacht's father, the young physics scholar had been opposed to the war and was in sympathy with "many of the discontents" on the campus. The bombing revolted most Americans who read of the tragedy, and some of the glamour surrounding the militants began to fade.* On February 16, 1972, Canadian authorities arrested Karleton L. Armstrong for the bombing. Armstrong was extradited and later convicted for his heinous crime.

A second major thrust against administration policies in Indochina was made by Senators George McGovern (D., S. Dak.) and Mark O. Hatfield (R., Ore.). In May the two senators had introduced an amendment to the defense-procurement bill that became known as McGovern-Hatfield, or the end-the-war amendment. The measure as sub-

---

[21] New York Times, July 2, 1970.

[22] New York Daily News, July 23, 1970.

* Even Senator McGovern became convinced that the violence may have become counterproductive and in a letter to congressional summer interns, the South Dakota Democrat cautioned them against "the folly of undisciplined radicalism" (Congressional Record, September 1, 1970).

mitted called for the establishment of a date beyond which funds would not be provided to support American troops in Indochina. Originally the withdrawal date had been set at December 31, 1970. But as congressional debate on the proposal continued through the summer, the date was extended by an additional year. The last formal discussions on the 1970 version of McGovern-Hatfield were held in the Senate on September 1, 1970. During the debate Senator Stephen M. Young (D., Ohio) urged that the measure be passed. In support of his position the senator said, "Of course, Mr. President, historically there has been no such thing as a North and a South Vietnam" (*Congressional Record*, September 1, 1970). Unfortunately, no one responded to Young's claim regarding the lack of historical precedent for the existence of a North and a South Vietnam.*

As the verbal contest continued, Senator Hatfield accused those who opposed his amendment as being guilty of "idolatry," in favor of "one-man rule," and opposed to the "wisdom of the constitutional process which is designed to guide this country" (*Congressional Record*, September 1, 1970). After several more emotional pleas to end the war, Senator Mansfield called for the yeas and nays on the measure. The final vote was 55 to 39, and McGovern-Hatfield was defeated (*Congressional Record,* September 1, 1970). In spite of the defeat of the end-the-war proposal, the defense procurement bill as passed by the Congress contained serious restrictions on the Commander in Chief's ability to maneuver in the war in Indochina. Under the terms of the legislation, Congress placed a financial restraint on United States aid to South Vietnamese and other free world units in Laos and Thailand:

> (a) (1) not to exceed $2,800,000,000 of the funds authorized for appropriation for the use of the Armed Forces of the United States under this or any other Act are authorized to be made available for their stated purposes to support (A) Vietnamese and other free world forces in support of Vietnamese forces, (B) local forces in Laos and Thailand. . . . Nothing in clause (a) of the first sentence of this paragraph shall be construed as authorizing the use of any such funds to support Vietnamese or other free world forces in actions designed to provide military support and assistance to the government of Cambodia or Laos.[23]

Congressional infighting continued throughout the fall, with the restrictive Cooper-Church amendment to the foreign military sales

[23] The defense-procurement bill was signed by the President on October 7, 1970, when it became Public Law 91-441.

* Historians familiar with Vietnamese events have often cited the division of the country throughout most of the seventeenth-century between the Nguyen and Trinh princes. The dividing line was marked by two high walls across the Vietnamese plain of Quang Tri near its narrow waist at Dong-Hoi.

bill remaining locked in committee. The impasse was broken when administration representatives agreed to the incorporation of a watered-down version of Cooper-Church in a foreign aid measure. The final version of Cooper-Church as embodied in the Special Foreign Assistance Act was signed by the President on January 5, 1971, and read:

> Sec. 7(a). In line with the expressed intention of the President of the United States, none of the funds authorized or appropriated pursuant to this or any other Act may be used to finance the introduction of United States ground combat troops into Cambodia, or to provide United States advisers to or for Cambodian military forces in Cambodia.[24]

And so in the final days of the 91st Congress, Cambodia was added to the zone where the American national leader was forbidden to use all the forces at his disposal in combating a tough and ruthless enemy. By congressional action, the area of operations which remained available for President Nixon to maneuver in had grown smaller and smaller. As for the other side, the space in which the NVA/VC forces could operate in relative safety had increased considerably. In declaring these combat zones off limits to American ground action, the legislators prolonged the war and in the end increased United States casualties. It should never be forgotten that the main supply routes for the war in Vietnam ran through Laos and Cambodia. And along these trails flowed the materials that were instrumental in the killing of more than 56,000 American troops and the wounding of an additional 300,000 United States fighting men.

[24] Public Law 91-652, January 5, 1971.

IV / Stalemate

On March 31, 1971, Congressman John E. Hunt (R., N.J.) addressed the House:

> Mr. Speaker, I feel it is again timely to draw attention to the so-called humanists who detest the killing in Vietnam so vehemently that their conduct may well be recorded in history as being responsible for prolonging the killing, and denounced as the reason we did not win the war. [*Congressional Record,* March 31, 1971]

Congressman Hunt's words proved to be prophetic. There is a considerable body of evidence that the constant attacks on the President's war policies by congressional liberals convinced the Hanoi leadership that the country was hopelessly divided. This conclusion only served to encourage the North Vietnamese and their Vietcong agents to continue the killing and prolong the war.

The Laos Raid

After the American withdrawal from Cambodia, the NVA/VC forces renewed their assault on the small Buddhist nation. The true nature of the Vietnamese attack on Cambodia was revealed by Lon Nol, who said, "This is a war of resistance against foreign invasion. Where the aggressors are not present, our nation is quiet and peaceful, and our administration functions smoothly."[1] Corroboration for the prime minister's estimate of the size of the native Cambodian Communist movement was received by a House committee in mid-

[1] *Far Eastern Economic Review,* September 5, 1970.

1974. In a statement before the House group Max Friedman of the National Student Coordinating Committee, who was in Cambodia in the fall of 1970, said:

> There was no real indigenous Communist movement in Cambodia. The refugees that I interviewed said that when the Communists came in they were North Vietnamese regular soldiers with Viet Cong guides. There were no individual Cambodians who were cooperating with the Viet Cong; they had to get the prisoners out of jail to act as interpreters and guards.[2]

In fact, he was convinced the Vietnamese were enemies of everything Cambodian. "The Communists have not come in as liberators, but as executioners and are perpetrating a policy of cultural genocide against the Cambodian people." In Friedman's judgment, the fierce animosity exhibited by the Vietnamese Communists against things Cambodian was due to the ancient enmity between the two peoples. This racial hatred was also greatly increased by an excess of Marxist zeal.

Near the middle of January 1971, the ferocity of the NVA/VC attack in Cambodia led Lon Nol to seek assistance in Saigon. When he arrived in the South Vietnamese capital, the prime minister and his twenty-two-man delegation met with President Thieu and other Saigon officials for the greater part of two days. Their meetings took on a particular significance because they coincided with an important government campaign then underway in Cambodia. A combined ARVN/CA (Cambodian army) assault had just been unleashed against North Vietnamese forces blocking strategic Route 4, the only remaining link between Phnom Penh and the Gulf of Thailand. By the end of the Cambodian leaders' visit to Saigon, the allied force succeeded in securing nine-tenths of the 120-mile route to the sea.

During the late winter of 1971, a South Vietnamese assault force struck into Laos.[3] This attack proved to be one of the most controversial events of the Vietnam War. The major point of disagreement was not whether the raid was necessary, but whether it had succeeded. On one side, the United States and Saigon governments claimed victory for the assaulting forces; and on the other side, the Communists, the media, and the antiwar forces maintained the assault had failed. From the data available it appears that there is considerable validity to the arguments of both points of view. If the attack had been undertaken to disrupt the North Vietnamese supply line along the Ho Chi

---

[2] Hearings Before the House Committee on Foreign Affairs, "Fiscal 1975 Foreign Assistance Request," 1974.

[3] Lao Patriotic Front, *Nixon's "Intensified Special War" in Laos: a Criminal War Doomed to Fail.* Lao liberated areas, July 1972.

Minh Trail, to destroy enemy equipment, and generally to set enemy planners off balance, it was a success. On the other hand, if the raid had been launched to prove that ARVN had grown to full adulthood, it did not fulfill its expectations.

The incursion began sometime near the beginning of February 1971. The actual dates of the early moves in the attack are somewhat obscured by an early news blackout. It appears, however, that on or about January 30, 1971, approximately 20,000 ARVN troops supported by 9,000 United States soldiers moved into northwestern South Vietnam. The assault force established a base of operations at Khesanh and pushed to the border of Laos.

On February 7, (Saigon time) and February 8 (Washington time), President Nguyen Van Thieu announced to his countrymen that he had ordered "the armed forces of the Republic of Vietnam to attack the Communist North Vietnamese bases on the Laotian territory along the Vietnam-Lao border." The president named the raid "Operation Lam Son 719." He stated that it was limited in time and space, with the clear objective of disrupting the enemy supply and infiltration network along the Ho Chi Minh Trail. The South Vietnamese leader added that his nation had no territorial designs on Laotian property. He also pledged that when the operation ended, South Vietnamese forces would be completely withdrawn from Laotian terrritory.

The initial ARVN assault element was composed of 5,000 men, who moved into Laos by various routes. The objective of the task force appears to have been the city of Tchepone, a major Communist supply center situated about twenty miles from the Vietnamese border. American units did not accompany their Vietnamese allies into Laos, since the 1969 Cooper-Mansfield-Church amendment forbade their doing so. Signs had been posted along the Laos-Vietnam border that read: WARNING, NO U.S. PERSONNEL BEYOND THIS POINT. The entire operation suffered undue hardship because of the congressional prohibitions. Owing to the language barrier between the American and South Vietnamese forces, ARVN troopers advancing into Laos were unable to adjust properly the supporting United States ground and air weapons. A great loss of life ensued.

On February 15, 1971, the South Vietnamese commander of the task force, Lieutenant General Hoang Xuan Lam, reported that his units had cut the Ho Chi Minh Trail. Following the general's announcement additional ARVN troops moved into Laos, swelling their numbers there to about 12,000.

In response to the South Vietnamese attack, NVA commanders gathered a strong force and moved against the ARVN troops on February 17–18. The fighting was severe and losses on both sides were great. On March 6, however, the South Vietnamese gained what appears to have been their objective—the city of Tchepone. By this time ARVN strength in Laos totaled about 20,000 men.

The South Vietnamese did not hold the city long, since North Vietnamese counterattacks grew almost irresistible. On March 12 Saigon's soldiers began to withdraw from Laos. Washington described the withdrawal as "mobile maneuvering," but news analysts said it was a full-scale retreat. By March 24 the greater part of the invasion force had fought its way back across the border with Communist troops in hot pursuit.

Upon the completion of Operation Lam Son 719, President Thieu announced that ARVN had won a total victory and that the raid had disrupted Communist attacks on South Vietnam for the balance of 1971. The Saigon command claimed that as a result of the incursion 1,160 government troops had been killed, 4,271 wounded, and 240 missing. The Associated Press stated that reliable sources with access to the real casualty figures had reported 3,800 men killed, 5,200 wounded, and 775 missing.

The news coverage of the raid, in the opinion of American and South Vietnamese government officials, had been less than fair. President Nixon, citing General Creighton W. Abrams, United States Commander in South Vietnam, said, "Of the twenty-two ARVN battalions, eighteen fought extremely well." Naturally, the Chief Executive added, the media concentrated their attention on the failures of the remaining four battalions. Saigon journalists were so disgusted with the American newsmen's coverage of the operation, as well as of the entire war, that one of them wrote:

> The Indochina conflict could have been terminated years ago had it not been for public opinion at home and abroad, supported by a largely negative and often hostile American press, exemplified by such dailies as the *New York Times* and weekly magazines like *Newsweek.* . . . if Hanoi ever gets around to issuing its version of the Pulitzer prize, *Newsweek* correspondents are sure to receive theirs.[4]

A final South Vietnamese tally of enemy losses due to Lam Son 719 included 9,043 killed, as well as 1,123 crew-served and 3,745 individual weapons captured. The report also stated that 110 tanks, 270 Moltava trucks, 13,630 tons of munitions, 15 tons of 122 mm rocket ammunition, and 7,010 meters of pipeline had been destroyed.

Admittedly it is true that South Vietnamese military units withdrew from Laos several weeks before they planned to do so. In evaluating the entire operation, however, one can see that the Saigon forces showed considerable progress. For just about the first time since

[4] *Vietnam Bulletin,* March 15, 1971.

1965, ARVN troops had attacked Hanoi's army on non-South Vietnamese territory. The very fact that they were not afraid to engage North Vietnamese regulars without their American advisers was a sure sign of maturation. There is no doubt that ARVN soldiers had stood toe to toe with the men from Hanoi and slugged it out. And finally, after reaching their main target, the South Vietnamese were still able to withdraw from the assault area in reasonably decent order. Certainly, during World War II the British/Canadian commanders at Dieppe would have been happy to say the same.

In the midst of the Laotian raid President Nixon delivered a nationwide foreign policy address. In his February 25, 1971 speech the Chief Executive described his program in Vietnam. According to Nixon, the United States had moved a long way toward "getting out" of the war since he had taken office. The President illustrated his point by citing the reduction in American personnel in Vietnam from a high of 550,000 in 1969 to a then-current total of 260,000. He attributed the ability to withdraw large numbers of combat troops from Vietnam to the success of the Cambodian operation in 1970. Midway through the broadcast Nixon reiterated his stand on the Paris negotiations:

> On October 7 we made a proposal that could open the door to that kind of peace; we proposed:
> - An immediate standstill cease-fire throughout Indochina to stop the fighting;
> - An Indochina peace conference;
> - The withdrawal of all outside forces;
> - A political settlement fair to both sides;
> - The immediate release of all prisoners of war.[5]

The following month, at a presidential news conference, the Chief Executive was questioned about the withdrawal of North Vietnamese and United States military forces from all of Indochina. The President answered that the removal of all outside troops from the Southeast Asian battlefields would be more than satisfactory to the American side. Nixon also said that he expected guerrilla warfare to continue in Laos and Cambodia, but expressed his willingness "to see whether or not they can handle their own affairs."[6]

The Democrats Vote to Withdraw

On March 24 the Democratic party's policy council voted unanimously to cut off all funds for United States military operations in Indochina and stated:

[5] *United States Foreign Policy, 1971: A Report of the Secretary of State*, 1972, p. 422.
[6] *Public Papers of the Presidents: Richard Nixon, 1971*, p. 391.

There should be a firm unequivocal declaration by the government that all American forces will be withdrawn by the end of this year. The Congress should share responsibility for this decision. An announcement for complete withdrawal this year should be used to negotiate the safe withdrawal of our troops and the speedy release of our men who are prisoners of war. [*Congressional Record,* April 23, 1971]

The council also opposed "any expansion of the war by American or South Vietnamese forces in Cambodia, Laos, or North Vietnam." The meeting was chaired by Senator Hubert H. Humphrey (D., Minn.), who voted for the funds cutoff. The Minnesota Democrat's support of the council's statement is surprising in view of his previous comments on the war, which included the statements:

We will not be defeated, we will not grow tired, we will not withdraw, either openly or under the cloak of a meaningless agreement. . . . He (North Vietnam) should know, too, that our objectives have not changed —and I will repeat them once more. The halting of aggression from the north; the opportunity for the people of South Vietnam to decide their own future; and the pursuit of a better life for the ordinary people in that part of the world. [*Congressional Record,* October 14, 1966]

A week later, by a vote of 138–62, House Democrats approved a resolution that called for the United States to terminate its involvement in Indochina by the end of the 92nd Congress (the beginning of 1973). The action represented a compromise between the moderate and radical elements among the Democrats. A stronger antiwar resolution had previously been drafted by Congressman Spark Matsunaga (Hawaii) and was supported by Bella Abzug (N.Y.), Ronald V. Dellums (Calif.), Sam Gibbons (Fla.), and Andrew Jacobs (Ind.). The Matsunaga proposal, which called for the withdrawal of all United States forces from Indochina by December 31, 1971, was narrowly defeated by a vote of 101–100. The more militant members of the caucus referred to the compromise resolution as a "victory for Nixon" and vowed to continue to exert pressure on the administration to end the war.

The President's response to the action of the opposition party was given by press secretary Ronald L. Ziegler, who commented that the measure "seems to be directed toward support of the President and his Vietnam policy." A more realistic appraisal was suggested by Congressman Gibbons, who accepted the fact that the antiwar forces had not gotten everything they wanted: "But you've got to consider where we came from. A month ago, we didn't stand a chance of getting any antiwar resolution through caucus."[7]

---

[7] *New York Times,* April 1, 1971.

After the publication of the Democratic policy statements on the war in Indochina, a supposedly unbiased national organization issued a report on the same topic. In its April 1971 newsletter, Common Cause urged:

> Congress must reassert its role. It must legislate an end to the war. It must enact into legislation the desire of the American people for a complete military withdrawal from Indochina and it must fix a date by which that process must be completed. Only this step can end American involvement in the war, free our prisoners, and permit the Vietnamese to determine their own future. [*Congressional Record*, April 23, 1971]

The close similarity between the Common Cause position on the war and the statement issued by the Democratic policy council prompted the Republican National Committee to conduct an investigation of the supposedly independent agency. As a result of this research, the Republican organization published two articles in *Monday*, their weekly newsletter.

In the press releases the Republicans clearly demonstrated that the nonpartisan position that the so-called neutral organization professed was a mere façade. Their conclusions were based on the public statements, activities, and political connections of John Gardner, the chairman of Common Cause, his staff, and the agency's policy council.

In its analysis of the chairman, the article stressed Gardner's strong opposition to the Nixon presidency and his accusations regarding the "widening" of the war in Indochina. He was also quoted as having accused the President of playing "Russian roulette," and a "deadly game" with the war.

As for the staff of the agency, the Republicans particularly directed their attention to Harold Willens, special adviser to Gardner. Willens was described as a Democrat and cofounder of the radical Business Executives Move for Vietnam Peace. *Monday* even quoted the *Washington Post* as reporting that Willens had blamed "American militarism" for the war in Vietnam. The Republican paper also revealed that the members of the policy council of Common Cause were overwhelmingly identified with liberal Democratic causes. It identified Georgia state representative Julian Bond; Texas state senator Joseph Bernal; Gary, Indiana mayor Richard Hatcher; Henry Santiestivan, husband of the editor of *ADA World*, a publication of the Americans for Democratic Action; Cleveland mayor Carl Stokes; and United Auto Workers president Leonard Woodcock as being Democratic members of the policy council.

As for issues themselves, a *Monday* reporter asked Thomas Matthews, special assistant to Chairman Gardner, to elaborate on the differences between ADA and Common Cause on important public matters. During the initial part of the interview Matthews hedged on his answers; however, when the newsman pressed the issue, Gardner's assistant exploded. After "yelling incoherently" for a while, Matthews calmed down and explained that when it came to questions regarding "our partisanship," he developed a "slight case of paranoia."

The Republican newspaper also incorporated other data that further damaged the claims of Common Cause to be politically unaligned. This information included the fact that the supposedly impartial agency had released its membership list to the Democratic National Committee for fundraising purposes.

In summation *Monday* commented that Common Cause and its leadership were entitled to campaign for, and to support, liberal Democratic causes. But the public organization did *not* have the right to claim to be an independent agency when in fact it adopted partisan positions on national issues.

Draft Extension

The main vehicle for congressional action against the war in 1971 was the draft-extension bill. The military conscription law was scheduled to end on June 30, 1971. This authority was allowed to expire and was not renewed until September 28, when the President signed a new extension of the draft. The major resistance to the passage of the compulsory service measure developed in the Senate, where the infighting was extremely vicious.

The House began its deliberations on the draft-extension bill on March 30. During the debate that followed, several propositions were offered that would have severely crippled or eliminated obligatory military service entirely. The author of one of these damaging revisions was Bella Abzug (D., N.Y.). On March 31 the congresswoman offered the following amendment:

That effective January 1, 1972 the Military Selective Service Act of 1967 is repealed and the President shall take such action as may be necessary before such date to insure an orderly winding up of the affairs of the Selective Service System. [*Congressional Record,* March 31, 1971]

If passed, Abzug's addition to the draft law would have extended conscription for six months and then dismantled the entire system. In opposition to her amendment Congressman F. Edward Hébert (D., La.) called the congresswoman's attention to the fact that without the draft there would be no manpower to defend the United States. The New York Democrat responded to Hébert's challenge by claiming that all mankind would welcome the day when international disputes would be settled through peaceful means "under the jurisdiction of a universal public authority." The congresswoman later clarified her meaning when she recommended "complete disarmament under a public international authority such as the United Nations." Hébert answered this idealistic daydream by saying:

I thank you for your observation, and may I say that I, too, share your desire for utopia and for everybody being in love with everybody else, and I hope for the elimination of evil from the world. But, unfortunately, we do not live in that atmosphere now, and we never will. [*Congressional Record,* March 31, 1971]

Following this lively exchage of opinions, the chairman called the issue to a vote. The amendment was rejected as Representative Abzug was unable to obtain the twenty supporters necessary to require recorded balloting.

Later in the day Harvard Law School graduate Michael J. Harrington (D., Mass.) offered an amendment that would have ended military conscription on June 30, 1971. His move to kill the draft bill was supported by Robert F. Drinan, S.J., a fellow Massachusetts Democrat. In his remarks the Jesuit politician stated:

I think it should be a matter of record [that] our churches are against this draft, just as our churches were in favor of continuing exemptions for seminarians. The Roman Catholic Church bishops, 200 of them, stated in very firm and unprecedented affirmation that they are against the draft we have today. [*Congressional Record,* March 31, 1971]

Drinan's comment implied that all the Catholic bishops opposed the compulsory service law, and one of the congressmen decided to confirm its validity. After investigating Drinan's statement regarding the bishops, Representative John Schmitz (R., Calif.) reported to the House as follows:

I have just made a phone call to the U.S. Catholic Conference to check on whether the Catholic bishops have ever come out unanimously against this bill which we are dealing with. Mr. William Ryan, of the Office of Information, tells me that they never made a stand on this bill we are dealing with. [*Congressional Record,* March 31, 1971]

The Harrington amendment was overwhelmingly defeated, and the next day the House passed the draft-extension bill 293–99 with 38 abstentions. On April 5 the legislation was referred to the Senate Committee on Armed Services, and the following month the full Senate began its deliberations on the measure.

Two days after the House had approved the compulsory service bill, President Nixon addressed the nation on television and radio. In his speech the President announced: "Between May 1 and December 1 of this year, 100,000 more American troops will be brought home from South Vietnam." He reported that the Cambodian and Laotian operations had been successful and urged Hanoi to enter into serious negotiations to end the war.

While the draft bill was being considered by the Armed Services Committee, another Senate group opened its hearings on other war-related measures. On April 20 the Senate Foreign Relations Committee began its deliberations on "Legislative Proposals Relating to the War in Southeast Asia."

The first witness was Senator George McGovern (D., S. Dak.), who appeared before the Committee as cosponsor of S. 376, the Vietnam Disengagement Act of 1971. The proposed legislation was merely an updated version of the old McGovern-Hatfield amendment, which had been presented in the Senate on January 27, 1971, and at that time was sponsored by the following senators:

George McGovern	(D., S.Dak.)	Jacob K. Javits	(R., N.Y.)
Mark O. Hatfield	(R., Ore.)	Edward M. Kennedy	(D., Mass.)
Alan Cranston	(D., Calif.)	Walter Mondale	(D., Minn.)
Harold E. Hughes	(D., Iowa)	John E. Moss	(D., Calif.)
Birch Bayh	(D., Ind.)	Gaylord Nelson	(D., Wis.)
Thomas F. Eagleton	(D., Mo.)	William Proxmire	(D., Wis.)
Mike Gravel	(D., Alaska)	Abraham A. Ribicoff	(D., Conn.)
Philip A. Hart	(D., Mich.)	John Tunney	(D., Calif.)
Vance Hartke	(D., Ind.)	Harrison Williams	(D., N.J.)
Daniel K. Inouye	(D., Hawaii)		

The disengagement proposal read:

Sec. 620(a). In accordance with public statements of policy by the President, no funds authorized to be appropriated under this or any other Act may be obligated or expended to maintain a troop level of more than two hundred and eighty-four thousand armed forces of the United States in Vietnam after May 1, 1971.

(b) After May 1, 1971, funds authorized or appropriated under this or any other Act may be expended in connection with activities of American armed forces in and over Vietnam only to accomplish the following objectives:

(1) to bring about the orderly termination of military operations there and the safe and systematic withdrawal of remaining American armed forces by December 31, 1971;

(2) to insure the release of prisoners of war;

(3) to arrange asylum or other means to assure the safety of South Vietnamese who might be physically endangered by withdrawal of American forces; and

(4) to provide assistance to the Republic of Vietnam consistent with the foregoing objectives. [*Congressional Record*, January 27, 1971]

As the inquiry continued, it presented the same old tired litany of support for the antiwar proposition that previous hearings had gained for other peace measures. By this time the procedure of the Committee hearings had become so familiar that it was even possible to predict their format as well as the outcome.

Knowledgeable observers of previous sessions of the Fulbright Foreign Relations Committee knew that certain procedures would be followed to present an aura of unbiased inquiry. These preparations included the selection of what appeared to be a number of so-called experts on the topic under discussion. When questioned, however, these "experts" usually revealed that they tended to support the chairman's previously expressed beliefs. An attempt was occasionally made to balance the presentations by the addition of a small number of professionals with opposing views. Unfortunately, these witnesses often turned into straw men whom the chairman badgered mercilessly when they expressed opinions that differed from his.

After the hearings had opened, one of the first witnesses was Senator McGovern. The senator spoke in defense of his bill and directed the attention of the Committee to how little trouble the French had with the Vietnamese in securing the release of their soldiers at the end of the Franco-Vietminh War. In his explanation, McGovern responded to a leading question asked by Chairman Fulbright in the following exchange:

> THE CHAIRMAN: There was no problem about the prisoners of war as soon as the agreement had been reached at Geneva; was there?
>
> SENATOR MCGOVERN: There was no problem. There were no French soldiers shot while they were trying to withdraw, there were no prisoners held permanently by the enemy once the decision was made to disengage.[8]

Both the chairman and Senator McGovern would have been well advised to have discussed the prisoner-of-war issue with the French. Article 21 of the 1954 Geneva agreement between France and the Vietnamese Communists reads in part:

> All prisoners of war and civilian internees of Vietnam, French, and other nationalities, captured since the beginning of hostilities in Vietnam during military operations or in other circumstances of war and in any part of the territory of Vietnam, shall be liberated within a period of thirty (30) days after the date when the cease-fire becomes effective in each theatre.[9]

[8] Hearings Before the Senate Committee on Foreign Relations, "Legislative Proposals Relating to the War in Southeast Asia," 1971.

[9] American Foreign Policy: 1950–1955, Documents. Vol. II, pp. 750–785.

This agreement was signed on July 20 and 21, 1954. Eight years later Radio Hanoi announced:

After a long period of negotiations between the DRV (Democratic Republic of Vietnam) Government and the Government of the Republic of France on the repatriation of French soldiers who had surrendered, on 25 October the representation of the Republic of France sent a message to the DRV Ministry of Foreign Affairs stating that it had been authorized to work out a plan for transporting, commencing November 1962, French soldiers who had surrendered and who had applied for repatriation. [*Congressional Record*, June 10, 1971]*

Additional support for establishing a date for withdrawal of United States troops from Vietnam was received from Professors Richard A. Falk, Princeton University, and John W. Lewis of Standord University. Former Senator Joseph Clark, president of the United World Federalists, also testified against the war as did a number of newsmen and students.

At one point in the hearings, the chairman allowed H. R. Rainwater, commander in chief of the Veterans of Foreign Wars of the United States, to appear before the Committee. The veterans' representative attempted to present the views of his organization. The chairman questioned Rainwater's right to speak for Vietnam veterans, since they formed such a small part of the VFW. He also attacked the commander's knowledge of Vietnamese affairs and attempted to correct his view of the Paris peace talks.

On the other hand, John Kerry of the Vietnam Veterans Against the War (VVAW) received the chairman's warm sympathy and "congratulations." Meanwhile former Navy Lieutenant John O'Neill, who disagreed with Kerry's position, was not allowed to appear before the Committee.

Two weeks after President Nixon's April 7 speech, Democratic presidential hopefuls gathered to criticize his major propositions. The condemnation was served up on prime television time by the American Broadcasting Company. The candidates were Senators Edmund S. Muskie (Maine), Hubert Humphrey (Minn.), George McGovern (S. Dak.), Birch Bayh (Ind.), Harold E. Hughes (Iowa), and Henry M. Jackson (Wash.).

* Apparently, someone forgot to tell Charles Lucet, French ambassador to the United States in 1972, that Radio Hanoi had admitted holding French prisoners of war in North Vietnam as late as 1962. This oversight is revealed by an exchange of correspondence between Lucet and Congressman Robert L. Leggett (D., Calif.). In 1972 Leggett wrote to Ambassador Lucet and inquired about the fate of the French POWs at the end of the Franco-Vietminh War. Lucet responded, we have "concluded that the last French prisoners were returned less than three months after the conclusion of the Geneva Agreements" (*Congressional Record*, June 30, 1972).

The half-hour program was opened and closed by Democratic National Chairman Lawrence F. O'Brien. With the exception of Jackson, all of the candidates were in accord that the President should set a date for the total withdrawal of American forces from Vietnam. The date they seemed to agree on was December 1, 1971, as called for in the McGovern-Hatfield resolution then being considered in the Senate.

Senator McGovern stated that Hanoi's terms for the resumption of negotiations included the setting of a withdrawal date and urged the Chief Executive to conform to this demand. Minnesota Democrat Humphrey discussed the possible repercussions of the abandonment of South Vietnam and said, "This is no time for recriminations. There will be risks in withdrawing. But there are greater risks in staying."*

The sixth senator, Henry M. Jackson, stated that he believed the President should not set a date for withdrawal. He based his support for administration policy on the fact that if Nixon gave a departure date, "we would be weakening the bargaining leverage we should be exerting on the governments of North and South Vietnam."

On the same day the Democratic rebuttal to the President's speech was broadcast, Senator Robert J. Dole (R., Kansas) offered an appropriate comment regarding the increasing calls for disengagement. In a speech before the Senate the Kansas Republican said:

> I am, Mr. President, somewhat amazed at the continued criticism of President Nixon's policies by the Democratic doves. Their silence during the sixties, when a Democratic President was shipping hundreds of thousands of young American men into combat, is testimony to the pure politics of their current dissent. [*Congressional Record,* April 22, 1971]

Following Dole's comments, Senator McGovern offered the "Thoughts of Chou En-lai" as guidance for his fellow senators when they were considering Asian problems. The ideas of the Chinese foreign minister were presented in the form of a discussion Edgar Snow had recently held with Chou in China.† The conversations were published in the March 21, 1971 issue of *The New Republic*. McGovern felt, however, that a wider number of Americans should have the opportunity to learn about "China's views," and he believed that pub-

---

* In his statement Senator Humphrey had also indicated that he had developed a change of mind about Vietnam. His about-face on the Vietnamese situation is perhaps more clearly revealed when his 1971 statement is contrasted with his warning in the Senate during 1955 that "if free Vietnam falls, or if the Communist elements take over, then, Mr. President, every country in the corridor of Southeast Asia will be in more difficulty, and we shall not be able to stop it" (*Congressional Record,* May 11, 1955).

† Edgar Snow is best known for his pro-Chinese Communist opinions as expressed in *Red Star Over China,* published in 1938.

lishing them in the *Congressional Record* would accomplish this purpose.

In the course of the interview, Chou had informed journalist Snow that American protection of Taiwan was the "crux of Sino-American difference which led to the Indochina War." He indicated that as a result of American encroachment in the Far East "China has now extended an umbrella of protection . . . to the . . . three Indochinese peoples against the United States." The foreign minister's solution for an end to the Vietnam War was for America to "recognize Taiwan as an inalienable part of the People's Republic of China" and to withdraw its "forces from Taiwan and the Taiwan Straits" (*Congressional Record,* May 22, 1971).

On June 4, 1971, the Vietnam Disengagement Act appeared in the Senate as Amendment Number 143 to the military conscription bill. The provision was worded slightly differently, but it still retained the basic features of the old McGovern-Hatfield legislation that had been defeated in 1970. Under the new version of the antiwar measure, funding for United States forces in Indochina was to be withdrawn on December 1971, with a sixty-day extension allowed.

During the debate on the amendment, Senator Dole (R., Kansas) criticized the bill as confusing and possessing a "pronounced tendency to change." In his attack on the measure, Dole referred to it as "as an amendment not to end the war, but an amendment to lose the peace." He was particularly disturbed by the fact that the champions of the new edition of McGovern-Hatfield had chosen to add the prisoner-of-war issue to their emotional appeals. According to the Kansas political leader, the advocates of Amendment Number 143 were attempting to persuade the general public that the only way the United States would be able to obtain the return of the POWs would be to set a date for withdrawal from Indochina. The fact that the admonitions of the supporters of the measure coincided with Hanoi's demands was ignored by its champions. Dole chastised the defenders of the proposal and said it was his belief that setting the date for withdrawal would destroy any chance for the prisoners to be released. In fact, he stated, it was this very "open-ended feature of our withdrawal timetable" that was expected to provide the impetus for the Communists to free the POWs (*Congressional Record,* June 10, 1971).

On June 16 the Senate defeated the McGovern-Hatfield amendment. Before the measure went down to defeat, however, Senator Margaret Chase Smith directed her attention to President Nixon's inheritance in Vietnam. According to the Maine Republican, the Chief Executive had acquired from previous administrations an "escalating, growing" war with a "built-in, no-win policy." She said that when the President had assumed the direction of the war, the American army had "one hand tied behind its back." Mrs. Smith added that these limitations on the United States armed forces included the granting of "enemy sanctuaries" and "an air war that precluded offensive operations against meaningful and lucrative enemy targets." The senator also mentioned the policy of using draftees to fight the war instead of calling up the reserves to do the job for which they were trained. She ended her listing of Democratic bequests by commenting that last, but not least, there was "the disenchanted press, which had already become more sympathetic to the enemy than our own national interest" (*Congressional Record,* June 16, 1971).

When Senator Smith finished her attack on the supporters of the McGovern-Hatfield amendment, John V. Tunney (D., Calif.) rose in defense of the measure. During his speech he introduced all the stale, tired arguments that liberals usually use when supporting a controversial issue. He claimed that the passage of McGovern-Hatfield would bring about the elimination of "poverty, hunger, and joblessness." Tunney maintained that the United States cannot continue to defoliate the jungles in Vietnam while we destroy our environment at home. He raised the issue of the burning of villages in Southeast Asia, which was turning our cities into "cauldrons of fear." And last of all, in his opinion, if the United States withdrew from Vietnam, Americans would somehow realize "equality" at home. Later in the day, when the Senate was polled on the McGovern-Hatfield amendment, the measure was defeated by a vote of 55–42 (*Congressional Record,* June 16, 1971).

Following the defeat of the controversial legislation, the Senate resumed its consideration of the selective service bill. As a result of an extended debate, the Senate adopted a rigorous end-the-war amendment that had been proposed by Senator Mike Mansfield (D., Mont.). The Mansfield amendment, as approved by the Senate on June 22, 1971, declared it was the policy of the United States that all American troops were to be withdrawn from Vietnam within nine months after the approval of the extension of the draft. The Montana Democrat's proposal was submitted to conference on June 24, where it remained for more than a month. During several heated discussions, the conferees softened the withdrawal requirement from "nine months from passage" to the "earliest practicable date."

The House accepted the conference report, but the Senate delayed its approval of the watered-down Mansfield provision. Finally, on September 21, Congress cleared the measure for the President's approval. A week later the military conscription bill was signed into law by President Nixon. The limiting clause of the Mansfield amendment in its final form read:

> *Title IV: Termination of Hostilities in Indochina*
> Declares it to be the sense of Congress that the United States terminate at the earliest practicable date all military operations of the United States in Indochina, and provide for the prompt and orderly withdrawal of all United States military forces at a date certain subject to the release of all American prisoners of war held by the Government of North Vietnam and forces allied with such Government and an accounting for all Americans missing in action who have been held by or known to such Government or such forces.[10]

The Marchers Again

On April 24, 1971, 200,000 people assembled in Washington, D.C. for a day of protest against the war in Vietnam. The preparations for this gathering, which took many months, are woven in with the history of the revolutionary movement in the United States.

At an undetermined point in June 1970, New Mobe had been torn apart by a struggle over the tactical direction the antiwar movement should assume. On the one hand the Trotskyites, who controlled the Socialist Workers Party (SWP), believed that the peace forces should maintain an undivided dedication to the single issue of the war. Their reasoning was based on the assumption that because the antiwar movement was composed of so many varied groups, only by concentrating on one focal point could any genuine unity of action be maintained. On the other hand, the policy of the CPUSA was directed to a multipurpose assault against the United States government. In the opinion of the Moscow-directed Communists, it was only by fusing the issue of Vietnam with that of political repression, racism, and poverty that a meaningful attack against the fabric of American society could be conducted. There was also the strong probability that the war would at some time come to an end, which of course, would be a disaster to a single-issue organization.

It appears that the tactical struggle had been developing for some time. The behind-the-doors conflict, however, did not surface until the middle of 1970. On June 19–21 of that year the Trotskyites called a conference in Cleveland under the auspices of the Cleveland Area Peace Action Council. At its meetings the council established the National Peace Action Coalition (NPAC) for the express purpose of

[10] Public Law 92–129, September 28, 1971.

86

directing the efforts of the American revolutionary movement into antiwar activities. The NPAC was under the firm control of the Socialist Workers Party.

A week later the CPUSA convened the Strategy Action Conference in Milwaukee (June 26–28, 1970). The Milwaukee gathering was by far the larger of the two conferences. There were more than 800 delegates at the Wisconsin meeting, representing such diverse organizations as CPUSA, the Southern Christian Leadership Conference (SCLC), National Welfare Rights Organization (NWRO), and the Black Panther Party. The official letterhead announcing the meeting contained the names of Charles R. Garry, CPUSA; Ron Dellums, Berkeley City Councilman; Ralph Abernathy, SCLC; David Hilliard, Black Panther Party; George Wiley, NWRO; Dr. Benjamin Spock, New Mobe honorary cochairman; and Trudi Young, Women Strike for Peace and New Mobe coordinator.

The Milwaukee delegates considered two approaches to disrupting the United States. One proposal was made by Professor Douglas Dowd of Cornell University, who had concluded that the success of the Cambodian raid would lead the administration to use nuclear weapons. This conclusion led him to say, "The only way you can bring the antiwar movement back to life is not by just repeating mass marches, but by creating chaos and upheaval." His program advocating violence was strongly supported by Cora Weiss of the New York Women Strike for Peace, who issued a call for "chaos."

The conference also considered a suggestion made by Arthur Waskow of the Institute for Policy Studies in Washington. Waskow proposed that a series of marches would begin at various locations, such as Kent State University, which carried symbolic value to the antiwar movement. According to Waskow, once the demonstrators had gathered in their symbolic sites, they would march toward Washington. On their way to the capital, the marchers would hold rallies related to local issues, and eventually all groups would end up in Washington for a period of mass civil disobedience.

Neither the Dowd nor the Waskow proposals were adopted; instead, conference spokesman William Douthard indicated the direction the conferees had taken when he said, "The treatment of the Vietnam War as a single issue has ended." He then described the close ties that had been developed during the assembly "between the antiwar movement, black organizations, and Mexican-American protest groups."

Delegates who agreed with the multi-issue program met after the Milwaukee conference in regional action gatherings. The most important of these unit meetings in 1970 were held in Chicago on July 20,

Philadelphia on August 28–30, and Wheeling, Illinois, from August 28–30. The Wheeling meeting was attended by representatives of CPUSA, Black Panther Party, Young Workers Liberation League, Women's International League for Peace and Freedom, Women Strike for Peace, American Friends Service Committee, and the National Committee for a Sane Nuclear Policy (SANE).

After the regional meetings, New Mobe leaders held a second Milwaukee gathering from September 11–13, 1970. At the conference eighty delegates formed the National Coalition Against War, Racism, and Repression (NCAWRR). At one of the sessions, Sidney Peck, a former member of the Wisconsin State Committee of the CPUSA, called for the holding of a massive protest in Washington, D. C., during May 1971. This time, however, instead of a peaceful assembly, he recommended massive civil disobedience and direct action in order to shut down the operations of the government. On the last day of the conference, the delegates also endorsed a national boycott of Standard Oil products. As a result of their meetings, NCAWRR issued a policy statement, which among other things, stated the need to unite to conduct a combined struggle against war, racism, poverty, repression, and the oppression of women.

A month later coalition coordinator Douthard announced that a rally in opposition to America's violent and racist acts against mankind would be held on November 21, 1970, in front of the United Nations. He stated that Mme Nguyen Thi Binh, foreign minister of the Provisional Revolutionary Government of South Vietnam, would be invited to address the gathering.

At the UN rally NCAWRR leader Rennie Davis addressed the 2,000 protestors. Davis threatened that if the government did not halt the war in Vietnam by May 1, 1971, "we are going to stop the Government." One of the methods he suggested to disrupt life in the city of Washington was to have cars conveniently "break down" in strategic locations on May 4.

After demonstrating at the UN, many NCAWRR stalwarts traveled to Stockholm to attend a World Conference on Vietnam, Laos, and Cambodia, which met from November 28–30, 1970. There the delegates adopted a program that endorsed the multi-issue concept of the NCAWRR and also ordered that from

May 1–16 the U.S. movement will mobilize massive nationwide action to end the war against Indochina during the first two weeks of May, one year after Nixon's invasion of Cambodia.

Following the Stockholm conference, NCAWRR held a meeting in Chicago, January 8–10, 1971. In a series of informal sessions the 365 delegates selected three primary areas of concentration for the coming year. The first event to receive their support was the string of nationwide demonstrations April 2–4 in honor of the memory of Martin Luther King. The second activity was the sponsorship of the "Joint Treaty of Peace Between the People of the United States, South Vietnam and North Vietnam." This so-called treaty had been signed in 1970 by a group of American students from the National Student Association (NSA) and representatives of the Vietnam Workers Party in Hanoi. The neutrality of the document is shown by its first formal paragraph, which reads: "The Americans agree to immediate and total withdrawal from Vietnam and publicly to set the date by which all American forces will be removed."[11] As their last major action the delegates endorsed the May 1971 protests in Washington. After the conference had adjourned, the NCAWRR had changed its name to Peoples Coalition for Peace and Justice (PCPJ).

While the CPUSA-dominated militants were organizing their movement, the Trotskyites had also been active. After a series of meetings in the latter part of 1970, the NPAC held a national convention from December 4–6 in Chicago. During the conference, the young Socialists set April 24, 1971 as the date for mass antiwar demonstrations in Washington and San Francisco. As this date did not agree with the day chosen by PCPJ for their demonstrations, Sidney Lens, the CPUSA coordinator between the two groups, tried to get the NPAC to change its mind as to the time of the protests. The Trotskyites were adamant, however, and held firm to the April 24 date.

The disagreement between the antiwar organizations continued into March with a great deal of vituperation on both sides. The inability of the two peace movements to agree on a common date for their activities alarmed the North Vietnamese greatly. Their fears caused Xuan Thuy, North Vietnam's ambassador to the Paris negotiations, to send the warring factions an urgent message on February 27, 1971. The Hanoi ambassador said: "Facing the serious situation now presented, I call upon the progressive American people and all antiwar organizations in the United States to unite closely."

Following Xuan Thuy's appeal, the leaders of the PCPJ called a news conference on March 2, 1971 in the Rayburn House Office building in Washington. Most of the major American antiwar organizations were represented at the press gathering. These groups and their representatives were: PCPJ—Dave Dellinger, Carol Evans, and Sidney Peck; NWRO—George Wiley; NSA—David Ifshin; Vietnam Veterans Against the War—Al Hubbard, and Cynthia Frederics of the

---

[11] Hearings Before the Senate Committee on Foreign Relations, "Legislative Proposals Relating to the War in Southeast Asia," 1971.

Committee of Concerned Asian Scholars. After the reporters arrived, the PCPJ leaders announced that they had arrived at an agreement with the NPAC on the date for a mass mobilization in Washington, and that day was April 24.

During the last two weeks of April and the first week of May, the nation's capital was the scene of various rallies against the war. In the week of April 19–23 an organization known as Vietnam Veterans Against the War appeared in the city and conducted a series of demonstrations against the continuation of the fighting in Vietnam. On April 24 the NPAC and PCPJ held a giant "March Against the War" followed by a rock concert. In the following ten days the PCPJ sponsored activities designed to "close down the government."

The tenor for the protests was set when the demonstrators received a message from Mme Binh. In her April 19 letter the Communist leader wrote:

DEAR AMERICAN FRIENDS,

I wish to extend my warmest greetings to all American friends of all social positions, political tendencies, and religious beliefs participating in the spring offensive. . . .

Mme Binh's instructions for her American associates were contained in the body of the message, where she demanded

. . . that Mr. Nixon set a reasonable date for the total withdrawal of American troops so we may have a cease-fire between the Liberation armed forces and the U.S. forces, and to discuss the question of ensuring safety for the withdrawing troops and the question of releasing military men captured in the Vietnam war.[12]

On April 18 members of the VVAW began arriving in Washington, D.C. Their announced purpose was to conduct a "limited incursion into the District of Columbia." By the next day the ranks of the veterans numbered a little over 900 men. Their spokesman was John F. Kerry, a former Navy lieutenant in Vietnam. The ex-servicemen conducted a march to the capitol and held a rally where they demanded "immediate unconditional and unilateral withdrawal of American forces from Vietnam." For the next few days the veterans visited their states' congressmen and conducted mock "search and destroy missions." Their most effective demonstration occurred on April 22, 1971, when 700 former members of the armed forces discarded medals in a protest gathering at the capitol. The veterans struck camp on the following day, with a few of them remaining in Washington to join the protest march scheduled for April 24. At their

[12] Ibid., p. 219.

rallies the former servicemen had heard speeches by Senators George S. McGovern (D., S.Dak.), Walter F. Mondale (D., Minn.), Philip Hart (D., Mich.), Edward M. Kennedy (D., Mass.), and Representatives Bella Abzug (D., N.Y.) and Charles A. Vanik (D., Ohio).

Three days after the VVAW had officially departed from Washington, Richard Wilson, editorial writer for the *Evening Star,* gave his evaluation of the entire affair. In Wilson's opinion, opponents of the war had succeeded in gaining the ear of the public. He believed that these detractors were making the most of the appearance in Washington of hundreds of crippled and wounded veterans of the war. The editorialist commented that he did not think the President was going to be swayed by the demonstrators and added:

> Nothing that the veterans did here brought the end of the war one hour closer, but their encampment did serve as a political backdrop for various Democratic presidential candidates who are trying to make the way out of the war as hard as possible for Nixon on the pretext that his commitments can't be relied upon. [*Congressional Record,* April 27, 1971]

On April 24 the NPAC–PCPJ–sponsored parade began its "March Against The War" down Pennsylvania Avenue in Washington, D.C. The lead group carried an American and a Vietcong flag. Among the contingents present were representatives of the Abraham Lincoln Brigade, one of the American Communist units that had fought in the Spanish Civil War. There was also a delegation from the Gay Liberation Front.

The demonstrators marched to the Capitol, where a five-hour rally was held. Among the various speakers who addressed the mass meeting were: Coretta Scott King (widow of Martin Luther King); George Wiley, NWRO; Ralph Abernathy of the SCLC; Dave Dellinger, PCPJ; Joseph Duffy of the Americans for Democratic Action; and journalist I. F. Stone.

The Congress was represented by Senator Vance Hartke (D., Ind.) who urged immediate withdrawal from Vietnam, and Herman Badillo (D., N.Y.), who said, "Friends, you've come to the right place, because I don't have much hope that President Nixon will take much action." Other congressional leaders who addressed the crowd were Abner Mikva (D., Ill.), John Conyers (D., Mich.), and Bella Abzug (D., N.Y.).

The rally received maximal news coverage from television stations WTOP, WMAL, WTTZ, and WETA. Entertainment was provided by singers Peter, Paul, and Mary. Pete Seeger and Country Joe McDonald led the demonstrators in their favorite antiwar songs. After the last speaker had made his presentation, the crowd moved in the direction of the Ellipse, where the demonstrators engaged in group discussions. In the evening PCPJ sponsored an all-night rock concert at the Sylvan Theater. By the next morning most of the protestors had left Washington; those who remained appeared to be hard-core militants who intended to "bring Washington to its knees."

The week of April 26–30, 1971 had been chosen by the PCPJ to convince government workers in the capital of the justness of the demonstrators' cause. The radicals had hoped to meet the government employees in their offices and discuss PCPJ demands for an end to the war, a guaranteed annual income of $6,500 for a family of four, and the release of all "political prisoners" then in jail. Unfortunately for the demonstrators, Federal officials decided against this procedure. Instead, the protestors were only allowed to meet with small groups of Federal employees.

By the end of the week-long "people's lobbying," the militants had not been very successful in convincing government workers that they should absent themselves from their jobs. Their irritation at this lack of success soon resulted in a new tactic, and the demonstrators attempted to block the entrance to government buildings so that employees could not enter their offices. Capitol police responded to these actions by arresting 300 PCPJ members who blocked the entrance to the Justice Department building on April 30.

As the "People's Lobby" ended, Washington girded itself for the second of May, when the extremists had promised "to close down the government." These threats had been made by a radical faction of PCPJ known as the Mayday Tribe. The militant Tribe members had chosen the American Indian as their symbol and were prepared to execute a major maneuver in Washington designed to halt traffic. The action is described in their manual, which read:

> Thousands of us with bamboo flutes, tambourines, flowers, and balloons [will be] moving out in the early light of the morning to paralyze the traffic arteries of the American military repression government nerve center.[13]

In answer to the threat posed by the radicals, government officials began moving military units into the city. By the afternoon of May 1, 1971, more than 50,000 protestors had gathered in Washington. The growing size of the crowd made Federal officials apprehensive about the possibility of violence. Their fears led them to take the offensive. On the morning of May 2 metropolitan police ordered some 30,000 demonstrators to vacate their encampment on the Potomac River. The unannounced raid surprised the protestors, who for the most part

---

[13] *New York Times,* May 3, 1971.

abandoned their canvas tents and moved to the campuses of Washington's universities.

The following day the militants moved out of their hiding places and attempted to tie up traffic in Washington at selected bridges and certain traffic circles. In answer to their disruptive actions, the police began arresting the protestors. By the end of the day more than 7,000 demonstrators had been arrested. Many of the activists had been detained in the Washington Redskins football practice field near the Robert F. Kennedy Memorial Stadium. Most of the demonstrators were freed when Federal judges ruled that they were being held in jail under "cruel and unusual" conditions. The three weeks of protest ended on May 6 when a march against the South Vietnamese Embassy drew only about sixty participants.

On June 13, 1971, the *New York Times* began publishing a series of classified documents relating to previous United States policy in Vietnam. The papers had been turned over to the newspaper by Daniel Ellsberg, a former government employee who opposed the war. These articles, documents, and position papers are known collectively as the Pentagon Papers.

The United States government tried to halt the publication of these confidential papers, but after several unsuccessful court battles was forced to admit defeat. The Pentagon Papers have since proven to be fertile ground for critics of the war.

The real value of these collected documents is best revealed in the letter of transmittal that accompanied the volumes, written by Leslie H. Gelb, director of the study task force. In Director Gelb's words: "Of course, we all had our prejudices and axes to grind, and these show through clearly at times."[14] It is worth noting that the classified study did not include any presidential papers and only a limited number of State Department publications.

President Nixon refused any direct public comment on the substance of the documents. He did, however, mention the fact that the activities described in the Pentagon Papers had primarily taken place during the Kennedy and Johnson administrations, and he could not vouch for their authenticity.* Nevertheless, to the President the publication of the official papers in the media revealed a close tie between

[14] *The Pentagon Papers: The Defense Department History of United States Decision-making on Vietnam* (Boston: Beacon Press, 1971).

* In July 1975, Nixon was questioned by United States government attorneys regarding his civil suit to regain possession of his presidential papers. In response to a question regarding his actions on the Pentagon Papers, the President said that members of the White House staff "were against my decision to litigate on the Pentagon papers matter, because it was no skin off our back ... all this reflects on the previous administration." *New York Times*, August 24, 1975.

disaffected members of the former Democratic administration and the Eastern liberal press.

Near the end of June 1971, a subcommittee of the House Committee on Foreign Affairs met in Washington. The House unit was conducting a series of hearings regarding "Legislation on the Indochina War." During their sessions, several members of Congress offered testimony regarding America's involvement in the Indochina War. Among these congressmen was John G. Dow (D., N.Y.). Representative Dow had formerly been a member of the International Peace Advisory Committee of the Episcopal Church. The congressman's opposition to the war was of long duration and relatively well known. Before he began his formal statement, the New York Democrat alluded to the increased usage of narcotics by American servicemen, the corruption of military officials in the PX stores, and the fact that officers received more medals in Vietnam than enlisted men. Warming up to his subject, he said:

> History will never charge those Vietnamese who came from the north into South Vietnam in the early sixties—many of them were born in the south—with committing aggression, while at the same time saying our American forces coming 10,000 miles from home were not aggressors.[15]

It is interesting to contrast Dow's observations on the source of the current "aggression" in Vietnam with the facts as they are known. In 1968 Nguyen Van Tiem, a member of the Central Committee of the NLF, was interviewed in Paris regarding Vietcong practices in the post-Franco-Vietminh war period. According to Tiem, upon the signing of the Geneva accords, large numbers of revolutionaries returned to their homes in South Vietnam with orders to resume what appeared to be a normal existence. At the same time thousands of southern Communist organizers were transported to North Vietnam, where they were placed in military training centers. In the late 1950s the trainees were sent back to their homes below the DMZ. They did not, however, return to till the land, but to join with their former Vietminh associates in the conquest of South Vietnam.

During the interview, the Communist leader discussed the methods the cadre used to foment revolution in the countryside. According to Tiem, when the former villagers returned to their homes, they did not talk about overthrowing the government. Instead, their contacts were used to stir up discontent among the people. The individual peasant's confidence was gained by talking about issues he could understand,

---

[15] Hearings Before the Subcommittee on Asian and Pacific Affairs of the Committee on Foreign Affairs, House of Representatives, "Legislation on the Indochina War," 1971.

such as land or livestock. At this point Tiem claimed: "You can do anything at all with them."[16]

When it came time for action, the peasants were encouraged to rid themselves of their village elders. In the process the government forces were obliged to resist, and the people would look to the Communist cadre for assistance. The revolutionary leader would then encourage armed revolt, and simple peasant dissatisfaction turned into deadly open warfare. It is worth noting that these events took place before American soldiers were committed to the defense of the Southern Republic.

President Nixon's July 15, 1971 announcement that he had accepted an invitation to visit the People's Republic of China the following year astounded a great many Americans. The surprise was probably greatest among the political conservatives who had supported Nixon through his many trials and tribulations. Their astonishment soon turned to chagrin, which then became a deep feeling of defeat and revulsion.

The bewilderment that the conservatives felt was based primarily upon the reversal of what had appeared to be the President's solid anti-Communist credentials. This record had been developed over a long period of time from Nixon's public statements and actions against the Communist movement throughout his entire career. The most galling part of the entire episode was that the President had won his first real acclaim as a member of the prosecution team that imprisoned Alger Hiss.

The conservatives need not have been surprised, had they merely read the revised doctoral dissertation of Henry Kissinger, the President's major foreign affairs adviser. Dr. Kissinger's scholarly magnum opus is entitled *A World Restored,* and it deals exclusively with the Congress of Vienna. Throughout this entire work the author's pragmatic approach to foreign affairs shines through. There is no question that Kissinger admired the work of the diplomats who had gathered in Vienna in 1815. While the handiwork of these statesmen was indeed admirable, their restoration of the balance of power in Europe was accomplished with little, if any, consideration for the wishes of the pawns. This formula, of course, has had a long and honorable tradition in European diplomatic circles. But it is not held in very high esteem among some Americans who approach their politics with a sense of ethics. For after all, what room is there in the practice of balance of power for principles, for morals, or even virtue? Though the Metternichs of the nineteenth century may have had no

---

[16] Interview with Nguyen Van Tiem by G. Chali in *Partisans,* January–February 1968.

problem in adapting to their former enemies, in this Age of Ideology accommodation often means the death of allies.

A month after Nixon's startling announcement, Secretary of State William P. Rogers announced that the United States had adopted a new policy regarding Chinese Communist representation in the United Nations. On August 2, 1971, the secretary stated that America would support action to seat the People's Republic of China in the Security Council of the international organization. At the same time, Rogers said, the State Department would do everything in its power to maintain representation in the UN for the government of the Republic of China.[17] Unfortunately for the Taiwan government, in spite of the "best efforts" of the United States, the Republic of China was excluded from the world organization, and on November 15 Communist China took its seat in the UN. The cold-blooded treatment and alienation of Nationalist China was one of the first results of the Kissinger policy of international pragmatism. In time, the tree of "practicalism in foreign affairs" would produce more bitter fruit for America.

Throughout the summer South Vietnamese political groupings had prepared for the presidential elections originally scheduled for October 17. At one point, both General Duong Van Minh (Big Minh) and Vice President Nguyen Cao Ky had declared their willingness to oppose Thieu for the nation's top office. Prior to the actual balloting on October 3, however, the two Vietnamese leaders claimed that the elections were rigged and withdrew their candidacy. There were rumors at the time that American foreign policy planners had attempted to bribe the South Vietnamese vice president to remain in the race. According to the reports, the United States officials believed it was desirable to have more than one candidate in what was supposed to be a democratic election.*

On October 31, 1971, President Thieu presented his second inaugural address and promised to:

- Protect the Fatherland
- Respect the Constitution
- Serve the interests of the Nation and the people
- Do his utmost to fulfill his responsibilities as the President of the Republic of Vietnam

[17] *United States Foreign Policy, 1971: A Report of the Secretary of State,* 1972, p. 63.
* Ky has recently confirmed the offer of monetary support, when he stated that in the fall of 1971 Ambassador Bunker "offered money" if he would "run against Thieu." *New York Times,* January 11, 1976, VI, p. 35.

While the words of the Saigon leader were primarily directed to the need for vigilance in the face of North Vietnamese threats, there was considerable attention given to domestic matters. The increased interest in internal affairs was based on an earlier decision by the South Vietnamese government to improve the economy as much as possible. Indeed, in the agricultural area alone, South Vietnam had made considerable progress during the year. This improvement was noted by Cao Van Than, Minister of Land Reform and Agriculture, in a report to the Agricultural Committee of the South Vietnamese Senate. Than told the committee members that as of July 15 the ministry had distributed 350,000 hectares of rice land to tenant farmers.* He added that from July to the end of the year the government anticipated distributing 400,000 additional hectares to the landless farmers.

While the South Vietnamese were participating in national elections, North Vietnam's most important front group prepared to hold its third meeting. In December the Vietnam Fatherland Front (Mat Tran To Quoc Vietnam) met in Hanoi. The front was established in 1955 as the successor grouping to the old Vietminh and Lien Viet organizations. Its honorary president had been Ho Chi Minh, who was succeeded by the aging Ton Duc Thang. The main goals of the front were to gain active support for the government, to encourage nationwide elections in which all Vietnamese citizens would participate, and to propagandize among the people. The front also ran a brotherhood movement between North and South Vietnam and maintained good relations with Communist organizations in Laos and Cambodia.[18]

During the third congress, the Fatherland Front sent greetings to the American friends of the Vietcong, which read:

> Our people endeavor to strengthen solidarity with the progressive people in the United States who are struggling to demand that the U.S. government stop its war of aggression in Vietnam and other parts of Indochina, and develop the friendly ties between the two peoples in the struggle against the common enemy—the state monopoly capitalists in the United States represented by Nixon and his clique.[19]

After four days of seemingly endless meetings, the Congress adjourned. Shortly after their final session, North Vietnam was rocked

---

* A hectare is equal to 2.47 acres of cultivated rice land.

[18] *Viet-Nam Fatherland Front and the Struggle for National Unity* (Hanoi: Foreign Languages Publishing House, 1956), pp. 16–23.

[19] *Third Congress of the Viet Nam Fatherland Front: Documents* (Hanoi: Foreign Languages Publishing House, 1972), p. 123.

by one of the most serious aerial assaults since the November 1968 bombing halt. Allied authorities said that the raids, which lasted for four days (December 26–30), were in retaliation for the "shelling of cities in South Vietnam" and as punishment for Hanoi's huge build-up of military supplies in Cambodia and Laos.

Other Congressional Limitations

Congress enacted additional legislation in 1971 that served to limit the courses of action available to the Commander in Chief in conducting a war against a ruthless enemy. Next to the draft extension, the most serious threat to Nixon's freedom of movement in the theater of war was another Mansfield amendment. This time it was tied to the defense procurement bill, which became Public Law 92-156. The new Mansfield amendment substituted the words "policy declaration" for the draft-extension wording that stated it was the "sense of Congress" that the United States withdraw from Vietnam "at the earliest practicable date."

The only other legislation that contained serious restrictive clauses on the President's ability to maneuver in Southeast Asia was the substitute Foreign Aid Authorization Act. Section 655 of the Act read:

> (a) Notwithstanding any other provision of law, no funds authorized to be appropriated by this or any other law may be obligated in any amount in excess of $341,000,000 for the purpose of carrying out directly or indirectly any economic or military assistance, or any operation, project, or program of any kind, or for providing any goods, supplies, materials, equipment, services, personnel, or advisers in, to, for, or on behalf of Cambodia during the fiscal year ending June 30, 1972.[20]

The year ended up as a disappointment to the President's opponents. While the administration was not free to conduct unlimited warfare in Indochina, antiwar legislation enacted by Senate doves had been largely negated by House action. For all intents and purposes a stalemate ensued, while both sides gathered their forces for the coming year.

---

[20] Public Law 92-226, February 7, 1972.

V / Election Year

When the North Vietnamese invaded South Vietnam in the spring of 1972, President Nixon took several steps to blunt the effects of the offensive. His efforts to halt the onslaught of the Hanoi forces met with bitter condemnation by American liberals and Democratic presidential hopefuls. In response to this criticism, Representative Bob Wilson (R., Calif.) said:

> Senator George McGovern apparently is the first to meet the hopes of the North Vietnamese Communists by declaring that the new Red offensive proves the Vietnamization program is a failure and that the war is a "hopeless venture."
>
> It is exactly this kind of reaction from America's liberals which has encouraged the Communists to continue their slaughter, and to persist in their war. [*Congressional Record*, May 9, 1972]

Happily for the South Vietnamese, the invasion of their country by conventional military forces was something the average American understood, and public opinion solidified behind the administration.

Secret Talks Revealed

On January 25 President Nixon revealed that the search for peace in Vietnam had been pursued privately since August 4, 1969. In a nationwide address, the Chief Executive disclosed that during the previous twenty-nine months, his national security adviser, Henry Kissinger, had met secretly with North Vietnamese negotiators a total of twelve times.

Nixon's motives for exposing the clandestine meetings were varied.

First and foremost among his reasons for divulging the secret negotiations was the fact that Le Duc Tho, the major North Vietnamese negotiator, had recently developed a case of diplomatic flu. Secondly, the President was in possession of intelligence data that revealed an enormous buildup of North Vietnamese forces north of the demilitarized zone. Lastly, antiwar forces in the United States had been able to gain considerable support due to what appeared to be the rigidity of the American position in the Paris peace talks.

During his speech Nixon disclosed the outline of a new plan to end the war. The key features of the President's proposal, which became known as the eight-point plan, were described as follows:

Within six months of an agreement
- We shall withdraw all United States and allied forces from South Vietnam.
- We shall exchange all prisoners of war.
- There shall be a cease-fire throughout Indochina.
- There shall be a new presidential election in South Vietnam[1]

On January 31, 1972, the North Vietnamese responded to Nixon's offer by presenting William J. Porter, the American negotiator in Paris, with a nine-point plant of their own. There were three major differences between the United States and North Vietnamese proposals:

1. While Nixon's call for United States withdrawal from Vietnam was based on a final settlement, Hanoi representatives insisted that a date for removal of American forces be established immediately.

2. The American offer also called for the withdrawal of all foreign military forces from South Vietnam, while the Communist plan mentioned only the removal of all United States and allied forces from Indochina.

3. The United States plan called for presidential elections in South Vietnam to be conducted by a commission which would include the Communists. The North Vietnamese demands envisioned the removal of the Thieu regime and the establishment of a new government that would include the Communists. This government would then run the elections.

The obvious discrepancy between the two propositions proved to be unsolvable, and the Paris meetings adjourned on February 10, 1972 at the request of the American side. When the negotiators returned to the bargaining table on February 24, the Communists walked out a few minutes after the meeting had convened.

[1] Department of State, *Current Foreign Policy,* "Vietnam: The Negotiating Process," 1972.

Near the end of January, an article appeared in the *Vietnam Bulletin*, a semimonthly publication of the South Vietnamese Embassy in Washington. The commentary described a dialogue held earlier in the month between Pham Kim Ngoc, the minister for economic affairs of the Southern Republic, and a reporter. The two-way conversation assumed the familiar newspaper format and provided an interesting insight into the thinking of an important Saigon official.

Pham had been asked about the minimum amount of money South Vietnam needed to survive. He responded that if the fighting subsided in 1973 as President Thieu had predicted, "then 1974 will be the turning point in aid, which means that United States economic assistance can gradually be reduced." The next question went right to the heart of the matter. When the economics minister was asked what effect it would have on the South Vietnamese economy "if the American Congress shut those funds off right now," Pham answered:

> I would say that it would prove fatal to the Vietnamization program, which is going so well . . . I hope the American Senate will not adopt an emotional attitude. The United States wants to get out of Vietnam not only militarily but also economically and we are trying to do just what will make that possible.

At this point the reporter asked, "You understand America's frustration, though?" The South Vietnamese official answered:

> Yes, I understand that the United States came here with the moral claim to foster democracy and fight Communism. When things do not happen as the purist American mind envisages they get mad. . . . We are fighting a big war with 1,100,000 people under arms and over sixty percent of the budget—twenty-five percent of the GNP—devoted to national defense. We cannot afford absolute democracy and still be efficient. I think that it is in the interest of both Vietnam and the United States to choose to be efficient rather than make this country an image of democracy.[2]

A Trip to China

After the People's Republic of China was safely seated in the United Nations, Richard Nixon traveled to Peking for talks with the rulers of the Middle Kingdom. The presidential party, in addition to Mrs. Nixon, included United States Secretary of State William Rogers, Special Assistant to the President Henry Kissinger, and more than a dozen senior advisers.

On February 17, 1972, following a brief departure ceremony on the White House lawn, the President moved by helicopter to Andrews Air

[2] *Vietnam Bulletin,* January 30, 1972.

Force base where he and his party emplaned for China. Four days later, after layovers in Hawaii and Guam, the party landed at Hung Chiao (Rainbow Bridge) Airport in Shanghai. After a brief pause for refreshments, they boarded Air Force One, which had been renamed the "Spirit of 76," and resumed their flight to Peking. At 11:30 A.M. the party arrived in the capital city of Communist China, where they were greeted by Chou En-lai and other Chinese dignitaries.

After their arrival in Peking, Nixon was granted an audience with Mao Tse-tung that lasted about an hour. While the interview was short in length, it marked a significant departure from the total animosity exhibited by both parties in their previous relationships. This variance from former diplomatic frigidity set off a minor ripple of criticism of the President's actions in the United States. Nixon and Kissinger viewed this opposition, however, as a small price to pay in their overall plan to create a counterweight against the growing power of Soviet Russia.

Chairman Mao's decision to negotiate with the United States also caused a limited amount of domestic controversy in the People's Republic. Disagreement with the Chairman's actions was reported in a collection of documents published by the Taipei Institute of International Relations in June 1974. According to the institute, the documents had been issued in Communist China by the Propaganda Division of the Political Department of the Kunming Military Region in March 1973.

The criticism, presented in a party information pamphlet, took the form of a question that allowed the writer an opportunity to instruct his comrades in the correctness of the Chairman's decision. The question read:

> There are some comrades who say that, in the past, we interpreted negotiations between the United States and the Soviet Union as United States–Soviet collusion, but now we, too, are negotiating with the United States. Hence, they asked whether we had changed our policy.[3]

The instructor's answer to this implied disapproval was based on the infallible wisdom of Chairman Mao. According to the author or authors of the documents, President Nixon's invitation to China had been sought in order to allow the Chairman to exhibit his known talent for "exploiting contradictions, winning over the majority, opposing the minority, and destroying them one by one." In no way was this modification in tactics to indicate any change in the policy of

[3] Michael Lindsay, "U.S. Relations with the People's Republic of China," *Asian Affairs, An American Review* (New York: American-Asian Educational Exchange, 1974), p. 22.

eventually overthrowing China's archenemies, United States imperialism and Soviet revisionism. Additional weight was added to the correctness of the Chairman's decision when the originators of the documents argued that the new contacts with America would allow the spread of the Maoist brand of Marxism-Leninism in the United States. The final benefit of the new relationship with America was that it increased the likelihood of the liberation of Taiwan by making the "Chiang gang" more willing to negotiate.

Following the historic meeting with the leader of mainland China, Nixon met for an hour in the afternoon with Chou En-lai in an exploratory session. That evening the President and the First Lady joined Premier Chou for dinner in the Great Hall of the People.

Over the next few days, Nixon met with various Chinese Communist officials in what has been described as a "frank exchange of views." At the end of his visit to Peking the President and his party flew to Hangchow, where they were given a tour of gardens first described to Westerners by Marco Polo. On the completion of their pleasure trip to the ancient Chinese city, the party left for Shanghai. It was in the burgeoning city of ten million inhabitants that the published results of Nixon's pilgrimage to China were revealed.

This 1,800-word joint communiqué issued on February 27, 1972 covered a wide range of topics. In the section concerning Indochina, the American side stated:

> The United States stressed that the peoples of Indochina should be allowed to determine their destiny without outside intervention; its constant primary objective has been a negotiated solution; the eight-point proposal put forward by the Republic of Vietnam and the United States on January 27, 1972, represents a basis for the attainment of that objective; in the absence of a negotiated settlement the United States envisages the ultimate withdrawal of all United States forces from the region consistent with the aim of self-determination for each country of Indochina.[4]

The Chinese expressed their

> firm support to the peoples of Vietnam, Laos and Cambodia in their efforts for the attainment of their goal and its firm support to the seven-point proposal of the Provisional Revolutionary Government of the Republic of South Vietnam.

As far as the Chinese Communists were concerned, the real substance of the meetings appeared in the later part of the communiqué when the United States side declared:

---

[4] *United States Foreign Policy, 1972: A Report of the Secretary of State,* 1973, p. 641.

The United States acknowledges that all Chinese on either side of the Taiwan Strait maintain there is but one China and that Taiwan is a part of China. The United States Government does not challenge that position. It reaffirms its interest in a peaceful settlement of the Taiwan question by the Chinese themselves. With this prospect in mind, it affirms the ultimate objective of the withdrawal of all United States forces and military installations from Taiwan. In the meantime it will progressively reduce its forces and military installations on Taiwan as the tension in the area diminishes.

The Nixon trip to China caused severe apprehensions among the Vietnamese Communists. Their anxiety was not without cause, since it was commonly accepted that the big Communist powers had sold out Hanoi's interest at Geneva in 1954.* The party newspaper *Nhan Dan* commented on February 24 that in his visit to Peking the American leader was guilty of "plotting to carry out continued United States neocolonialist war in South Vietnam and throughout the Indochina peninsula." The editor added:

> Never before has a president gone to an international meeting in an area which before was a very strange place for a great majority of all American people.

The growing fear of a possible United States/China accord, had been expressed earlier in *Thong Nhat* (Unite), another Hanoi publication. In a November 1971 issue, the paper had published a letter from a southern compatriot who expressed concern over the expected Nixon visits to China and Russia. The writer said that the American President's forthcoming trips created "hot problems" within the Vietcong movement. He also expressed "the worries of a number of associates in Saigon as to whether international support for our movement will weaken." The editors attempted to reassure the author of the letter and told him that China and Russia would not desert the Vietcong. At the same time, however, they urged him and his friends to become more self-sufficient.

The southern Communists were not the only ones to be upset by Nixon's visit to China. America's Asian allies were visibly disturbed by what could turn into a major disaster for their countries. Marshall Green, assistant United States secretary of state, visited these na-

---

* In 1954 Pham Van Dong, the North Vietnamese negotiator at the Geneva Conference, strongly desired to establish a separate "Pathet Lao" government in Laos and believed that he had the ability to do so. When he discovered that Chou En-lai had previously agreed not to support this position, Dong was furious. He is reported to have been reduced to such "suppressed" fury at Chou's "betrayal" that subsequent relations between the North Vietnamese and Chinese delegations remained embittered for the rest of the negotiations. See Donald Lancaster, *The Emancipation of French Indo-China* (New York: Oxford University Press, 1961), p. 334.

tions in early March and attempted to calm their fears. During his trip to Saigon, he conferred with President Thieu and other members of the government. In his discussions with the Saigon leaders, Green assured them that nothing had changed and that America would continue its strong support for South Vietnam. As he left Tan Son Nhat airport, the secretary commented that he was glad that the government of the Southern Republic continued to show "understanding toward the United States policy in the Pacific."

The Easter Offensive

The view from Hanoi in early 1972 must have appeared ominous indeed. The South Vietnamese were exuding confidence in the growing success of the Vietnamization program. Peking seemed to be more interested in the future of Taiwan than in the war in Vietnam, and the American "peace" movement had slumped into a lethargic state. The picture, however, was not an entirely gloomy one. Luckily for the Vietnamese politburo leaders, their Russian allies remained steadfast and the United States was entering a presidential election year.

The combination of these factors, plus the unsatisfactory results of the negotiations in Paris, led the North Vietnamese Communists to unleash a conventional invasion of the Southern Republic on March 29–30, 1972. The major thrust of the campaign was directed through the demilitarized zone that divided North and South Vietnam. The invaders appeared to be well-armed and moved into combat behind T-54 medium tanks supported by 130 mm artillery pieces. These supplies had, for the most part, only recently arrived in Haiphong from the Russian supply base in Vladivostok. In addition to sending the increased armaments, the Soviets had also provided high-ranking advisers for the invasion. The Russian delegation, which had arrived in Hanoi on March 26, was led by Marshal Pavel F. Batitsky, a member of the Central Committee of the Communist Party of the Soviet Union; Lieutenant General A. N. Sevchenko, representing the General Political Department of the Soviet Air and Naval Forces; Lieutenant General of Artillery F. M. Boldarenko, Soviet AA Missile Forces, and Lieutenant General M. T. Beregaroy, Head, Soviet AA Radar Forces. After their arrival, the visitors spent their time visiting "various air force missile, navy and infantry units."[5]

The attacking North Vietnamese forces were identified as major elements of the 304, 308, and 324 B Divisions, supported by three artillery regiments, several antiaircraft units, and one tank regiment. While the strongest push was aimed at Quangtri City in the

[5] Hanoi: International News Service in English, March 29, 1972.

northernmost province of South Vietnam, fighting soon broke out at Kontum, An Loc, and Hue. The T-54 tanks were much bigger than anything the Americans had prepared the South Vietnamese to fight. Initially, the enemy armored units pushed through the outposts of the defending ARVN forces. Before the NVA/VC troops had penetrated too far into the South Vietnamese positions, however, the United States and South Vietnamese air forces came to the rescue. Flying through the overcast skies, the allied planes bombed and rocketed the Soviet-made tanks until the North Vietnamese units were forced to halt their advancing elements. At this point the fighting became a brutal war of numerous infantry battles scattered across the face of South Vietnam.

The intensity of the combat caused severe dislocation of South Vietnamese residents and almost one million people fled before the Communist juggernaut. It is worth noting that they fled from and not toward the Hanoi conquerors.

The flagrant disregard of their borders caused the Joint Committee of South Vietnamese Political Parties to issue a resolution condemning the invasion. The committee appealed to Great Britain and the Soviet Union, the cochairmen nations of the 1954 Geneva Conference, to halt the North Vietnamese aggression. The resolution also called for all South Vietnamese to back their heroic fighting men. The appeal was signed by representatives of the Vietnam Restoration Party, Social Democratic Buddhist Force, Humanist Revolutionary Party, Popular Force for National Construction, Popular Republican Party, National Union Party, and the Vietnamese Restoration Alliance.[6]

The key battle of the Easter offensive centered on An Loc, a city about forty miles north of Saigon on Route 13. In the beginning days of the invasion, approximately 15,000 men of the ARVN 5th Infantry Division had moved into the city. They were almost immediately surrounded by superior North Vietnamese forces. On April 13, 1972, the NVA assaulted the defending positions with a task force of 3,000 men assisted by more than 40 tanks. The initial attack was halted by a massive United States/SVN air strike. For the next several weeks, the North and South Vietnamese soldiers stood toe to toe on the battlefield and slugged it out.

As the invasion army moved south, President Nixon ordered the resumption of the bombing of North Vietnam. United States Secretary of Defense Melvin Laird warned Hanoi that the air strikes would continue until the invading troops were withdrawn across the demilitarized zone.

The North Vietnamese attack prompted Democratic presidential

[6] *Vietnam Bulletin*, April 20, 1972.

hopefuls to issue frantic appeals for America to withdraw from the war. One candidate, Senator Edmund S. Muskie (Maine) speaking at a Democratic fund-raising dinner, accused the President of "doing irreparable harm" to our country and "undermining our sense of decency" by increasing the bombing. The senator's audience did not respond too favorably to his speech and held its applause to the end when he promised to stay in the race "until Richard Nixon is defeated." Hubert Humphrey (Minn.), then on the campaign trail, called the accelerated bombing a "dangerous retaliation." His appeal for caution in the war met with only scattered applause among the small crowds that had gathered to hear the senator speak.

A few days later, the House Democratic caucus voted to support legislation that would set a date for American withdrawal from the war in Vietnam. The resolution was directed to the House Foreign Affairs Committee and instructed Democratic members of the Committee to report a full withdrawal proposal to the House within thirty days.

The initial shock of the North Vietnamese assault had pushed the ARVN defenders out of their forward positions. This retrograde movement and the consequent necessity for more United States assistance worried Henry Kissinger greatly. Strong American countermeasures, coming only a few weeks before President Nixon's visit to Moscow, could endanger the proposed summit talks. In order to forestall any complications in the projected Nixon-Brezhnev talks, the President's national security adviser flew to Moscow on April 20. After a series of conversations with Chairman Brezhnev, Kissinger agreed to accept an "in-place" cease-fire in South Vietnam. In return, he asked that the North Vietnamese troops who had entered South Vietnam since March 30 be withdrawn.[7]

The true meaning of this offer was not lost on Chairman Brezhnev, who agreed to recommend its acceptance to the North Vietnamese. For the first time in the long and arduous war, the Americans had signaled their willingness to cease demanding that Hanoi remove all its troops from South Vietnam in exchange for a peace treaty. When Le Duc Tho was informed of Kissinger's offer, he knew that the Easter offensive had secured an unexpected dividend. A few days after receiving the in-place cease-fire message, the Communist negotiator offered to meet with Kissinger on May 2. When the two emissaries met in Paris, their positions proved to be irreconcilable and the fighting continued.

As the North Vietnamese divisions penetrated South Vietnam's

[7] *China News Analysis,* March 21, 1975.

defenses, their killer teams, known as *Dich Van,* went into action.* These well-trained specialists operated in a manner familiar to all students of totalitarian methods. As the regular military units entered a town the fighting men would mingle with the inhabitants, and in the process, identify the "top ring leaders." These individuals included the local village officials, "policemen, spies, pacification agents, and security agents." After identifying the suspects, the soldiers turned their names over to the *Dich Van.* The execution teams then conducted a house to house search and arrested the suspected "criminals." After a short and meaningless hearing, the officials were placed before a firing squad. The total number of South Vietnamese citizens who were eliminated in this fashion will probably never be known, but even the lowest estimates run into the tens of thousands.

As North Vietnamese intransigence left no room for movement at the peace table, on May 8, 1972, President Nixon announced over nationwide television that he had ordered the mining of North Vietnam's harbors and rivers. The President also stated that "rail and all other communications will be cut off to the maximum extent possible" and "air and naval strikes against military targets in North Vietnam will continue."

Nixon also confirmed Kissinger's offer to the North Vietnamese to withdraw the American demand for the removal of their troops from South Vietnam. The President's new peace terms included the following:

> First, all American prisoners of war must be returned. Second there must be an internationally supervised cease-fire throughout Indochina.
> Once prisoners of war are released, once the internationally supervised cease-fire has begun, we will stop all acts of force throughout Indochina, and at that time we will proceed with a complete withdrawal of all American forces from Vietnam within four months.[8]

Democratic response to the Nixon broadcast was immediate, but not unexpected. In a party caucus, Senate Democrats voted 29–14 to disapprove "the escalation of the war in Vietnam." In the Senate, William Proxmire (Wis.) called the President's actions "reckless and wrong." His accusations were based on the fear that Nixon's strong measures had moved the country into a "direct collision course with the Soviet Union." In order to halt what he envisioned as a threat of general war, the senator recommended that Congress cut off all fu-

---

[8] *United States Foreign Policy, 1972: A Report to the Secretary of State,* 1973, p. 651.

* These North Vietnamese Army units are very similar to the elite *Einsatzgruppen* (Special Action Groups) of the German National Socialist *Schutzstaffel* (SS). The sole purpose for their existence is to serve as executioners of the politically or socially undesirable.

ture financial support for United States forces in Southeast Asia (*Congressional Record*, May 9, 1972). Vance Hartke (Ind.) cautioned the Senate that "Armageddon may be only hours away" and urged his colleagues to halt the President from arming the mines in Haiphong harbor.

House Democrats also reacted strongly to the President's May 8 speech. John G. Dow (N.Y.) accused the Chief Executive of "leading us down the road of evil" and of "acting like a despotic monarch." Bella Abzug (N.Y.) issued a call for impeachment, charging Nixon "with that high crime and misdemeanor." Jonathan Bingham (N.Y.) referred to the President's "drastic action" and stated that it was the work of a "dictator" (*Congressional Record*, May 9, 1972).

The *New York Times* response to Nixon's action was presented in a long article by Tom Wicker. The editorialist referred to the President as an "unchecked Caesar" who in "his majesty chose to speak to the American people last night about his intentions in Southeast Asia." Wicker questioned Nixon's authority as Commander in Chief to take such positive steps. In ending the condemnatory editorial, the *Times* writer assured his readers that the President did not need to be "psychoanalyzed" for the world to know his actions were unpredictable.[9]

The Soviet answer to the threat to mine Haiphong harbor and interdict supplies moving to North Vietnam was distributed by Tass, the official Russian news agency, on May 11. The statement included a charge that "the measures taken by the United States are a gross violation of the generally recognized freedom of navigation." It also called on the United States to raise the blockade of the North Vietnamese coast. Generally speaking, the Soviet note was couched in language that did not seem to threaten an open rupture with America over the increased bombing and mining. There is a good probability that Brezhnev continued to be strongly irritated by North Vietnam's reluctance to come to terms with the Americans. Strong evidence for this assumption was presented later in May when the Soviet representatives in Washington visited President Nixon and assured him that his visit to Moscow was still very much alive. These officials, Ambassador Anatoly Dobrynin and Foreign Trade Minister Nikolai S. Patolichev, were questioned by newsmen as they left the President's office. One of the reporters asked if Nixon's trip to Russia was still scheduled. Patolichev replied: "We never had any doubts about it. I don't know why you asked this question. Have you any doubts?"

The Chinese Communists in their official newspaper *Jenmin Jih Pao* called Nixon's actions a "dangerous move." They also stated their

---

[9] *New York Times*, May 9, 1972.

support of the people of North Vietnam in their war against the "aggressor" forces.

On May 10 the Democrats on the House Foreign Affairs Committee voted 10 to 1 in favor of a proposal that would require the withdrawal of all American personnel from Vietnam by October 1, 1972. Under the terms of the resolution, the only requirement the North Vietnamese would have to fulfill would be to return the American prisoners of war. A full committee hearing on the proposed legislation was scheduled for May 16.

Other action against the strong response to the North Vietnamese attack was taken when a number of House Democrats filed a resolution of impeachment against Richard Nixon. The charges were read by John Conyers, Jr. (Mich.), and supported by Bella Abzug (N.Y.), Shirley Chisholm (N.Y.), Ronald Dellums (Calif.), and William Ryan (N.Y.). In effect, the congressmen charged that the United States was not in a declared war, yet the President was committing warlike acts. In their view, this was an impeachable offense (*Congressional Record,* May 10, 1972).

The following day, twenty-three Democratic legislators brought a suit against Richard Nixon and other top administrative officials. The action was filed in the United States District Court for the District of Columbia. The legislators claimed that the President and his subordinates were conducting and expanding an illegal war. The plaintiffs were:

> Senator Mike Gravel (Alaska)
> Senator Fred R. Harris (Okla.)
> Representative Bella Abzug (N.Y.)
> Representative Herman Badillo (N.Y.)
> Representative Jonathan B. Bingham (N.Y.)
> Representative Philip Burton (Calif.)
> Representative William Clay (Mo.)
> Representative Shirley Chisholm (N.Y.)
> Representative John Conyers (Mich.)
> Representative Ronald V. Dellums (Calif.)
> Representative Charles C. Diggs, Jr. (Mich.)
> Representative Don Edwards (Calif.)
> Delegate Walter Fauntroy (D.C.)
> Representative Michael J. Harrington (Mass.)
> Representative Augustus Hawkins (Calif.)
> Representative Henry Helstoski (N.J.)
> Representative Robert W. Kastenmeier (Wis.)
> Representative Parren Mitchell (Md.)
> Representative Thomas Rees (Calif.)

Representative Benjamin Rosenthal (N.Y.)
Representative William F. Ryan (N.Y.)
Representative Louis Stokes (Ohio)
[*Congressional Record,* May 11, 1972]

In the middle of May, the proposal of the Democratic caucus to withdraw from Vietnam by October 1 became the main subject of a series of hearings conducted by the House Foreign Affairs Committee. During the second day of testimony, Clark M. Clifford, a former Secretary of Defense in the Johnson administration, presented his observations of the withdrawal proposal. In the main, the secretary supported the resolution; however, he opined that it had not gone far enough. When questioned as to what he meant by this remark, Clifford offered his own design for peace, which he said would have "extricated us from the war at any time in the last three and one-half years." The secretary's plan consisted of four parts:

The United States would agree to two actions:
(1) Withdraw all United States military personnel from South Vietnam, Laos, and Cambodia on a date certain.
(2) End all ground, air and naval activity by United States forces in South Vietnam, North Vietnam, Laos, and Cambodia by the same date.

North Vietnam and the National Liberation Front would also agree to:

(1) Return all United States prisoners held by North Vietnam and the National Liberation Front as United States troops withdrew.
(2) Refrain from attacks that would threaten the safety of United States military personnel during the period of withdrawal.

In addition to the four-part proposal, Clifford said:

It is my firm conviction that if this plan were agreed to, political forces would surface in South Vietnam that would institute negotiations between the Vietnamese leading to an overall settlement.[10]

The former defense secretary's proposition clearly ignored any American commitment to the embattled South Vietnamese. The plan was also a refutation of his former warlike stance when he had been an official in the Johnson administration. Clifford's complete about-face on the issue of the war caused committee member Vernon W. Thomson (R., Wis.) to doubt his credibility as a witness. Thomson's misgivings were partially based on a statement which had been issued by the secretary at an earlier date. The quotation appeared in

---

[10] Hearings Before the House Committee on Foreign Affairs, "Termination of Hostilities in Indochina," 1972.

the October 15, 1969 issue of the *Washington Star* and was entered in the record of the committee hearings by the Wisconsin Republican; it read:

> Former Defense Secretary Clark Clifford said today Senator Goodell's proposal to withdraw all American troops from South Vietnam by December 1, 1970, is both immature and impractical and would result in a bloodbath in that country. He said that Goodell's plan would result in the collapse of the military and the collapse of the government in that country.

Clifford's newly-adopted dovish position regarding the war was also questioned by John H. Buchanan, Jr., (R., Ala.). The Alabama minister commented that when he first heard the secretary's testimony, he thought he was hearing the voice of the Kremlin, then he thought maybe it was the "voice of Hanoi," or perhaps the voice of George McGovern. However, upon reflection, Buchanan said, "I realized it was the voice of the Honorable Clark Clifford, who had somehow undergone a miraculous conversion."

During his testimony Clifford had asserted that as the United States forces withdrew from Vietnam, peace forces in both the northern and southern portions of the country would surface and reach harmonious accord. He also stated that if a cease-fire in Vietnam was agreed to by both parties, he would

> inform Hanoi where the American troops were after this matter had been agreed to, and we were in the process of withdrawal and getting our prisoners back. We would inform them of the locations of American troops, and part of the agreement would be that those troops would not be attacked.

This testimony stunned Paul Findley, an Illinois Republican, who questioned its naïveté and indicated his concern for the safety of the American troops if the plan were adopted. When the House panel adjourned, Jonathan Bingham (D., N.Y.) apologized to Clifford for any "nasty" comments other committee members may have made during the day.

The following month the committee voted to shelve the October 1 withdrawal proposal and substituted a resolution presented by Representative Buchanan. The accepted measure was a close paraphrase of what the President had offered the North Vietnamese on May 8. The Buchanan proposal was not brought to the floor in the House, nor was it considered in the Senate.

For several weeks, Congressman Robert F. Drinan (D., Mass.) had been extremely troubled by the President's response to the North

Vietnamese invasion of South Vietnam. During this time he had received several communications from his constituents regarding the "escalation" of the war. The congressman had hastened to answer these letters and felt it was his duty to share these "thoughts with" his Senate colleagues.

According to Drinan, he told his supporters that George McGovern had predicted some fifteen months ago the war in Vietnam would be the key issue in the 1972 elections. He noted that the mining of Haiphong harbor had yielded little on the battlefields of Vietnam and characterized this act as being "militarily unsound." Drinan charged the electorate with bearing the ultimate responsibility for United States intervention in Indochina "because of their political illiteracy." He referred to the House of Representatives as the silent "House of Hawks." His solution for those who were opposed to the war was to "work patiently but persistently in all of the ways available" to end the fighting in Indochina (*Congressional Record,* May 22, 1972).

By the end of the first week in June 1972, the North Vietnamese forces had been routed at Kontum and the siege of An Loc had been lifted. Near the end of the month, the North Vietnamese defeat formed the basis for a new set of instructions from Le Duan, first secretary of the Vietnam Workers Party, to the Southern cadre. In his communication the politburo leader called on Vietcong forces to concentrate on winning land and not on conquering cities. He referred to the prospect of the creation of uprisings in urban centers as hopeless, and the Communist command in South Vietnam was ordered to suspend attacks on cities and towns.[11]

Additional confirmation of the magnitude of the Saigon victory was given by Joseph Alsop in early July, when the syndicated columnist wrote:

> The great North Vietnamese offensive of 1972 must now be seen as a vast and unqualified disaster. The dimensions of this disaster have largely been kept from the American public.

Alsop described "once tough North Vietnamese units throwing away their weapons and running like rabbits." He attributed the poor reporting of the Hanoi defeat to reporters who had predicted the demise of South Vietnam for so long that they had a vested interest in a North Vietnamese victory. (*Congressional Record,* July 27, 1972).*

[11] *China News Analysis,* September 13, 1974.

* Alsop continues to believe the North Vietnamese lost a major battle when their 1972 invasion of South Vietnam collapsed. However, he contends that "losing battles does not matter . . . if your adversary lacks the will to exploit his successes." Letter to the author, January 5, 1976.

The Senate Passes the War Powers Resolution

While South Vietnam had been engaged in a desperate fight for survival, the United States Senate passed a bill designed to limit the President's military authority. The measure, known as the War Powers Resolution, was approved in the Senate on April 13 by a vote of 68–16. In spite of the efforts of Senator Mike Gravel (D., Alaska) to make the bill currently applicable, the resolution specifically excluded the Vietnam War from its provisions. Under its terms, during a national emergency the President was allowed to commit American troops to combat. At the end of thirty days, however, the Chief Executive must cease such action unless Congress approves it. There were also special situations when the President would be allowed to take military action beyond the thirty-day limit. These allowances were, however, limited to the protection of United States troops and of United States nationals on the high seas.[12]

Case-Church, 1972

During the late spring, Senate doves attempted to use the Foreign Relations Authorization Act of 1972 as the vehicle for an end-the-war amendment. The Act contained the 1973 appropriations for the Department of State and other Federal agencies engaged in international relations. The end-the-war measure was sponsored by Senators Clifford P. Case (R., N.J.) and Frank Church (D., Idaho). As initially proposed, the amendment contained a withdrawal date of December 31, 1972. After the President ordered the mining of Haiphong harbor, its sponsors changed the wording to read:

Title VII—Termination of hostilities in Indochina

Sec. 701. Notwithstanding any other provision of law, none of the funds authorized or appropriated in this or any other Act may be expended or obligated for the purpose of maintaining, supporting, or engaging United States forces, land, sea, or air, in hostilities in Indochina, four months after reaching an agreement for the release of all prisoners of war held by the Government of North Vietnam and forces allied with such Government and an accounting for all Americans missing in action who have been held by or known to such Government or such forces. [Congressional Record, May 9, 1972]

After extended discussions on May 9, Senator Robert C. Byrd (D., W. Va.) proposed that the terms "a cease-fire and" be inserted after the word "reaching." The next day, Byrd changed his wording to read "an internationally supervised cease-fire."

[12] Congressional Quarterly Almanac, 1972, p. 842.

The Senate voted 47–43 in favor of the Byrd addition to the Case-Church amendment. As the new words defeated the purpose of the end-the-war clause, the entire amendment was defeated on May 31. Following the elimination of the Case-Church proviso, the bill was approved in the Senate by a vote of 76–23. Both chambers agreed to a joint conference committee report near the end of June, and the President signed the measure into law on July 13, 1972, when it became Public Law 92-352.

A Visit to Moscow

As a part of his plan to return international affairs to a more balanced position, and only incidentally to end the Vietnam War, Richard Nixon journeyed to Moscow. He was the first American President to visit the Soviet capital in his official capacity.

After a number of serious discussions during the period May 22 to May 31, the two heads of state arrived at several important agreements. The most significant of these areas of cooperation embodied the signing of the Treaty on the Limitation of Anti-Ballistic Missile Systems and an Interim Agreement on Certain Measures with Respect to the Limitation of Strategic Offensive Arms. These treaties have collectively become known as the SALT agreements. Under the terms of the nuclear accords, the parties to the agreements placed major strategic armaments under formal limitations. Both sides were limited to one anti-ballistic missile (ABM) site to protect the nation's capital and one additional location to defend an ICBM field. A limitation was set on the number of offensive missiles each side could possess, but none was placed on the number of warheads the weapons could carry. The two signatory powers agreed that the 1972 nuclear accords were only a temporary agreement and agreed to resume Phase II of the SALT talks in Geneva at a later date.

On May 29 the two governments issued a joint communiqué entitled "Basic Principles of Mutual Relations Between the United States of America and the Union of Soviet Socialist Republics." Among the "basic principles" contained in the agreement was a section regarding Indochina. In these paragraphs both sides reaffirmed support for their Vietnamese allies. The one item they agreed on was that the United States military forces should leave South Vietnam. The major area of disagreement concerned the conditions under which they should leave. The American side continued to press for the return of all prisoners of war, and an internationally supervised cease-fire prior to the withdrawal of its troops. There was no mention of the necessity for the removal of North Vietnamese military forces from South Vietnam.

One interesting difference, however, appeared in the mutual statements regarding Indochina. The Soviet Union demanded that America and her allied military forces withdraw from South Vietnam "so that the peoples of Indochina would have the possibility to determine for themselves their fate without any outside interference." The United States side stated that "the political future of South Vietnam should be left for the South Vietnamese people to decide for themselves, free from outside interference."[13] The key elements in each of these statements may be found, first, in the Soviet demand that the "peoples of Indochina" solve South Vietnam's problems, and also in the American proviso that the situation be resolved by "the South Vietnamese people." The difference between the two wordings was, of course, the crux of the entire war. For if the South Vietnamese people had been allowed to determine their own future there would not have been a second Indochina War.

While the two world leaders were negotiating their differences, Henry Kamm, a *New York Times* reporter, spent three weeks interviewing the people of South Vietnam. During his extended tour of Saigon and environs, he was accompanied by Nguyen Ngoc Long, a Vietnamese journalist-interpreter.

In his travels reporter Kamm conversed with dozens of South Vietnamese citizens from all walks of life. Among the people interviewed he found a growing weariness of the war, accompanied by a willingness to continue fighting. In response to a question about the war, a pedicab driver answered, "If we make peace with them we have to let them form a government, and then they'll kill us." A young woman, when asked what she would do about the war said, "If I were a man I'd become a pilot to bomb the North." After further questioning, she added, "If the Communists capture Saigon, I'll go right to the Saigon River and drown myself." Kamm expressed his general reaction to what the people of Saigon were thinking about when he wrote, "Their fear of a Communist victory remains as strong as their weariness with the war."[14]

Campaign Promises

By the beginning of June 1972, the presidential campaign was encouraging the Democratic candidates to outbid each other with unrealistic promises. This situation caused the *Wall Street Journal* to run a column on June 1 entitled "A Fantasized Condition." In the editorial the writer noted that "Mr. McGovern has told us that his $32

[13] *United States Foreign Policy 1972: A Report of the Secretary of State,* 1973, p. 602.
[14] *New York Times,* May 23, 1972.

billion defense-budget cut is based on the world being 'as we know it.' " If the United States were attacked tomorrow, however, "all bets are off . . . we'll have to prepare for it." On the other hand, according to the author of the commentary, we have "Mr. Humphrey, who a few years ago was glorifying 'the wonderful American adventure in Vietnam,' " and now this same man is stating that he and McGovern have "parallel" records on the war.

The constant promises of the Democratic presidential candidates had a devastating effect on America's servicemen. One of these young men, Richard J. Wira, who was serving on the USS *Sterett,* directed a complaint to the *Cincinnati Post and Times Star* regarding these statements. In his letter to the editor, which the newspaper published on June 1, Wira stated that every time he read a paper either McGovern, Muskie, Humphrey, or Fulbright were attacking the President's Vietnam policy. Wira added:

> This has two effects on the American serviceman over here: one, it degrades us and what we are trying to achieve and two, it saddens/ angers [us] to think that a few Democrats are willing to let the Communists overrun the South . . . .
>
> These . . . Democrats have done more for the Communists effort in Southeast Asia than Russia will ever do in supplying arms and supplies.

The candidates' promises became so absurd that even responsible Democrats were forced to issue condemnations of their party leaders. Near the end of May, Charles Sawyer, who had served as ambassador to Belgium under Franklin D. Roosevelt and secretary of commerce in the cabinet of Harry Truman, was compelled to issue a statement criticizing the presidential hopefuls. Roasting the candidates for their undesirable declarations, Sawyer said:

> Mr. Nixon's decision to bomb North Vietnam has evoked some frightening statements from some of our Democratic candidates for President. These statements disclose an incredible naïveté about the world and the enemies or potential enemies with whom we deal. I am being kind in describing their attitude as naïve. In so important a matter, I would hope that politics was not the motive which brought about this reaction.
> [*Congressional Record,* June 1, 1972]

Following several months of vigorous infighting, Senator George McGovern (D., S.Dak.) won the Democratic presidential nomination in Miami Beach on July 12. The senator's campaign had been primarily based on his opposition to the war in Vietnam and the American economic system. Prior to the convention, McGovern had told a group of South Carolina delegates that he "would go to Hanoi and beg" if he thought it would release the POWs one day earlier. This statement had earned the senator several strong denunciations. One opponent viewed McGovern as "the darling of the advocates of American retreat and defeat," whose policies contained "the seeds of the downfall of our great Republic." Two days after his nomination, the senator pledged:

> Within 90 days of my inauguration, every American soldier and every American prisoner will be out of the jungle and out of their cells and back home in America where they belong.[15]

His vow to withdraw American military personnel from Indochina in 90 days was a relatively conservative promise when compared with the Democratic party's platform plank:

> If the war is not ended before the next Democratic administration takes office, we pledge, as the first order of business, an immediate and complete withdrawal of all United States forces in Indochina.

The Second Break-In at Watergate

At 2:00 A.M. on the morning of June 17, five men were arrested by Washington police in the Watergate offices of the Democratic National Committee.* These individuals were in possession of burglar tools and electronic listening equipment. It was obvious that the intruders had entered the committee headquarters to engage in political espionage and to place listening devices on key telephones. After their arrest, it was discovered that some of the burglars were ex-CIA personnel and former White House aides employed by the Committee to Reelect the President (CREEP).

As the news of their arrest spread across the nation, most Americans regarded the activities of the CREEP employees as forming a normal part of the electoral process. When Barry Goldwater learned of the Watergate arrests, he was reminded of the time the Democrats had placed a "spy" in his mobile headquarters. The event occurred in 1964 when Moira O'Conner, a Democratic spy, was placed on Senator Goldwater's campaign train. The pretty twenty-three-year-old woman posed as a reporter and used her good looks to uncover confidential information. After Goldwater's aides discovered O'Conner's identity, she freely admitted her connection with the Democratic party. The

---

[15] McGovern's promises to end the war on Hanoi's terms were classed as "irresponsible" by knowledgeable East European diplomats. See Morton Kaplan, in *Vietnam Settlement: Why 1973, not 1969?* (Washington, D.C.: American Enterprise Institute for Public Policy Research, 1973), p. 41.

* This event is known as the "second break-in." During the period May 26–28 there had been at least two other attempts to effect an entrance into the Democratic national offices. The first successful break-in had been completed on May 28.

118

young woman even identified the source of her operating funds as California Democratic strategist Richard Tuck (*Congressional Record,* July 20, 1972).

Most of the men taken into custody after the Watergate break-in were placed on trial following the national elections. The usual plea was guilty and the sentences were relatively mild. During the trial, however, their testimony revealed that further investigations would disclose a close connection between Watergate and top administration officials in the White House.

The failure of the amateurish attempt to gain Democratic party secrets played a minor role in the contest for the number-one spot on the 1972 Republican ticket, and on August 23 Richard Nixon was chosen as the GOP standard-bearer. Nixon's renomination also took place in Miami Beach in a convention that held few surprises. In his acceptance speech the President stressed that there were three things on which he differed with the Democrats:

We will never abandon our prisoners of war.

We will not join our enemies in imposing a Communist government on our allies—the seventeen million people of South Vietnam.

And we will never stain the honor of the United States of America.

While the Democrats and Republicans had been fighting over their party's top position, Prime Minister Lon Nol was elected on June 4 to the position of President of Cambodia. The new Cambodian leader immediately issued orders for his countrymen to "improve their vigilance" in the face of a determined enemy attack.

Lon Nol's calls for renewed determination in fighting the invaders of his country were issued to an army in retreat. The drastic change in the fortunes of the government military forces resulted from a significant improvement in the Communist position inside Cambodia. This increase in enemy capabilities had been brought about by the recent infiltration into Cambodia of several thousand Cambodian expatriates.[16] These men had been residing in North Vietnam since the signing of the Geneva Armistice Agreements in 1954. They were returned to the country of their birth for the express purpose of participating in its conquest.

Fonda and Clark in Hanoi

When the North Vietnamese realized the Easter offensive had failed, they decided to concentrate their efforts on increasing the

[16] *Asian Affairs,* January–February, 1975, p. 192.

scope of the antiwar effort in the United States. For some time, the politburo leaders had sponsored visits to North Vietnam by various American "peace" personalities. During their stay in Hanoi, the visitors were normally taken on a guided tour of bombed-out villages, hospital wards containing war casualties, and an occasional damaged dike. Following the trip to the countryside, the guests were invited to discuss the "war crimes of the Americans" over Radio Hanoi.

By mid-1972, approximately fifty Americans had made a total of eighty-two broadcasts over the North Vietnamese radio system. However, the greater number of these visitors were either Communists, known sympathizers, or other leftists who lacked an extended audience. Probably the best known performers had been Stokely Carmichael, Dagmar Wilson, Tom Hayden, Rennie Davis, Noam Chomsky, Eldridge Cleaver, David Ifshin, and Pete Seeger. This lack of prominent "stars" failed to gain the Communist war effort the widespread support its psychological warfare experts desired. The inability to obtain a wide following caused the politburo leaders to extend their propaganda net. Fortunately for the North Vietnamese, their efforts were highly successful and during 1972 they were able to obtain the services of Jane Fonda, the Hollywood actress, and Ramsey Clark, a Texas Democrat.

It was only by a stroke of luck that Hanoi sympathizer Tom Hayden had met Jane Fonda at an antiwar rally in the late 1960s. The chance meeting blossomed into an avid romance and led to the conversion of the actress from a gullible peacenik to a conscious partisan of Communist causes throughout the world. Evidence of Fonda's newfound advocacy for left-wing ideas was presented on November 22, 1969, when she told a student group at Michigan State University, "I would think that if you understood what Communism was, you would hope, you would pray on your knees that we would some day become Communist."[17] The direction that Fonda's new militancy would take was indicated on July 18, 1970, when she told an interviewer for the *People's World:* "To make a revolution in the United States is a slow day-by-day job that requires patience and discipline."

It was not until she became deeply involved with Hanoi's effort to defeat United States forces in Vietnam, however, that Fonda's hatred for America really reached its greatest depths. Her opportunity to contribute to the demise of the country she so detested arrived when the actress was invited to visit Hanoi in the summer of 1972.

Fonda arrived in North Vietnam on July 8 in the possession of American passport number C1478434, which had not been validated

[17] Hearings Before the House Committee on Internal Security, "Hearings Regarding HR 16742: Restraints on Travel to Hostile Areas," 1972.

for travel in that country.* Over the next few days, she was taken on the standard tour, which included visits to "war museums" displaying evidence of alleged American "war crimes," trips to hospitals containing war casualties, and a bomb-damaged dike.

Following her visits to the countryside, the actress made a series of broadcasts over Radio Hanoi. These speeches included a strong condemnation of the United States and the American war effort in Vietnam. The first broadcast was made on July 14 over the Voice of Vietnam Radio. In this address, she appealed to United States servicemen who were engaged in bombing North Vietnam and said:

> All of you in the cockpits of your planes, on the aircraft carriers, those who are loading the bombs, those who are repairing the planes, those who are working on the Seventh Fleet, please think what you are doing.
> Are these people your enemy? What will you say to your children years from now who may ask you why you fought the war? What words will you be able to say to them?

Three days later, she made another broadcast particularly directed to "servicemen who are stationed on the aircraft carriers in the Gulf of Tonkin . . . and in the Anglico Corps in the south of Vietnam." In this speech Fonda said:

> I don't know what your officers tell you that you are dropping on this country. I don't know what your officers tell you, you are loading, those of you who load the bombs on the planes . . . . The men who are ordering you to use these weapons are war criminals according to international law, and in the past, in Germany and in Japan, men who were guilty of these kind of crimes were tried and executed.

She continued:

> Now I know you are not told these kind of things, but, you know, history changes. We've witnessed incredible changes, for example, in the United States in the last five years. The astounding victory that has just been won by George McGovern, for example, who was nominated by the Democratic party, is an example of the kind of changes that are going on —an example of the overwhelming, overwhelming feeling in the United States among people to end the war. McGovern represents all that is good to these people. He represents an end to the war, an end to the bombing.

To several congressmen, Fonda's statements smacked of high treason, and on September 19 and September 25, 1972, the House Committee on Internal Security conducted hearings regarding her activi-

* While entry by United States citizens into certain countries without government approval is forbidden by law, Communist authorities have bypassed this regulation by not stamping the visitor's passport and merely issuing visas at the port of entry.

ties in North Vietnam. During the testimony concerning Fonda's disloyalty, the Committee listened attentively while William Olson, a Department of Justice lawyer, defined the term "treason." In Olson's opinion:

> The treason statute, 18 U.S.C. 2381, provides that whoever levies war against the United States or adheres to their enemies, giving them aid and comfort, is guilty of treason. Additionally, Section III, Article 3 of the constitution provides that no person shall be convicted of treason except on the testimony of two witnesses to the same overt act or a confession in open court.

He further stated that "a country with whom the United States is engaged in open hostility would qualify as an enemy." However, Olson directed the Committee's attention to the procedural difficulties the Justice Department would have in prosecuting Fonda. These legal technicalities were based on the simple fact that the government was unable to produce two witnesses who had seen her make the broadcasts.

Later in the hearings Edward Hunter, a former propaganda specialist with the OSS during World War II, was questioned as to the value of Fonda's actions to the enemy. The psychological warfare veteran answered that in his opinion, her broadcasts had produced an effect on American military morale in Vietnam that was "bad to devastating." Hunter added that the Fonda performance was merely a part of an overall "black" propaganda effort of the Communists to destroy the defenses of the United States. He described the first goal of this operation as the elimination of the legal means to combat subversion in America. According to the former intelligence officer, once these laws have been removed or rendered ineffective, Communist propaganda experts would be free to ply their trade.

The actual method by which the antisubversive laws or organizations are to be eliminated, as he described it, was simple and direct. The process included the recruitment of prominent American personalities who were to be used to deliver the Communist message both within and without the United States. These statements are developed by propaganda experts and were designed to alienate the American fighting man, or the average citizen, from the legitimate goals of his country. However, the subversive comments are also carefully designed to fall within the legal limits of American laws on espionage and treason.

The full effect of this technique would be felt when an aroused populace demands that a Jane Fonda be punished and finds it is not legally possible to do so. At this point, the soldier or citizen's anger will turn to resignation and apathy. Once the citizenry have been shown the ineffectiveness of the existent laws, it will be a relatively easy matter to remove even these protective arrangements.

The unusual success the enemy propaganda experts have gained in the United States may easily be recognized by the recent elimination of the Subversive Activities Control Board and the House Committee on Internal Security, and the emasculation of the Senate Internal Security Subcommittee. These accomplishments mean that in the global contest for power, the average American faces domestic enemies whom he otherwise views as outstanding representatives of his system. While at the same time, those whom he is fighting are being portrayed as friendly "agrarian reformers" or misguided Vietnamese patriots.

One of the strangest phenomena of the entire Vietnam War was the appearance of a former United States attorney general in Hanoi investigating the alleged war crimes of his own country. The North Vietnamese visit of Ramsey Clark lasted from July 29 to August 12, 1972. Clark, the son of a former Supreme Court justice, traveled to Hanoi under the sponsorship of the Stockholm-based International Commission of Inquiry, a Communist "peace" front.[18]

After the former attorney general arrived in Hanoi, he was driven through bombed-out villages, hospitals containing war casualties, and the damaged dikes at Namcuong. A few days later, he visited the heavily bombed port city of Haiphong. When Clark returned to Hanoi, he was interviewed by North Vietnamese reporters. He said, "There is absolutely no excuse for bombing North Vietnam and there never has been." The newsmen, who had recorded the interview, played the tape on Radio Hanoi three days later. Following his recording session, Clark met with a number of American prisoners of war whom he found to be in good health and reported their living conditions "could not be better."

Clark returned to the United States on August 13, and the following day he told newsmen that the Communist leaders in Hanoi had promised to release some prisoners of war when George McGovern was elected to the presidency. In the middle of August, he appeared before the American Bar Association, which was meeting in California, and reported the excellent treatment American prisoners were receiving in North Vietnam. Clark even suggested that those who claimed that American men were mistreated held "other motives" and were more interested in supporting "the Thieu government than getting the boys home."

The absurdity of Clark's claims was clearly shown when some of these men were released from their North Vietnamese prisons

[18] *Congressional Record,* March 18, 1974.

and the truth about their mistreatment became public knowledge. One of the former prisoners, Air Force Colonel James H. Kasler, was interviewed by the Pacific edition of *Stars and Stripes*. When asked about the antiwar protesters who visited North Vietnam during the war, Kasler said, "Efforts were made to force me to see these people. When I went to extremes to avoid that, I was tortured." He added:

> We can thank the war protestors for prolonging the war. Undeclared or not, what they did was treason. They gave aid and comfort to the enemy. Their hands are stained with the blood of American GIs."[19]

The Peace Talks Resume

The summer of 1972 was a time of great agony for the politburo leaders in Hanoi. Their invasion army had been defeated, the major ports of North Vietnam were closed to friendly shipping, and their supporters in Moscow and Peking were urging them to go back to the conference table. After a considerable amount of soul-searching, the North Vietnamese leadership decided to return to the negotiations in Paris.

The peace talks resumed on July 13, when both sides restated their positions. The American terms were recited by Deputy Ambassador William Porter, who summarized President Nixon's May 8 proposals. Xuan Thuy rejected these conditions and again demanded the overthrow of the Thieu regime.

On July 15 Le Duc Tho arrived in Paris for secret talks with Henry Kissinger. Four days later, the two negotiators met in private for more than six hours. During the next few weeks, Kissinger continued to negotiate with Tho, while he shuttled back and forth between Paris, Washington, and Saigon.[20]

At one point General Alexander M. Haig, Kissinger's deputy, was sent to Saigon to exert pressure on Thieu to accept several concessions the American side had already agreed to. Haig's mission was doomed to failure as the irate South Vietnamese president remained adamant in his stand against at least two of these proposals. Thieu stated that his government would never accept the establishment of a tripartite electoral body or the right of North Vietnam to maintain its troops in South Vietnam. After Haig left South Vietnam, United States Ambassador Ellsworth Bunker was assigned the undesirable task of softening up the reluctant Saigon leader.[21]

---

[19] *Indianapolis Star*, March 9, 1973.
[20] *Washington Post*, August 2, 1972.
[21] *China News Analysis*, March 21, 1972.

While the American ambassador was consulting with Thieu, Kissinger flew to Moscow as part of a series of previously arranged United States/Soviet consultations. On September 11, while the presidential adviser was in the Russian capital city, Radio Hanoi announced:

A solution to the internal problems of South Vietnam must proceed from the actual situation—that there exist in South Vietnam two administrations, two armies and other political forces.

After receiving news of the North Vietnamese broadcast, the American negotiator asked his hosts if the radio announcement meant that Hanoi had ceased demanding that the United States remove Thieu on its way out of South Vietnam. The Russians responded that they believed that this interpretation of the radio announcement was correct. Kissinger immediately returned to Paris, where he conferred again with Le Duc Tho on September 15. The next day, the presidential adviser emplaned for Washington, where he engaged in a series of discussions with other administration officials. At the end of the month, Kissinger journeyed again to Paris for further meetings with the North Vietnamese negotiator.

On October 8 Le Duc Tho placed a draft of a peace agreement on the table, which the presidential adviser has described in rather positive terms.* In spite of Kissinger's initial reaction, the North Vietnamese proposal contained several items that were unacceptable to the American side. These differences did not appear to be major, however, and a counterproposal was soon offered. After several working meetings, a fifty-eight-page document was developed that both groups felt was acceptable. The only remaining obstacle to the complete acceptance of the accords was the consent of the home governments of the parties involved in the negotiations. As this approval seemed a mere technicality, Kissinger and Tho agreed that the signing of the agreement would take place on October 31, just before the American national elections. When the presidential adviser returned to Washington, senior administration officials found the document to be a workable arrangement.

After securing approval in Washington, Kissinger traveled to Saigon with a stopover in Paris. He was determined to convince President Thieu that the draft peace proposal was acceptable. The South Vietnamese chief executive was adamantly opposed to the agreement and is reported to have stated that he would not accept "any two-part, three-part, or four-part government." Kissinger reportedly tempered Thieu's resistance to the accords by assuring him the United States

* In his speech before the *Pacem in Terris* conference on October 8, 1973, Henry Kissinger referred to Tho's draft agreement as the "breakthrough."

had an "understanding" with Moscow and Peking that would reduce the supply of arms to Hanoi and would cause the North Vietnamese to limit their future military activities.[22]

In spite of the Saigon leader's protest, the presidential adviser, who had returned to Washington, stated on October 26 that "peace is at hand." Three days later President Nixon, who apparently disagreed with Kissinger, announced that he would not go through with the signing of an agreement that would only bring a "temporary and not a lasting peace."

On November 7 Richard Nixon and Spiro Agnew were reelected in a victory of historic proportions. The Republican duo won every state in the Union with the exception of Massachusetts and the District of Columbia.* A week after the victory at the polls, the President directed a stern letter to his counterpart in Saigon. Nixon's message of November 14 was sent in response to a communication he had recently received from President Thieu. In his correspondence the American Chief Executive assured the Saigon leader that he was considering the changes that Thieu had suggested on November 11. However, Nixon left no doubt about who was in charge of the negotiations with the North Vietnamese when he wrote: "I cannot overemphasize the urgency of the task at hand nor my unalterable determination to proceed along the course we have outlined." The President cautioned Thieu:

In order to do this effectively it is essential that I have public support and that your government does not emerge as the obstacle to a peace which American public opinion now universally desires.

But the warnings were accompanied by a pledge of strong support for ᴖouth Vietnam in the event the Communists violated the peace arrangements. This assistance the American leader promised by saying, "You have my absolute assurance that if Hanoi fails to abide by the terms of this agreement, it is my intention to take swift and retaliatory action." There is every reason to believe that Nixon meant these words when he wrote them. Thieu, for his part, took immediate steps to perfect the formation of a new political grouping known as the Democracy party, which he had started in 1971. The South Vietnamese president also began forming "Peoples Anti-Communist Political Struggle Committees" throughout South Vietnam.

By the middle of November it appeared to Kissinger that the only obstacle to peace was a matter of language changes in the draft ac-

---

* The Nixon-Agnew team received 521 electoral votes against McGovern's 17. It was the worst defeat ever suffered by a Democratic presidential candidate.

[22] New York Times, April 7, 1973.

cords. This conclusion led him to reenter negotiations with Le Duc Tho on November 20 in a favorable frame of mind. After Kissinger had presented what he viewed as minor modifications in the format of the agreement, the North Vietnamese negotiator requested that the deliberations be recessed for eight days. The special adviser's reason for requesting the temporary cessation of negotiations was that he wanted to return to Hanoi for consultations. The North Vietnamese politburo's reaction to the proffered changes in the agreement was ominous indeed, for on December 3 they issued an order that all children be evacuated from Hanoi.[23]

While Le Duc Tho was in North Vietnam, Kissinger returned to the United States and held hurried discussions with President Nixon and other governmental officials. When the talks resumed in Paris on December 4, the Communist side insisted that the United States accept the October draft accords intact. After a week of fruitless negotiations, Tho presented Kissinger with a new set of "protocols" that contained sixteen alterations in the original agreement.

Having returned to Washington on December 15, the presidential adviser described these changes to newsmen the following day:

> These protocols were not technical instruments, but reopened a whole list of issues that had been settled, or we thought had been settled in the agreement. They contained provisions that were not in the original agreement, and they excluded provisions that were in the original agreement.[24]

Kissinger also pinpointed a major area of disagreement between the two parties when he discussed the machinery for supervising the accords. According to the American negotiator, the North Vietnamese believed that the administrative force should be limited to 250 men. In his opinion, this number was extremely inadequate, as he envisioned several thousand monitors.

The next day President Nixon, who had not been able to gain Thieu's complete agreement to the terms of the agreement, addressed another letter to the South Vietnamese leader. This time he wrote: "I am convinced that your refusal to join us would be an invitation to disaster—to the loss of all that we together have fought for over the past decade."

The stalled negotiations caused Nixon's advisers to search for a way to break the deadlock. After an extended series of meetings, they arrived at an answer which seemed to solve a multiplicity of prob-

---

[23] *U.S. News and World Report,* January 1, 1973.

[24] Department of State, Bureau of Public Affairs, "Vietnam Peace Talks: Status of Negotiations," 1972.

lems. This solution was the Christmas bombings of 1972.* For a period of twelve days, from December 18 to 30, North Vietnam was subjected to one of the most intensive bombings in the history of warfare.[25] B-52s operating from bases in Guam and Thailand, and other warplanes from the decks of the Seventh fleet in the China Sea, flew over 1,400 strikes in the first week of the aerial assault. The President ordered a thirty-six-hour halt in the bombing over Christmas and the attack was resumed with increased ferocity on December 26.†

As a result of the air raids, approximately eighty percent of North Vietnam's electrical power was knocked out. Major military installations were reduced to rubble and about twenty-five percent of the country's petrol supplies were wiped out. The extreme losses forced the Communist leaders to agree to a resumption of the peace talks, and on December 30 President Nixon ordered a halt to the bombing above the 20th parallel. At the same time, he announced that Kissinger and Le Duc Tho would meet again in Paris on January 8, 1973.

While the aerial destruction had convinced the North Vietnamese that negotiations were preferable to living under a hail of bombs, President Thieu was still not prepared to agree to the terms Kissinger had negotiated. The South Vietnamese leader's views on the peace agreement, as it existed on December 30, were expressed in a personal interview with Italian journalist Oriana Fallaci: "Accepting the presence of North Vietnamese troops by juridicial agreement, ratified by an international conference, is absolutely unacceptable."[26]

At the end of the year, it appeared that congressional antiwar forces had won several minor victories. Public support for the President's Vietnam policies, however, was rather widespread. This general attitude, plus an unwillingness to challenge the authority of the Chief Executive in the conduct of foreign relations, effectively disposed of all serious end-the-war legislation during the 92nd Congress.

[25] *The Late December 1972 US Blitz on North Vietnam* (Hanoi: Foreign Languages Publishing House, 1973).

[26] *New Republic,* January 20, 1973.

* The December 1972 bombings were designed to force the North Vietnamese to return to the conference table. They also served to convince Thieu that the United States would stand by him in time of need.

† One top military planner said that "if the United States had bombed North Vietnam as heavily years ago as it did between December 18 and December 30, 1972, the war would have been over in 1967."

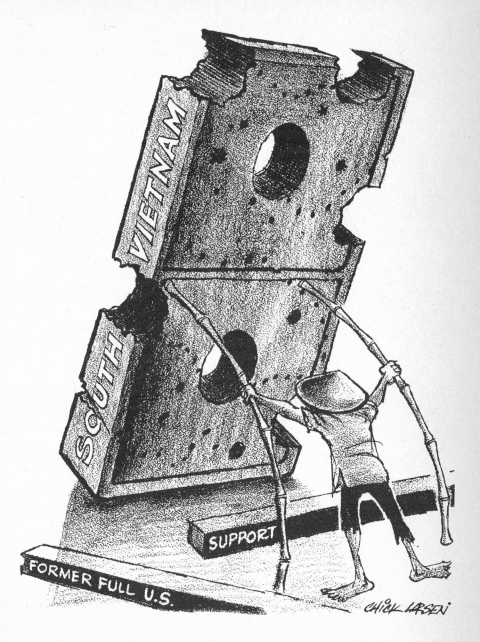

—*Richmond Times-Dispatch*

VI / The Peace That Could Have Been

During the summer of 1973 the war in Indochina continued to smolder and Watergate became a congressional fixation. One of the sources of contention in the continued Indochinese fighting was Hanoi's attempt to infiltrate its soldiers into South Vietnam through Cambodia. The President had managed to halt or at least to slow down the entrance of these troops into the Southern Republic by bombing Cambodian sections of the Ho Chi Minh Trail.

Congressional opponents of the war seized upon the continued aerial assaults and the President's Watergate-induced weakness as an opportunity to eliminate all American military activities in Indochina. In a series of bitter battles in the Senate, the antiwar members demanded that the bombing of Cambodia stop on June 30. As a result of a compromise between administration forces and Senate doves, the President agreed to halt all United States military activities in Indochina on August 15.

When the President's compromise agreement reached the Senate, the man who led the fight for the extension of the cutoff date was Senator Fulbright. The senator's reason for supporting the administration's proposal was based on a well-grounded belief that the President would continue to veto any other antibombing legislation. Since the Senate had previously refused to override the presidential veto on this issue, Fulbright concluded it was August 15 or nothing. The Arkansas Democrat further clarified his motives for supporting the extended date on June 29, when, in describing the situation of the President, he said:

> From his point of view, he is in a very difficult position today on account of the hearings in the committee under the leadership of the

distinguished senator from North Carolina. [Sam J. Ervin, Jr. of North Carolina was Chairman of the Senate Watergate Committee]

The Congress proceeded to pass this legislation, which was signed into law on July 1, 1973.

The Peace Accords

President Nixon's announcement of the resumption of negotiations in Paris on January 8, 1973 was received with strong misgivings in Saigon. The South Vietnamese leadership indicated that no agreement could be developed which would meet the requirements of Hanoi, Washington, and Saigon. President Thieu was reported to have stated at a New Year's Eve reception that he wanted a "durable, long-lasting peace, not just an armistice which the Communists can exploit to renew their aggression." The primary resistance of the Saigon regime to the October accords was based on their very real desire for the North Vietnamese troops to return to North Vietnam. They also demanded that any final arrangements grant the government of the Republic "sovereignty" over the entire South Vietnamese nation.

Thieu's continued fight against the accords prompted President Nixon to exert additional pressure on the Saigon leader. The new coercion came in the form of another urgent communication informing the South Vietnamese president that if the Communists went along with "our concerns . . . we will proceed to conclude the settlement." The message continued: "The gravest consequences would then ensue if your government chose to reject the agreement and split off from the United States." The letter obviously represented a threat. Thieu must support the American position in the negotiations, or else. As a further means of encouraging the South Vietnamese leader to sign the accords, Nixon wrote:

> You have my assurance of continued assistance in the post-settlement period and that we will respond with full force should the settlement be violated by North Vietnam.[1]

This guarantee, coupled with the memory of the Christmas bombings of North Vietnam, lessened Thieu's resistance to signing the agreement.[2]

[1] *New York Times,* May 1, 1975.

[2] Nguyen Cao Ky has described Thieu's dependence upon the guarantee in the following words: "Before he signed it, Mr. Thieu was fully aware that it was not popular so he just passed the word around that, well don't be afraid. We had that guarantee from President Nixon." Ky has also stated: "So I think without Watergate maybe Mr. Nixon could have kept his promise"; see *Firing Line,* guest: Nguyen Cao Ky, PBS, October 4, 1975.

Henry Kissinger and Le Duc Tho resumed their negotiations in Paris on January 8 in a less than "cordial atmosphere." By the morning of the next day, however, it was apparent to the presidential adviser that both sides were determined to make a serious effort to break the "deadlock in negotiations."

For the next week the two diplomats worked on resolving their major disagreements, while a combined team of American and North Vietnamese subordinates worked out the details. After completing what he viewed as the essential issues, Kissinger returned to Washington, while Deputy Ambassador Porter remained behind to complete the agreements.

On January 14 General Haig flew to Saigon to discuss the accords with President Thieu. Four days later, following an announcement of the suspension of all offensive actions against North Vietnam, Kissinger left Washington for Paris "for the purpose of completing the text of the agreement."

At 10:01 P.M. on January 23, President Nixon addressed the nation on radio and television and issued a formal statement announcing the end of the war:

> At 12:30 Paris time today, January 23, 1973, the agreement on ending the war and restoring peace in Vietnam was initialed by Dr. Henry Kissinger on behalf of the United States, and Special Adviser Le Duc Tho on behalf of the Democratic Republic of Vietnam.
>
> The agreement will be formally signed by the parties participating in the Paris Conference in Vietnam on January 27, 1973, at the International Conference Center in Paris.
>
> The cease-fire will take effect at 2400 Greenwich Mean Time, January 27, 1973. The United States and the Democratic Republic of Vietnam express the hope that this agreement will insure stable peace in Vietnam and contribute to the preservation of lasting peace in Indochina and Southeast Asia.[3]

The following day Kissinger released the text of the cease-fire agreement at a news conference in Washington. The settlement was entitled "Agreement on Ending the War and Restoring the Peace in Vietnam."[*] There were four protocols accompanying the document. Because the Republic of South Vietnam was unwilling to grant recognition to the Vietcong, the agreement and three protocols were drafted in two versions. Both renditions were almost identical. The heart of the accords was the cease-fire article, which stated that when the agreement went into effect the armed forces of both sides were to

[3] U.S. Department of State, Bureau of Public Affairs, "Address of the President as Delivered on Live Radio and Television, January 23, 1973," 1973.

[*] See Appendix A.

"remain in place." Other key features of the settlement involved the withdrawal of all American armed forces from Vietnam and the release of captured military personnel. It also created several committees to supervise or implement the various military and political provisos that the negotiating parties had agreed to.

At the end of the presentation, Kissinger indicated his willingness to accept questions from the newsmen. One of the reporters asked about the North Vietnamese troops that remained in the south. The presidential adviser responded that there were approximately 145,000 of these regular soldiers, but that "nothing in the agreement established the right of North Vietnamese troops to be in the south." He added that due to various restrictions contained in the treaty there would eventually be a "reduction of North Vietnamese troops in South Vietnam." Kissinger was also asked how he had been able to sell the agreement to President Thieu; he answered:

> President Thieu, after examining the totality of the agreement, came to the conclusion that it achieved the essential objectives of South Vietnam, of permitting his people to bring about self determination and of not posing a security risk that he could not handle with the forces we have equipped and trained.

As a general rule, Americans seemed to accept the settlement with relief and a desire to move on to other things. There was, however, considerable criticism of the presidential adviser for having negotiated an agreement that appeared to have little chance of success. On the other hand, several veteran observers of the affairs of Southeast Asia had come to a different conclusion. Former Brandeis University Professor John P. Roche and Morton Kaplan of the University of Chicago were convinced that the settlement was better than might have been hoped for under the existing conditions. Within three weeks after the signing of the accords, Kaplan said, "That the South Vietnamese have reasonable opportunity to maintain their independence and resist totalitarian rule is a remarkable outcome."[4] Two days later Roche stated: "The Paris accords, if successfully implemented, do constitute the fundamentals of peace with honor."[5]

The signing of the documents in Paris provided an opportunity for the Cambodian president to declare a unilateral cease-fire on January 28, 1973. At first the truce seemed to open up some "promising" contacts with Cambodian Communist leaders. But this initial response disappeared when the rebels launched scattered attacks against government posts near Phnom Penh. The Communist as-

---

[4] *Vietnam Settlement,* p. 164.
[5] Ibid., p. 13.

saults were met by Lon Nol's forces, who requested that the Americans resume the bombing of their country.

In spite of the renewal of fighting in Cambodia in the early part of February, United States naval forces began clearing the mines from the harbors and rivers of North Vietnam. At the same time, the North Vietnamese released the first group of American POWs. These actions were viewed by interested observers as indications of the peaceful intentions of both sides.

Sad to say, peace did not reign on the South Vietnamese battlefront. Under the terms of the accords, the future of the various areas into which South Vietnam was to be divided was left undecided. The negotiators had stated that it would be better for the "two parties" (the Vietcong and the Saigon government) to decide the exact dimensions of their zones of control. When the agreement was signed the "two parties" immediately rushed their political action teams into the contested areas and sporadic fighting erupted.

The minor violations of the settlement had been expected by Henry Kissinger, who made little mention of these incidents when he visited Hanoi February 10–13, 1973. The presidential adviser had flown to the former enemy capital for the purpose of arranging postwar American financial assistance to North Vietnam. This economic aid had formed an important part of the negotiations in Paris, and the North Vietnamese were counting strongly on its immediate delivery.*

After meeting with North Vietnamese Premier Pham Van Dong and other members of the politburo, Kissinger agreed to the establishment of a joint economic commission. The new organization was to be staffed with an equal number of members from both sides. Its mission was to "develop economic relations" between the United States and North Vietnam. As Kissinger left Hanoi, his hosts reminded him that they would soon meet again in Paris.

When the two parties met again in the capital of the French Republic, they were both members of an international assembly. Under the terms of the Paris accords the negotiators had agreed to invite other powers to help "guarantee the ending of the war."

In accord with this agreement, twelve political groupings gathered in Paris on February 26, 1973, for an international conference. The participants were Canada, the People's Republic of China, the United States of America, the French Republic, the Provisional Revolutionary Government of the Republic of South Vietnam, the Hungarian People's Republic, the Republic of Indonesia, the Polish People's Republic, the Democratic Republic of Vietnam, Great Britain, the Republic

---

* The sum most often mentioned by administration representatives that was eventually destined for North Vietnam amounted to $2.5 billion.

of Vietnam, The USSR, and the secretary general of the United Nations. The delegates included United States Secretary of State Rogers, Soviet Foreign Minister Andrei A. Gromyko, French Foreign Minister Maurice Schumann, and British Secretary of State Alec Douglas-Home.

After several days of diplomatic speech-making, the representatives signed a statement on March 2 that, in effect, was meant to guarantee the Paris agreements. During the discussions regarding the settlement, the North Vietnamese had succeeded in having the Vietcong designated as a government in the opening paragraphs of the act. The United States, in order to counter this minor Communist achievement, was able to have a phrase inserted in the declaration that stated, "Signature of this act does not constitute recognition of any party in any case in which it has not previously been accorded."[6] In retrospect, the conference appears to have provided a place for diplomats to issue solemn statements of support for the Paris accords. In the long run, however, it proved to be merely another exercise in public showmanship by the parties concerned.

During the time the delegates were meeting, the continued struggle between North and South Vietnamese military and political units had caused the release of American POWs to be temporarily interrupted. Accordingly, President Nixon ordered a halt to the clearing of the mines and ceased withdrawing American troops from Vietnam. These strong measures had the desired effect, and on March 1 the North Vietnamese announced that they would start releasing the prisoners again. In return, the President ordered the navy to continue removing the mines and the United States troops to leave Vietnam by the end of the month.

On March 29, 1973, the last sixty-one Americans were freed by the North Vietnamese. Their return brought the total number of United States prisoners released to 587. During the period the exchange was taking place, the POWs had not commented on their life in prison. The silence was based on the fear of retaliation against those Americans still remaining in North Vietnam. Once the last of their numbers had been released, the ex-prisoners began to tell how they had been treated in Hanoi's prisons.

The tales revealed that the North Vietnamese had tortured, starved, and in some cases executed prisoners in what appeared to be a systematic pattern of brutal behavior. The men reported that they had been beaten and shackled, that their wounds had remained untreated, and that they were denied basic medical care.

[6] United States Department of State, "Text of the Act of the International Conference on Viet-Nam," March 5, 1973.

A random sampling of the stories reveals how the men had been abused. Navy Lieutenant Commander Rodney A. Knutson, in describing his imprisonment, said that after he was captured in 1965:

> I was beaten to the point of near unconsciousness, my nose was broken, both my eyes were swollen shut. My teeth were broken. I was then turned over on my stomach in the stocks while my ropes were still tying my arms together. . . .

Knutson concluded, "It has been said by the North Vietnamese that we had received lenient and humane treatment. Lenient and humane? Not on your life!"

Air Force Colonel Robinson Risner, who was captured in 1965, reported that North Vietnamese guards

> would tie your wrists behind you, make your arms pull out of their sockets, bend you until your toes were in your mouth, then leave you in this manner until you acquiesced in whatever they were trying to get you to do.[7]

According to the former captives, one of the most galling experiences they had to endure was the intellectual anguish caused by enemy psychological warfare experts. This mental torture occurred when the North Vietnamese guards subjected the prisoners to daily propaganda lectures regarding the war and the evils of the American system of government. At first the Communists were forced to use their own material. After 1967, however, an ever-increasing supply of American newspapers and magazines containing antiwar statements allowed the guards to use the new publications. Nick Rowe, who had escaped from captivity in 1968, has described this development:

> It was no longer a matter of manufacturing propaganda; they had only to scan our publications, find a prominent American who had said what they wanted to use and hit us with it. The most damaging material was that drawn from our *Congressional Record* in which our goals and efforts were condemned.
>
> Because we refused to comply with the demands of our captors, we suffered. Three of my people died of starvation and disease, and three were executed.[8]

These reports of calculated abuse were in strong contrast to the treatment that North Vietnamese and Vietcong prisoners of war received in South Vietnamese camps. During the war International Red Cross supervisors, as well as several Western newsmen, were allowed to enter the enclosures where the enemy soldiers were imprisoned.

[7] *U.S. News and World Report*, April 9, 1973.
[8] *New York Times*, February 12, 1975.

One of these reporters, Martin Gershen of the *Long Island Press*, visited the POW compound in Pleiku during the month of December 1967. At that time the NVA/VC soldiers were detained in Da Nang, Pleiku, Quinhon, Bien Hoa, Can Tho, and on the island of Phu Quoc, which was reserved for the more troublesome prisoners.

The inhabitants of the camps had arrived there after being screened by South Vietnamese intelligence personnel. Following the interrogation, the POW had been placed in one of four categories: (1) innocent civilians—these were returned immediately to wherever they came from; (2) Chieu Hoi—a Vietnamese term meaning "returnees" or defectors; these men were placed in separate camps where they are trained for service in the South Vietnamese army or given a civilian job; (3) civil defendents—these were spies, saboteurs, or terrorists; they were turned over to civilian authorities and classified as political prisoners; and (4) military prisoners of war—men and women who have been captured in combat and are clearly legitimate soldiers; these were placed in POW camps.

After Gershen had passed the multiple strands of barbed wire that stretched endlessly around the compound at Pleiku, he inspected the barracks, the medical building, and the mess hall. When he had completed his visit, the New York journalist wrote:

> Captives are quartered in wooden barracks, in comfortable bunks with mosquito netting and blankets. They get three meals a day, totaling 3,200 calories. The average prisoner gains about 25 pounds in the first two months. Each camp also has a doctor or a medic provided by the South Vietnamese army.

Three years later, two dozen newsmen accompanied Texas millionaire H. Ross Perot as he inspected four of the six prison centers in South Vietnam. Perot's inspection tour was part of an attempt to get the North Vietnamese to release information about captured United States servicemen.

One of the reporters was Charles H. Wickenberg, Jr., executive editor of *The State* and the *Columbia Record* newspapers in Columbia, South Carolina. As Perot visited the POW enclosures, the newsmen followed closely behind him and observed the condition of the prisoners. On April 2 editor Wickenberg filed a story with his newspapers from Pleiku that fairly well substantiated what Gershen had previously reported. His report contained a description of clean barracks, decent food, medical treatment, and an observation from Perot, who stated, "The International Red Cross indicates that these camps here are some of the best run. I'd say that if I were a POW, I'd rather be here than in the North" (*Congressional Record*, May 6, 1970).

On March 29, 1973, the last United States troops left Vietnam and the American Military Assistance Command in Saigon was deactivated. These events provided the occasion for President Nixon to make a nationwide address. In his speech the Chief Executive indicated satisfaction with the American withdrawal from Vietnam. He directed the attention of his audience to the fact that under the terms of the treaty the South Vietnamese people still "had the right to choose their own government without outside interference." The President admitted, though, that problems still remained, particularly North Vietnamese violations of the clause in the agreement that prohibited "infiltration from North Vietnam into South Vietnam." Nixon ended his talk with a call for national unity.

The withdrawal of the United States troops also gave the administration an opportunity to reassign Ellsworth Bunker, the American ambassador to South Vietnam. Following the announcement of Bunker's impending transfer, the White House revealed on March 30 that his replacement would be Graham Martin, a veteran diplomat.

Several days before the ambassadorial reassignments were announced, the specter of Watergate began to haunt Richard Nixon's actions. The increased intrusion on the President's conduct was due to the fact that his attorney, John W. Dean III, had been directly connected to Watergate affairs by L. Patrick Gray.* The implications contained in Gray's testimony forced Nixon to remove Dean from all Watergate related activities on March 30. The same day, the former presidential attorney hired a criminal lawyer.

Hanoi's 1973 Spring Offensive

When the politburo leaders looked at North Vietnam's position in early 1973, it was obvious that the attempt to conquer South Vietnam would have to shift into a combined political-military effort, with an emphasis on the political. This conclusion was based on a realistic appraisal of their resources. The army was still weak from its 1972 losses, and the home front had been badly damaged by the December bombings. However, the situation was far from lost: the United States navy was clearing the harbors through which new war materials could be imported, the American command in Saigon had departed, and a North Vietnamese army of about 145,000 men was still in South Vietnam.

Unfortunately, and much to the Hanoi leadership's dismay, Presi-

* On March 22 during the hearings regarding his confirmation as director of the FBI, Gray testified that Dean had probably lied to agents investigating the Watergate incident.

dent Thieu was proving to be a strong adversary. His organization of the Democracy Party and subsequent political and military actions had denied the Communists the ability to assume control over several disputed sections of Vietnam. Their failure to capture these areas was primarily based on the simple fact that there was a lack of southern Communists in South Vietnam. The Vietcong movement had been so decimated during Tet in 1968 that it had never fully recovered its previous strength. The South Vietnamese police had also played a significant role in reducing the number of available revolutionaries. After several long and stirring sessions of self-criticism, the Communist leaders arrived at what appeared to be an easy solution to their problem—they would free their cadre from the South Vietnamese jails.

The political prisoners captured during the war still remained incarcerated when negotiations between the "two parties" for their liberation broke down. Under the terms of the Paris accords, the return of United States military personnel and foreign civilians (North Vietnamese) had been accomplished. The question of the release of Vietnamese civilian personnel had, however, been delegated to the "two parties," who were currently not talking to each other.

The retention of the South Vietnamese terrorists was a perfectly normal desire on the part of the Saigon authorities. Any government that wishes to survive must, out of sheer necessity, arrest those who work for its destruction. The concept of the friendly neighborhood guerrilla is a creation of the Western news media. There is nothing friendly about being on the receiving end of several pounds of plastic explosives or having your throat slashed in the night. To classify these enemies of society as political prisoners and place them beyond responsibility for their actions is to grant all terrorists anywhere a license to maim and kill.

Even great democracies have had to restrict some civil liberties in time of war. During World War I, Great Britain suspended the Magna Carta, the Petition of Right, and the Bill of Rights by enacting the Defense of the Realm Act (DORA) on August 8, 1914.

Under the terms of DORA, the British government granted military authorities the right to

> arrest without warrant any person whose behavior is of such a nature as to give reasonable grounds for suspecting that he is acting or has acted or is about to act in a manner prejudicial to the public safety or the defense of the realm.[9]

---

[9] Clinton Rossiter, *Constitutional Dictatorship: Crisis Government in the Modern Democracies* (New York: Harcourt, Brace and World, Inc., 1948), p. 252.

Later in the century, when Hitler's legions were poised to invade Poland, the British enacted a rejuvenated DORA known as the Emergency Powers Act on August 24, 1940. The new law allowed government authorities to arrest and imprison some 1,428 persons for political offenses, including Captain Archibald Ramsay, a member of the House of Commons.

In times of war the United States has not been without restrictive legislation of its own. During the Civil War, Abraham Lincoln suspended the writ of habeas corpus and is known to have jailed thousands of persons who could probably best be described as political dissidents. Woodrow Wilson successfully prosecuted more than 1,000 United States citizens for violating various censorship laws during World War I. Franklin Roosevelt had his emergency proclamations, and Harry Truman acted under the Internal Security Act of 1950.

Once the politburo leaders had realized they were losing the political war in South Vietnam, they launched an international campaign to "free the political prisoners in South Vietnamese jails." The organization chosen to direct the worldwide effort was the National Liberation Front.[10]

Within days of the establishment of the new program, letters were pouring in to editors in every country in the world describing the plight of the political prisoners of South Vietnam. News analysts featured interviews with prominent personalities regarding Saigon's prisons, and magazines set aside sections of their foreign news columns for discussions of "Thieu's tiger cages." A representative sampling of these activities follows:

"Thieu must be Pressured to Free Political Prisoners"—*Ann Arbor News,* February 22, 1973

"Political Prisoners in South Vietnam"—NBC Nightly News, Interview by Dennis Troute with David and Jane Barton in Saigon, Washington Report, February 28, 1973 (6:30 P.M.)

"Many New Tiger Cages"—John Champlin, *Washington Post,* March 3, 1973

"Shackled in the Tiger Cages of Con Son"—Anthony Lewis, *Irish Times,* Dublin, March 7, 1973[11]

[10] *The Thieu Regime Put to the Test: 1973–1975* (Hanoi: Foreign Languages Publishing House, 1975), p. 33.
[11] Additional entries may be obtained from a listing presented to a House Subcommittee by Representative Bella Abzug (D., N.Y.). Hearings Before the Subcommittee on Asian and Pacific Affairs of the House Committee on Foreign Affairs, "Political Prisoners in South Vietnam and the Philippines," 1974. To date Mrs. Abzug has not published a report on political prisoners in North Vietnam, even though this state has been at the bottom of the Freedom House "political rights" and "civil rights" surveys since its founding. *Freedom at Issue* (New York: Freedom House, January–February 1976), p. 15.

The success the NLF campaign enjoyed in the media was, however, vastly overshadowed when the House of Representatives of the United States set aside one hour for the condemnation of President Nguyen Van Thieu of South Vietnam. This development is almost without precedent. There is probably no other time in history when one warring nation has manipulated the legislature of its mortal enemy into setting aside an hour for the censure of that nation's ally.

The condemnation session opened on April 2, 1973, while Thieu was visiting President Nixon in San Clemente, California. The first accusations against the South Vietnamese leader were made by Robert F. Drinan (D., Mass.). The political priest charged Thieu with being "crafty," "cunning," a "panhandler," and a "self-appointed dictator." During his verbal assault on South Vietnam's president, Drinan criticized the Vietnamese national election of 1967 and complained about the treatment of Trung Trinh Dzu, who had come in second in the contest.[12]

John F. Seiberling (D., Ohio) lamented the case of two French teachers, Pierre Debris and Andre Menras, who, while guests of the South Vietnamese government, participated in political demonstrations against their hosts. These men were subsequently arrested and placed in prison. Seiberling continued:

. . . until finally the International Red Cross came in, and there was such a hue and cry raised in France that the regime finally, in December 1972, released them and they were sent back to France.*

Jerome R. Waldie (D., Calif.) spoke of the dangers contained in the Phoenix program and stated that it was his belief the United States should not have engaged in activities "whose primary objective was to prepare the country for the political struggle to ensue at the conclusion of the military hostilities."[13]

[12] Dzu, a Saigon lawyer with a shady reputation, had won five provinces in the election. All of these areas were considered to be at least under nominal Vietcong control. Howard R. Penniman, *Elections in South Vietnam* (Washington, D.C.: American Enterprise Institute for Public Policy Research, and Stanford, California: The Hoover Institution on War, Revolution, and Peace, Stanford University, 1972), pp. 69, 74.

[13] The Phoenix program was an American-sponsored pacification plan designed to remove the Vietcong terrorist network that threatened the daily lives of the Vietnamese people. When Max Clos of *Le Figaro* visited the village of Long Thoi in South Vietnam during 1972, he noted the extent that peace had returned to the area. He was informed by the local chief, "That is the work of the Phoenix operation, which is very efficient here."

* There is every probability that if two American Nazis had participated in political demonstrations in favor of their cause in New York City during World War II, they might not have made it to the police station. It should also be noted that the International Red Cross was able to enter the situation. This is not the case in most so-called democracies in the world, nor is the Red Cross even allowed to enter North Vietnam.

George E. Brown, Jr. (D., Calif.) discussed the "horrors" of prison life for the political prisoners in Vietnam. He then entered into the *Congressional Record* a document from the Indochina Resource Center entitled "Vietnam: What Kind of Peace?" The report, as expected, contained a strong attack on the South Vietnamese government. Among other things, the article mentioned "Thieu's repression" and "Thieu's political prisoners."

The Indochina Resource Center was a political action group very similar to the old Institute of Pacific Relations, which conditioned the American people to abandon mainland China to the Communists. Only this time, the activities of the new grouping were directed to convincing the public to forsake the South Vietnamese nationalists. Gareth D. Porter and Fred Branfman were codirectors of the center.[14] Porter has been known to cite Hanoi's propaganda publication, *The Vietnam Courier,* when discussing the areas the Communists claimed as their own in South Vietnam.[15] He also believes it was simple Vietnamese mountain tribesmen known as Montagnards and not North Vietnamese regulars who captured the South Vietnamese city of Ban Me Thuot in 1975.[16] Branfman's sympathies are revealed by his reference to the Communist attempt to conquer South Korea as a "local insurgency."[17]

Congressman Brown also raised the issue of the total number of political prisoners in South Vietnamese jails when he said:

> And now that the conflict is slowing down, Mr. Thieu is buying his respect with the bodies of 200,000 men, women, and children he keeps locked away as political prisoners.

There has understandably been considerable controversy over the exact prison population in South Vietnam at this time. Estimates have varied from 300,000 to none. The more likely figure is in the neighborhood of 35,000 prisoners of all types.[18] This fairly precise number was arrived at by the investigators for the American Mission in Saigon, who also concluded that in mid-1973 the entire prison capacity of South Vietnam was under 50,000 persons.

---

[14] In testimony before a House committee, Branfman stated, "We are sponsored by the Board of Social Concern of the United Methodist Church, United Church of Christ, and the United Presbyterian Church." Hearings Before the House Committee on Foreign Affairs, "Fiscal Year 1975 Foreign Assistance Request," 1974, p. 671.

[15] House Subcommittee Hearings, "Political Prisoners in South Vietnam and the Philippines," 1974, p. 41.

[16] *New York Times,* January 11, 1976.

[17] House Subcommittee Hearings, "Political Prisoners in South Vietnam and the Philippines," 1974, p. 18. A further indication of Branfman's political persuasions may be inferred by his membership on the advisory board of *Counter-Spy,* the publication of the Fifth Estate.

[18] Ibid., p. 98.

As the condemnation hour proceeded, Representative Don Edwards (D., Calif.) complained indignantly about the toilet facilities in an Operation Phoenix establishment located near Saigon. According to the congressman, when he visited the compound in 1971, he discovered that the prisoners had to sleep on the floor, "with a small hole in the center" for sanitary purposes.*

Elizabeth Holtzman (D., N.Y.) attempted to show how the Thieu government had not lived up to the terms of the Paris accords. In a statement before the House the Brooklyn Democrat directed the attention of her associates to the fact that American POWs had been released, yet Vietnamese civilians still remained imprisoned. These actions were, in her opinion, interconnected, and revealed the utter depravity of the South Vietnamese government. Holtzman's actual words were:

> The cease-fire accords—under which our prisoners of war were returned—provide for the release of "Vietnamese civilian personnel captured and detained in South Vietnam"—Article 8.

This partial quotation, taken from Article 8 of the agreement, could lead the unwary to connect the two events. Research reveals, however, that the accords provided for the release of these two groupings at different times. Article 8(a) of the agreement required the return of the American POWs within sixty days. Article 8(c) only provided for the "resolution" of the Vietnamese civilian prisoner question within ninety days.[19]

As the accords had been signed on January 27, 1973, the "two South Vietnamese parties" had until April 27 to resolve the release of the Vietnamese civilians. When Holtzman addressed the House, some twenty-five days remained under the terms of the agreement for the negotiators to "resolve" their difficulties.

Five other members of the House spoke in the hour-long attack on Thieu on April 2, 1973. For the most part, they accused the South Vietnamese government of being repressive and not releasing the civilian prisoners. The representatives, all Democrats, were Bella Abzug (N.Y.), Patricia Schroeder (Colo.), Jonathan Bingham (N.Y.), Michael Harrington (Mass.), and Ralph H. Metcalfe (Ill.).

Meanwhile, the South Vietnamese leader and President Nixon had been meeting at the Western White House. On April 3 the two leaders issued a joint communiqué reporting that a "full consensus" had

[19] See the text of the accords in Appendix A.

* It would be interesting to know what kind of accommodations the congressman enjoyed when he visited South Vietnam. A small hole in the floor for sanitary purposes is standard equipment throughout Asia. Only westernized establishments are equipped with ceramic toilet fixtures.

been reached. Among the statements that indicated the tone of the conference were the following:

> Both presidents . . . viewed with great concern infiltrations of men and weapons in sizable numbers from North Vietnam into South Vietnam in violation of the agreement on ending the war, and considered [that] actions which would threaten the basis of the agreement would call for appropriate vigorous reactions.
>
> * * *
>
> They expressed their grave concern at the fact that Article 20 of the agreement, which calls for the unconditional withdrawal of all foreign forces from Laos and Cambodia, has not been carried out.
>
> * * *
>
> President Nixon affirmed that the United States, for its part, expected to continue, in accordance with its constitutional processes, to supply the Republic of Vietnam with the material means for its defense consistent with the agreement on ending the war.[20]

Following the issuance of the joint statement, President Thieu flew to Washington, where he addressed the National Press Club. In his speech he stated that he was ready to release 5,000 Communist "agents" if North Vietnam would only release the 67,500 South Vietnamese officials it still detained. Later in the day Thieu went to Capitol Hill, where he met with congressional leaders.

A few hours before the South Vietnamese leader met with the legislators, the Senate voted 88–3 to forbid any reconstruction aid to North Vietnam unless President Nixon obtained the prior approval of Congress. The lopsided vote was a clear message to the Chief Executive that Congress wanted to be consulted on any postwar assistance to Indochina.

Surrender in Washington

The Senate action against aid to North Vietnam had been taken at a time when United States air forces were conducting virtual round-the-clock bombing in Cambodia. The air attacks were in response to Hanoi's failure to observe Article 20, section (b), of the Paris accords, which read:

> Foreign countries shall put an end to all military activities in Cambodia and Laos, totally withdraw from and refrain from reintroducing into these two countries troops, military advisers, and military personnel, armaments, ammunition, and war materials.

While the majority of the B-52s and F-111 fighter-bombers were engaged in helping Lon Nol's forces, a sizable number of bombs were

[20] *New York Times*, April 4, 1973.

144

dropped on the Cambodian section of the Ho Chi Minh Trail where it entered Vietnam. The necessity for this bombing was revealed in a 43-page report issued on July 19, 1973 by the Canadian representatives to the International Commission for Control and Supervision (ICCS). The ICCS is the organization that was supposed to supervise the implementation of the Paris accords.

The study was entitled ICCS Investigation R7/106, and it described what the Canadians believed to be the source of the breakdown in the cease-fire agreement. According to the report, the continuing infiltration required an on-the-spot investigation of the accusations. The Canadian team, in compliance with their duties, prepared to examine the evidence to discover which side was at fault. The Hungarian and Polish members of the ICCS refused to participate in the inquiry, so the Canadians and Indonesians conducted the investigation on their own. The section of the accords that the Canadians were particularly interested in enforcing reads:

> From the enforcement of the cease-fire to the formation of the government provided for in Articles 9(b) and 14 of this Agreement, the two South Vietnamese parties shall not accept the introduction of troops, military advisers, and military personnel including technical military personnel, armaments, munitions, and war material into South Vietnam.

As part of their investigation of the infiltration charges, the Canadians questioned four captured members of Hanoi's "2006 infiltration group," who had entered Vietnam after passing through Cambodia in June 1973. Following the interviews, a report was prepared.

> From the testimony of the captured North Vietnamese Army soldiers, it can be concluded there never was the slightest indication during the four and one-half months following the cease-fire that the Democratic Republic of Vietnam has modified its infiltration policy. This policy of unrelenting infiltration down the Ho Chi Minh Trail system is graphically illustrated by the piling up of 7, 12, or even 20 infiltration units of approximately 500 men each in Cambodian rest stations when the infiltration pipeline was blocked for 15 days during the month of April.*

The North Vietnamese soldiers also described how they had changed from their regular army uniforms to the blue-green pajamas of the Vietcong before entering South Vietnam. One of the troopers said that he had seen trucks headed south loaded with ammunition, rice, and supplies. According to the NVA soldier, the convoys were no longer restricting their travel to nighttime as the bombing in Laos

---

* The reason the North Vietnamese troops were "piling up" in Cambodia was that United States bombers had virtually closed the trail where it enters lower South Vietnam.

had been halted. While the infiltrators had observed war materials moving south, they had also seen large groups of North Vietnamese civilians heading in the same direction.

The high level of infiltration of North Vietnamese troops into South Vietnam was of great concern to President Nixon. As an indication of his annoyance, on April 7 he sent General Haig on a whirlwind tour of Laos, Cambodia, South Vietnam, and Thailand. After the general had returned to Washington, United States warplanes stationed in Thailand bombed Laos-based NVA units that had seized a small Laotian town near the Plain of Jars. President Nixon also ordered the navy to stop removing mines from the North Vietnamese coast. In addition to these retaliatory acts, the United States on April 24 circulated a warning notice to "members of the International Conference on Vietnam." The note condemned the illegal movement of war materials and troops from North Vietnam into Laos, Cambodia, and South Vietnam. It also questioned the failure of the Communists to release the thousands of civilian prisoners in their prison camps.[21]

The importance that American foreign policy planners attached to the continued North Vietnamese aggression was revealed by Henry Kissinger at a later date. On April 29, 1975, at a news conference, the presidential adviser was asked if there had been any plans to renew the bombing of North Vietnam in the spring of 1973, and if Watergate had "intruded" on these arrangements.

Kissinger responded that "options" had been prepared in April 1973 by the Washington Special Action Group. However, the President had never made a final decision between these choices, and consequently, "the effect of Watergate is a psychological assessment that one can only speculate about."[22]

The obvious failure of the cease-fire agreement became the major topic of conversation before a congressional hearing in the early days of May 1973.[23] The hearings were held for the purpose of examining the foreign military sales and assistance bill as submitted by Senator Fulbright to the Senate on April 3. When Senator Fulbright had introduced the measure it did not contain any provision for aid to Indochina. This deletion was not an oversight, but was in the chairman's words "held in abeyance pending presentation of the administration's case for its policy in Indochina."

[21] United States Department of State, "Note Verbale Circulated to Members of the International Conference on Vietnam," April 24, 1973.

[22] United States Department of State, Bureau of Public Affairs, "Press Conference of the Secretary of State, Major Topic: Viet-Nam," April 29, 1975.

[23] Hearings Before the Senate Committee on Foreign Relations, "Foreign Military Sales and Assistance Act," May 2, 3, 4, and 8, 1973.

The Foreign Relations Committee accepted statements from its usual one-sided claque. Declarations came from, among others, Dr. Julius Iossifides, executive director of SANE; John N. Plank, University of Connecticut, on behalf of the Friends Committee on National Legislation; D. Gareth Porter, research associate, international relations of East Asia project, Cornell University; and Paul C. Warnke, a Washington attorney who formerly served as assistant secretary of defense for national security affairs and chairman of the Democratic party's national security panel.

The most important part of the hearings concerned the testimony of Secretary of Defense Elliot L. Richardson. Appearing before the Committee on May 8, the Secretary stated that he did not support the bill because "it does not provide for . . . an effective security program." During the discussion period that followed this comment, Senator Stuart Symington (D., Mo.) asked the secretary a number of questions about American assistance to Southeast Asia. Most of the dialogue between Symington and Richardson explored the extent of American aid to Cambodia. Symington asked the secretary "if the Cambodian government was entirely dependent upon United States air support for its survival?" Richardson responded, "I think that is a fair statement, yes, Senator."

A few days after the secretary's testimony, two amendments were passed by the House of Representatives. These additions to a minor financial bill would, in time, mean the death of non-Communist Cambodia. Each year, in addition to monies appropriated under regular agency programs, federal agencies find they need supplemental funds to continue essential services. The administration also asks the Congress for approval to transfer dollars between various special accounts. These transactions are usually lumped together in a supplemental appropriations bill. For the year 1973 this legislation was known as the second supplemental appropriations bill (H.R. 7447).

When the measure was originally submitted, it contained a request for $2.85 billion in extra funding for items such as military retirement pay, fire-fighting costs, and military mail privileges. In addition to the new monies requested, the administration had asked for permission to transfer $143 million between various military accounts. According to the previous testimony of the comptroller of the Air Force before a defense appropriations subcommittee, some $80 million of the transfer monies would be used for combat operations in Cambodia.

In order to stop this expenditure, Representative Joseph P. Addabbo (D., N.Y.) submitted an amendment to the bill that would deny the military the ability to transfer any funds within the supplemental accounts. In addition to the New York Democrat's action, Clarence D. Long (D., Md.) presented another amendment, which read:

> None of the funds herein appropriated to the Department of Defense under this act shall be expended to support directly or indirectly combat activities in, over, or from off the shores of Cambodia by United States Forces.

The Addabbo measure was passed by a vote of 219-188, and Long's amendment was also approved 224-172.

Following the passage of these proposals, the House acted favorably on another insertion in the bill, which read:

> Sec. 304. No funds appropriated in this Act shall be expended to aid or assist in the reconstruction of the Democratic Republic of Vietnam (North Vietnam).

H.R. 7447 was approved by the House of Representatives on May 10 by a vote of 284-96. These actions marked the first time in six years that the House had voted in favor of end-the-war legislation. The shift in the voting patterns strongly suggested the growing influence of the Watergate hearings.

The dramatic change in the attitude of the congressmen toward the renewal of American military activities in Southeast Asia had a strong effect on the nation's diplomatic arm. After the representatives had voted against the transfer of funds to finance the bombing of Cambodia, Secretary Rogers conceded that "there are violations on both sides." He also stated a belief that the "North Vietnamese fundamentally want the agreement to work." His comments represented a distinct switch in the administration's vocal representations regarding the war in Southeast Asia. This transformation was in evidence when Henry Kissinger returned to Paris for further consultations with Le Duc Tho on May 17, 1973. When the two negotiators met, each side presented its list of grievances and some "preliminary conclusions" were drawn. As a result of their first meeting the participants agreed that additional negotiations to "strengthen the peace" were needed.

While the two delegations continued to meet in Paris, the Senate resumed its deliberations on the Second Supplemental Appropriations bill. During the course of debate on this measure, Senator George McGovern (D., S. Dak.) recommended on May 30 that:

> We should condition further aid of any kind to South Vietnam on the release of all political prisoners and the release of all restrictions on civilian movement. Such legislation should require verification of the International Control Commission that the conditions have been met.

If the senator's recommendation had been approved, it would have had the immediate effect of halting all assistance to South Vietnam. The basis for this assumption may be found in the Paris accords themselves. The teams of the International Commission for Control and Supervision (ICCS) were composed of representatives from Hungary, Poland, Indonesia, and Canada. The purpose of the Commission was to supervise the cease-fire in Vietnam, official reports of the ICCS groups being "made with the unanimous agreement of the representatives of all the four members." The Communist members of the ICCS played a blatantly partisan game. On March 10, for instance, the Hungarian and Polish members refused to investigate the installation of missiles by the North Vietnamese at Khe Sanh, because there was "no proof" that they existed. This in spite of the fact that United States intelligence had provided photographs of the missile facilities the previous week. And the Khe Sanh incident is only one example of the noncooperation exhibited by the Communist members of the ICCS. There is every reason to believe that when it came to reporting the release of political prisoners in South Vietnam, their response would have also been of a negative nature.[24]

When the senators received H.R. 7447 on May 18, 1973, it contained an amendment that had been approved unanimously by the Senate Committee on Appropriations. The measure, proposed by Senator Thomas Eagleton (D., Mo.), read:

> Sec. 305. None of the funds herein appropriated under this Act or heretofore appropriated under any other Act may be expended to support directly or indirectly combat activities in, over or from off the shores of Cambodia or in or over Laos by United States forces.

This paragraph, known as the Eagleton amendment, was immediately attacked in the Senate for having been placed in a supplemental appropriations bill. The senators who opposed the measure claimed that the phrase "or heretofore appropriated under any other act" was in actuality an attempt to place new legislation in an appropriations bill. As this practice was forbidden under Senate rules, it was their judgment that the amendment was out of order.[25] During the debate

[24] Further confirmation of the weakness of McGovern's proposal is found in the words of the Canadian representatives to the ICCS who reported: "The Khe Sanh request illustrated that the Poles and Hungarians, when confronted with an issue they regard as truly crucial, will not hesitate to block ICCS action." *Viet-Nam: Canada's Approach to Participation in the International Commission of Control and Supervision, October 25, 1972–March 27, 1973,* by Mitchell Sharp, Secretary of State for External Affairs, Ottawa, Canada, May 1973.

[25] On May 29, 1973, Senate Rule XVI read: "If an appropriation bill is reported to the Senate containing amendments proposing new or general legislation or any such restriction, a point of order may be made against the bill, and if the point is sustained the bill shall be recommitted to the Committee on Appropriations.

on the legality of the paragraph, Senator Mike Mansfield (D., Mont.) attacking the bombing of Cambodia, said:

> Mr. President, let these people decide their own destinies. Let them plan their own futures. Let them look out for their own countries, their cultures, their civilizations, their societies.

Senator John Tower (R., Texas) responded:

> The distinguished majority leader has rightfully suggested that we let these people work these things out for themselves. Well, let us get the North Vietnamese out of there so the Cambodians can work it out for themselves. [*Congressional Record*, May 29, 1973]

As the senators continued to discuss the appropriateness of the measure, Edward W. Brooke (R., Mass.) asked the legislators to consider the germaneness of the amendment instead of the "question of the point of order." He also informed his associates that adding Laos to the area where bombing would be prohibited was his idea. Brooke claimed that he was convinced the proper targets for the B-52 would "be industrial plants—certainly—manufacturing plants, railroads, and the like." He said that Cambodia does not have these facilities and consequently, the United States was bombing the countryside. In his opinion, this type of bombing was not very effective and therefore "I attempted to persuade my colleagues that this bombing in Cambodia and Laos should stop."

Later in the day Birch Bayh (D., Ind.) supported the antibombing legislation when he said:

> The administration has also justified its action on the basis of article 20 of the Vietnam cease-fire agreements. But the fact is that article 20 states with absolute clarity that all outside forces must refrain from intervening in the conflict. It is difficult for me to understand how the fact that one side may be violating these agreements by deploying forces inside Cambodia, whether they are involved in combat or not, can be turned around and used as a justification for the United States to violate its accords.*

As the end of the debate approached the presiding officer announced: "The question before the Senate is: Is the amendment germane to the House-passed language of the bill?" When the votes were counted, there were 55 yeas, 21 nays, and 24 not voting. On May 31, 1973,

* This line of reasoning presents interesting possibilities when related to the current armed truce existing between the United States and the Soviet Union. One could only assume that if Birch Bayh were President of the United States that the following scenario could ensue: A. The Soviet Union would launch its missiles against targets in America; B. The United States would not be free to respond because it had signed the SALT agreements and would be violating "its accords."

H.R. 7447 containing the Eagleton amendment was approved in the Senate by a vote of 73–5.

While the congressmen had been debating the bombing cutoff, the negotiators in Paris continued their discussions. Finally on June 13, 1973, over strong objections from South Vietnamese President Thieu, a joint communiqué implementing the Paris accords was issued by Kissinger and Tho. The supplementary agreement was drawn up in a "Four-Party Version" and a "Two-Party Version." The two versions were again required because the Saigon administration did not want to grant recognition to the Provisional Revolutionary Government.

On the day the "Implementary Agreement" was signed, Kissinger held a news conference. During his presentation the presidential adviser stated: "We believe we have achieved a satisfactory conclusion of the points that were of principal concern to the United States." Among these points was the question of the growing infiltration from North Vietnam, which, he said, the new proposals clearly prohibited. The situation in Cambodia, Kissinger went on, depended "on the solemn decisions of other parties." The most difficult problem facing the disputants appears to have been left unresolved. This was the dilemma posed by the political future of South Vietnam. The only comment contained in the communiqué regarding the country's political evolution was:

> The South Vietnamese people shall decide themselves the political future of South Vietnam through genuinely free and democratic general elections under international supervision.

Tran Van Lam, South Vietnam's foreign minister, said that he "believed" the supplementary agreement was an improvement over the original accords. In his opinion, however, too many basic areas of disagreement still remained. The problems he referred to were the organization of the general elections and political control of the contested areas. Lam also repeated his demand that several thousand Saigon troops be released from their North Vietnamese prisons as the accords stated.

Following the announcement that the Paris agreements had been strengthened, the Senate approved a sweeping cutoff of funds for the war. The action was taken when a vote was called on the Department of State appropriations authorization bill for financial year 1974 (July 1, 1973–June 30, 1974). The legislation, as passed, contained an amendment which had been submitted by Senators Clifford P. Case (R., N.J.) and Frank Church (D., Idaho). The antiwar paragraph, as it appeared on June 14, 1973, forbade the expenditure of monies to finance the use of United States forces "in or over or from off of the shores of North Vietnam, South Vietnam, Laos, or Cambodia unless specifically authorized by Congress." The Case-Church amendment was passed by a vote of 67–15 with 18 members not voting. No Democrats voted against the measure.

As the Democrats prepared their forces for the coming battle, Leonid Brezhnev arrived in Washington on an official visit. The Nixon-Brezhnev meetings formed a part of the cautious cooperation that was developing between Russia and the United States. After seven days of bargaining, which began on June 18, 1973, the two leaders of the world's superpowers announced that they had arrived at several areas of agreement. These topics of mutual accord were placed in a joint comminiqué that included a vow to discuss conflict situations before launching nuclear weapons, an understanding that another summit meeting would be held in Moscow during 1974, and several principles that each side would try to follow when the SALT talks were resumed in 1974. As the Soviet leader departed from Washington's Andrews Air Force Base he described his talks with President Nixon as a "further milestone" in improving relations between the two countries.

While the two national leaders were holding their discussions, the House of Representatives considered the adoption of the conference report on H.R. 7447, the supplemental appropriations bill. According to George H. Mahon (D., Texas), the House manager of the bill, there was a lively discussion when the congressional conferees met to reconcile the differences. One of the key issues in contention, according to the Texas Democrat, concerned the funding for the bombing of Cambodia and Laos. The Senate delegates had tended to favor the Eagleton amendment, which excluded monies "heretofore appropriated," and added Laos to the bombing restrictions. On the other hand, the House conferees supported the less stringent Addabbo-Long proposals. When Mahon submitted the conference report to his colleagues, he recommended that Laos be added to the "no bombing zone," but that otherwise the original House version remain unchanged.

Representative Robert N. Giaimo (D., Conn.) moved that the House abandon its position, which in effect would have meant the adoption of the harsher Eagleton amendment. Majority Leader Thomas P. O'Neill, Jr. (D., Mass.) rose in support of the Giaimo proposal and said, "Let us vote to stop the pipeline of funds for bombing in Cambodia." Gerald R. Ford (R., Mich.) pleaded with his fellow congressmen to vote against the Giaimo amendment. He added that because of President Nixon's actions "we have a cease-fire in South Vietnam, a cease-fire in Laos, and we are practically at the point of putting the last piece in the puzzle, the last link in the chain."*

* While the House was deliberating the bombing halt, secret negotiations were being conducted that would have established a coalition government in Cambodia.

When the vote was called, a large number of representatives were evidently not in the House. Informed that balloting was being conducted, these individuals came to the House floor with only the vaguest idea of what was at issue. In the words of Representative Samuel S. Stratton (D., N.Y.):

> As I stood in the door as people were coming in to vote . . . and were asking what the vote was on, some of my colleagues were saying that they should vote "yes" so as to end the war in Cambodia.

The final vote was 235 in favor of the Giaimo measure with 172 opposed, 1 "present," and 25 not voting.

After the House had adopted the Connecticut Democrat's proposal, Mahon made an attempt to salvage some form of negotiating room for the administration. His action took the form of submitting a motion which read:

> Sec. 305. After September 1, 1973, none of the funds herein appropriated under this Act or heretofore appropriated under any other Act may be expended to support directly or indirectly combat activities in, over or from off the shores of Cambodia or in Laos by United States forces.

What he had attempted to do was to add sixty days to the Eagleton amendment. When the vote was initially recorded, it favored Mahon's proposal 205–204, and the Republicans were jubilant. Their joy was short-lived, however, for K. Gunn McKay (D., Utah), who had voted in favor of the motion, announced that he had paired his vote with that of John E. Moss (D., Calif.), who was absent and against the motion. This action had the effect of reducing the count to 204 in favor and 204 against the measure. Speaker Carl Albert quickly announced the motion had failed on a tie vote and the Democrats burst into loud cheers. And so, at the end of the day, the only antibombing legislation contained in the supplemental appropriations bill was the Eagleton amendment. Following the action of the House, H.R. 7447 was sent to the Senate, where it was approved and forwarded to the President on June 26.

The passage of the antibombing legislation was not the only cruel blow dealt to Richard Nixon on June 25. This was also the day that John W. Dean III began his testimony before the Senate Watergate Committee. Dean's statements proved to be extremely damaging to the Nixon administration. For five days the former presidential lawyer accused his previous employer of participating in the Watergate cover-up. He also asserted that the President had been involved in a conference that involved the use of "hush money" and had offered executive clemency to one of the burglars in exchange for legal silence.

The next day the House began its deliberations on House Joint Resolution 636, which provided continuing appropriations for the fiscal year 1974 (July 1, 1974—June 30, 1975.) The monies contained in this bill were "necessary for continuing activities" that had been conducted the previous year and had been approved for 1974. These projects included the funding of special units in the Departments of Agriculture, Defense, Commerce, State, Transportation, Health, Education and Welfare, as well as other federal agencies.

In short, if the continuing appropriations were not approved by July 1, 1973, there was a good chance that a significant part of the United States government would grind to a standstill. The resolution was, however, designed to expire on September 30, at which time other funds would become available to the eligible units. The floor manager of the bill was George H. Mahon (D., Texas), chairman of the House Appropriations Committee.

After the resolution had been presented to the House, Joseph P. Addabbo (D., N.Y.) offered an amendment, which read:

> Sec. 108. None of the funds under this Joint Resolution may be expended to support directly or indirectly combat activities in or over Cambodia, Laos, North Vietnam, and South Vietnam or off the shores of Cambodia, Laos, North Vietnam and South Vietnam by United States forces without the express consent of Congress. [*Congressional Record*, June 26, 1973]

Chairman Mahon countered Addabbo's actions with a substitute amendment of his own that would have extended the cutoff date to September 1, 1973, and eliminated the two Vietnams from the combat restrictions. Clarence D. Long (D., Md.) moved to modify Mahon's proposal by extending the funds cut to monies "heretofore appropriated" and by striking the words "after September 1, 1973."

Following this flurry of activity, Jack Kemp (R., N.Y.) spoke in opposition to the Addabbo and Long amendments. His position appears to have been partially based on the need to maintain America's credibility in an increasingly hostile world. After pursuing his main argument for several minutes, he said:

> What I am suggesting here to my colleagues today on the floor of the House is this: America and the President as our leader has to be credible all over the world. You cannot ask him to be credible in the SALT talks or the mutual balanced forces reduction talks if you will not allow him to be credible and enforce the negotiations that were so difficult to achieve at Paris.

A few moments later, Congressman Wayne L. Hays responded to Kemp's pleas to support the President. The extent to which the Watergate hearings had permeated the mood of the House was shown when the Ohio Democrat said,

> The preceding speaker made a great argument which really left me a little bit cold about the credibility of the White House. Apparently he has not been watching television in the last few days.

As the procedural battle waxed hotter, there were demands to limit the debate to fifteen or twenty minutes. When the votes were finally taken, both the Mahon and Long proposals were passed. The effect of their passage meant the Addabbo amendment was also accepted but in a revised version. The new Addabbo-Mahon-Long measure did not contain a September 1 cutoff date, nor did it restrict United States combat activities in the two Vietnams. It did however, cut off funds "heretofore appropriated."

The day after the House had passed the joint resolution for continuing appropriations (H.J. Res. 636), President Nixon vetoed the supplemental appropriations bill. In his message to the Congress conveying his disapproval of the measure, the President said:

> I am returning today without my approval H.R. 7447, the Second Supplemental Appropriation Act of 1973.
> I am doing so because of my grave concern that the enactment into law of the "Cambodia rider" to this bill would cripple or destroy the chances for an effective negotiated settlement in Cambodia and the withdrawal of all North Vietnamese troops as required by Article 20 of the January 27 Vietnam agreement.

At the close of his communication, the Chief Executive emphasized the importance of preparing new legislation in place of H.R. 7447. He added:

> By June 28, nine government agencies will have exhausted their authority to pay the salaries and expenses of their employees. The disruptions that would be caused by a break in the continuity of government are serious and must be prevented. For example, it will be impossible to meet the payroll of the employees at the Social Security Administration which will threaten the flow of benefits to 25 million persons.

When the rejected legislation was received in the House, its supporters could not muster the votes to override the veto and H.R. 7447 died a natural death.*

The veto infuriated the antibombing forces, and in the House Congressmen Giaimo and Long questioned the President's sense of responsibility. Elford A. Cederberg (R., Mich.) answered these charges:

---

* The vote to override the veto was 241–173 with 19 not voting, which was 35 votes short of the two-thirds majority necessary.

I think we ought to put this matter in its proper perspective. If they want to have a clear-cut issue on the question of bombing in Cambodia, they ought to bring out a bill from the Committee on Armed Services or the Committee on Foreign Affairs. The only reason they put it in the continuing resolution and in the supplemental is they did not think the President had guts enough to veto it, and his veto message clearly sets forth his reasons. [*Congressional Record*, June 27, 1973]

Congressman Mahon's first reaction to the veto was to recommend that a modified bill be developed by the Committee on Appropriations. On the morning of June 29, the Committee placed a revised supplemental appropriations bill before the House known as H.R. 9055. The new measure contained a clause that would halt the bombing in Cambodia and Laos on August 15, 1973. As he spoke in support of the changed date for the bombing cutoff, Mahon stated that the language of the proposal was acceptable to the administration. House Minority Leader Gerald Ford rose to support the new proposition. He said that a White House spokesman had told him that the President would go along with the new supplemental appropriations bill and declared:

I have communicated directly with the spokesman at the White House last night and again today and I am authorized to say the following: Number one, the President will definitely accept a bill that contains the language in Section 307. Number two, if military action is required in Southeast Asia after August 15, the President will ask congressional authority and will abide by the decision that is made by the House and the Senate, the Congress of the United States.

Several Democrats, though not questioning Ford's honesty, suggested they would prefer the President's word on the issue to that of a "spokesman." While the debate on H.R. 9055 continued, the Minority Leader left the floor of the House and placed a call to the President regarding the new proposal. Upon returning to the chamber, Ford stated:

I have just finished talking with the President himself for approximately ten minutes, and he assured me personally that everything I said on the floor of the House is a commitment by him.

The fact that the President had agreed to include North and South Vietnam in the bill was a great surprise to the House antiwar leadership. This unexpected dividend led to a demand that these two areas be added to the proposed legislation. After some Republican resistance, Frank E. Evans (D., Colo.) was successful in having North and South Vietnam added to the prohibited areas.

The August 15 date continued to provoke strong resistance from

House Democrats who wanted the bombing in Cambodia stopped immediately. In response to this demand, Congressman John J. Flynt, Jr. (D., Ga.) offered an amendment that read:

> Sec. 307. None of the funds herein appropriated under this Act or heretofore appropriated under any other Act may be expended to support directly or indirectly combat activities, in over or from off the shores of Cambodia or in or over Laos by the U.S. forces.

Representatives Bella Abzug (D., N.Y.), Robert F. Drinan (D., Mass.), Robert N. Giaimo (D., Conn.), Gilbert Gude (R., Md.), Elizabeth Holtzman (D., N.Y.), Clarence D. Long (D., Md.), Frank E. Moss (D., Utah), David R. Obey (D., Wis.), Henry S. Reuss (D., Wis.), and Patricia Schroeder (D., Colo.) spoke in favor of the new proposal.

Roger H. Zion (R., Ind.) indicated displeasure with his colleagues' lack of compassion for the free peoples of Southeast Asia, adding:

> It is possible that as a result of an action today, millions of people may be slaughtered because they do not want to live under godless Communism. The people of Cambodia, Thailand, and perhaps all of Southeast Asia could fall under the cancer of Communism.

John J. Rhodes (R., Ariz.) voiced strong opposition to the measure; however, he let the antiwar forces know they had successfully forced the first real surrender in the history of the United States. "I think it is time to let my friends on the other side of the Chamber in on a secret. They won. They have won."

From this point forward, the actual date that the Commander in Chief was forbidden to use American Forces in Southeast Asia was immaterial. The groundwork had been laid for total surrender. The end was merely a matter of time.*

When the vote was called on the Flynt amendment, it appeared that the antibombing forces had won a clear victory and funds for the war would be immediately curtailed. The count had been taken by voice vote and the chairman announced that "the ayes appear to have it." Representative Gerald Ford called for a recorded vote, and the Flynt proposal was defeated with 206 noes, 169 ayes, and 28 not voting. The House immediately considered the passage of the entire bill, and on a roll-call vote of 278–124 with 2 voting "present" and 29 abstentions, H.R. 9055 was approved and sent to the Senate.

On the same day that the House passed the new supplemental

---

* Sir Robert Thompson, a former presidential adviser on Vietnam, had this to say about the congressional actions: "The American Congress, completely overriding the administration, has laid down its new policy line. If you surrender, the killing will stop. That may be all right for their allies, but it also heralds the abject surrender of the United States."

appropriations bill (H.R. 9055), the Senate gave final consideration to the continuing appropriations resolution (H.J. Res. 636). After adopting a proposal to deny financial assistance to North Vietnam, the Senate was startled when Senator Fulbright asked for the consideration of an amendment that read:

> Sec. 109. Notwithstanding any other provision of law, on or after August 15, 1973, no funds herein, heretofore or hereafter appropriated may be obligated or expended to finance the involvement of United States military forces in hostilities in or over or from off of North Vietnam, South Vietnam, Laos, or Cambodia.

The chairman of the Committee on Foreign Relations explained that this paragraph had been approved by his Committee by a vote of 15–2. Fulbright added that the present amendment was the result of a compromise between the Committee and the White House.

The new wording of the measure, which contained an August 15 cutoff date, was strongly opposed by several liberal senators. Speaking in opposition to the proposal, Senator Mansfield said:

> What we are doing, if we approve this substitute is agreeing to the policy of this administration past, now, and in the future, at least until August 15. I cannot in good conscience accede to the diminution of the constitutional power of Congress. That has been happening in this institution since the days of Franklin Delano Roosevelt.

Adlai E. Stevenson III spoke in favor of the compromise:

> For eight years I have opposed U.S. involvement in the Indochinese War . . . now for the first time I have a chance to support a deadline which will not fail. There is no other way.

When the votes were counted, the Fulbright amendment was passed with 64 in favor, 26 opposed, and 10 not voting. A few moments later the entire resolution was approved and sent to a joint House-Senate conference.

Following the passage of the continuing resolution (H.J. Res. 636), the Senate received and acted favorably on the new supplemental appropriations bill (H.R. 9055), which was immediately sent to the President. The next day, the House endorsed the Senate's action on H.J. Res. 636 and directed the resolution to the White House.

On July 1, 1973, President Nixon signed into law H.R. 9055 and H.J. Res. 636, which became Public Laws 93-50 and 93-52, respectively. Both of these legislative acts contained prohibitions on the expenditure of funds to support American military forces in Indochina. It was PL 93-50, the Second Supplemental Appropriations Act, however, that forced the President's hand. The surrender section of this law reads:

Sec. 307. None of the funds herein appropriated under this Act may be expended to support directly or indirectly combat activities in or over Cambodia, Laos, North Vietnam and South Vietnam or off the shores of Cambodia, Laos, North Vietnam and South Vietnam by United States forces, and after August 15, 1973, no other funds heretofore appropriated under any other Act may be expended for such purpose.[26]

With the passage of these two appropriation measures, the administration's ability to maintain a credible position in the face of North Vietnamese aggression was considerably lessened.

For several months before the Congressional surrender in Southeast Asia, the Russian and Chinese Communists had withheld certain military supplies from Hanoi. The delivery of these items of war had been suspended in exchange for American promises of détente, trade, and recognition. When the North Vietnamese had complained about the interruption in the flow of arms, the Communist leaders in Peking and Moscow had been able to raise the issue of cost, loss, or hopelessness.* After June 30 and the public announcement by the United States Congress that South Vietnam was being virtually abandoned, it became almost impossible for Brezhnev or Mao to refuse Hanoi's request for what was beginning to appear an easy victory.

The dangers inherent in the congressional actions were emphasized in a letter from President Nixon to Speaker of the House Carl Albert and Senate Majority Leader Mike Mansfield. In his message to the congressional leaders, the Chief Executive wrote:

> The incentive to negotiate a settlement in Cambodia has been undermined, and August 15 will accelerate this process.
>
> This abandonment of a friend will have a profound impact in other countries ... and I want the Congress to be fully aware of the consequences of its action ....
>
> I can only hope the North Vietnamese will not draw the erroneous conclusion from this congressional action that they are free to launch a military offensive in Indochina.[27]

The President's warning did not fall on deaf ears, and the North Vietnamese drew the only conclusion that could be drawn from the congressional action, which was that Cambodia and South Vietnam were ripe for conquest. In keeping with this belief, the Hanoi strategists ordered a significant increase in the movement of equipment, supplies, and men into South Vietnam. Most of the material and

---

[26] Public Law 93-50, July 1, 1973.

[27] *Congressional Quarterly Almanac,* 1973, p. 862.

* When the Congress removed the Commander in Chief's ability to use American forces in Vietnam, there were at least 200 B-52s in Guam and Thailand, about 350 Air Force and 45 Marine fighter-bombers in Thailand, and a Navy aircraft carrier cruising the South China Sea.

personnel were directed into areas the Communists had seized along the Cambodian–Vietnamese border.

The northern tier of the North Vietnamese enclaves was connected by new roads that were eventually intended to link all Communist-held territory in South Vietnam together. Intelligence sources believed that the road system was used by some 4,500 trucks per week. There were also reports that a fuel pipeline ran alongside the section of the road extending from Khe Sanh into the Central Highlands.

This large-scale movement of people and the extended road-building program formed a major part of the Communist activities in South Vietnam during the month of July. These efforts were intended to give physical substance to the Vietcong claim of popular support in South Vietnam.

On August 15, 1973, the American bombing in Cambodia came to an official end. In spite of the bombing halt, the war ground on and the Communists expanded their zones of control throughout the countryside. By the end of August the Hanoi-directed insurgents had extended their authority to over eighty-five percent of the rural areas of Cambodia. Government forces, however, maintained their control over Phnom Penh and the other major cities. Despite the large number of soldiers in Lon Nol's army (estimates ran over 100,000), the advantage belonged to the insurgent forces, which consisted of about 50,000 men organized into 200 combat battalions.* The reason for rating the rebel forces over the government troops was the existence of 43,000 North Vietnamese support and advisory personnel inside Cambodia. In spite of the heavy infusion of NVA troops, the insurgents failed to perform particularly well in battle, and Lon Nol's forces were given a good chance to muddle through. But the halt in United States aerial support had hurt the government army, and the rebels began to move into areas they had not previously controlled.

These new Communist moves were the subject of a White House press conference conducted by Gerald L. Warren, deputy press secretary, on August 15, the day the bombing cutoff became effective. In his statement to the press Warren said:

> It should be clearly understood in Hanoi that the President will work with Congress in order to take appropriate action if North Vietnam mounts an offensive which jeopardizes stability in Indochina.

The secretary's message had little effect on the Congress, which asked that previous restrictions on the President's Indochina options be confirmed. The additional limitations were placed in H.R. 7645,

---

* The reason for the estimated figure for government forces is the relatively high number of phantom payrollers in the Cambodian army.

the Department of State authorization bill, which the President signed into law on October 8. This was the legislation containing the Case-Church amendment, which in its final form read:

> Sec. 13. Notwithstanding any other provision of law, on or after August 15, 1973, no funds heretofore appropriated may be obligated or expended to finance the involvement of United States military forces in hostilities in or over or from off the shores of North Vietnam, South Vietnam, Laos, or Cambodia, unless specifically authorized hereafter by the Congress. Notwithstanding any other provision of law upon enactment of this Act, no funds heretofore or hereinafter appropriated may be obligated or expended for the purpose of providing assistance of any kind, directly or indirectly, to or on behalf of North Vietnam, unless specifically authorized hereafter by the Congress.[28]

The passage of the new appropriations bill had taken place during a time of trial for the President and his chief administrative officer. On October 10, 1973, Spiro T. Agnew resigned as Vice-President after pleading no contest to charges of evading federal income taxes. Richard Nixon immediately appointed Representative Gerald Ford to fill the nation's second highest office.

The War Powers Resolution

The embattled presidency came under further attack when the Senate approved a conference report and sent the War Powers Resolution (H.J. Res. 542) to the White House for signature. The new legislation imposed severe restrictions on the ability of the Commander in Chief to command the nation's armed forces. President Nixon vetoed the measure on October 24 and returned it to the Congress. In his rejection letter the Chief Executive said, in part:

> The restrictions which this resolution would impose on the authority of the President are both unconstitutional and dangerous to the best interests of our nation.
>
> *   *   *
>
> I am also deeply disturbed by the practical consequences of this resolution. For it will seriously undermine this nation's ability to act decisively and convincingly in times of international crisis.[29]

The reason Nixon had not returned the resolution any earlier than October 25 was that he was again busy with the Watergate problem. On July 16 FAA administrator Alexander P. Butterfield, a former White House aide, had revealed that the President routinely taped

---

[28] Public Law 93-126, October 18, 1973.
[29] *Weekly Compilation of Presidential Documents*, October 24, 1973.

conversations and phone calls in the White House and Executive Office buildings. This information caused Archibald Cox, the special Watergate prosecutor, to issue a subpoena against Richard Nixon for the release of the tapes. The ensuing struggle erupted into what has become known as the "Saturday Night Massacre."

On October 20 (a Saturday night) at 8:25 P.M., Ronald Ziegler, the White House press secretary, announced at a news conference that Cox had been fired and that the office of special prosecutor had been abolished. He also said that Attorney General Elliot L. Richardson had resigned and Deputy Attorney General William D. Ruckelshaus had been fired because they had refused to terminate Cox.

When the Congress received the rejected War Powers Resolution, both chambers began discussions on overriding the veto. While the President had declared the law to be both unconstitutional and unwise, backers of the measure claimed the resolution would merely restore the balance of power between the legislative and the executive branches of government.

On November 7 after a short debate, the Congress voted to override the presidential veto. The vote in the House was 284–135, with 14 not voting. In the Senate there were 75 yea's and 18 nay's, with 7 abstentions. And so finally, at the end of a three-year effort, the President's war-making powers had been curtailed.

While some congressmen viewed the outcome of the voting with great pride, others believed the action reflected personal motives rather than consideration for the future of America. Those who opposed the legislation primarily believed that the "action" branch of the government (the executive) should have the ability to select the appropriate manner in which to respond to an enemy initiative. From this day forward, America's wars were to be fought by a Committee of 500.

The War Powers Resolution, also known as Public Law 93-148, stated in part:

> The constitutional powers of the President as Commander-in-Chief to introduce United States Armed Forces into hostilities, or into situations where imminent involvement in hostilities is clearly indicated by the circumstances, are exercised only pursuant to (1) a declaration of war, (2) specific statuatory authorization, or (3) a national emergency created by attack upon the United States, its territories or possessions, or its armed forces.

> Consultation

> Sec. 3. The President in every possible instance shall consult with the Congress before introducing United States Armed Forces into hostilities or into situations where imminent involvement in hostilities is clearly

indicated by the circumstances, and after each such introduction shall consult regularly with the Congress until United States Armed Forces are no longer engaged in hostilities or have been removed from such situations.

The congressional action limiting the President's ability to respond to warlike acts came at a difficult time for American foreign-policy planners. Intelligence sources had reported a significant buildup of North Vietnamese military forces in South Vietnam, and Pentagon officials were hesitant about what course of action to follow. Any doubt that politburo leaders in Hanoi were still resolved to conquer South Vietnam was laid to rest by Ellsworth Bunker at a luncheon meeting in Washington sponsored by the American Security Council on November 25, 1973. Speaking to a distinguished audience composed of representatives from the press and prominent government personalities, the ambassador said, "North Vietnam is still determined to gain political power in South Vietnam and by force if necessary." In his closing comments he declared that peace in Indochina depended on continued American support for South Vietnam and that "clearly, if we do not maintain our support, there is no incentive for the Soviets and Chinese to cut back on their support."[30]

Congress Imposes Its Will

In the middle of November the President signed the Department of Defense procurement bill that authorized expenditures for the research, development, and purchase of special weapons systems in fiscal 1974 (July 1, 1974–June 30, 1975). During the previous year the department had been authorized to expend $2.5 billion in procurement for military assistance to South Vietnam and Laos. Because of the reduced level in the fighting on South Vietnamese battlefields, however, the administration had only requested the sum of $1.6 billion in the budget item for the two countries during 1974.

As the bill worked its way through Congress, antiwar advocates successfully reduced the final amount authorized to $1.126 billion.[31] The $474 million decrease represented a severe blow to the defensive capabilities of the South Vietnamese. It also provided an insight into the direction Congress was prepared to move on future military expenditures in Southeast Asia. The President signed the bill into law on November 16, 1973, with great reservation.

The curtailment of these funds seemed to act as some kind of signal to Hanoi, and Communist activity increased throughout the Southern

[30] *Washington Report*, December 1973.
[31] Public Law 93-155, November 16, 1973.

Republic. On December 3 the Vietcong set fire to an oil storage depot near Saigon and destroyed more than twenty million gallons of oil. Several sharp battles broke out in the Mekong Delta, and the Central Highlands were the scene of renewed fighting. But an even more ominous development was the construction or rebuilding of eighteen airfields in Communist-controlled areas of South Vietnam by North Vietnamese labor battalions.

In spite of what appeared to be a resurgence in NVA troop aggressiveness, the Communists had not turned the war around in any real sense. The South Vietnamese military units were still strong and perhaps even more aggressive than they had been in the spring. The closest estimates that could be made of the comparative fighting strength of the two sides placed NVA strength in South Vietnam at about 240,000 fighting effectives, assisted by a guerrilla force of unknown size. In opposition to the Communists, ARVN numbered about 360,000 regulars, supported by an air force of 63,000 men, a small navy, and a half-million paramilitary forces of varying capabilities.

It would appear on a simple numbers-comparison test that South Vietnamese military forces outnumbered NVA/VC elements by almost two to one. It must be remembered, however, that fully one-half the manpower available to the Saigon command were regional/self-defense forces. These local militiamen were by and large well armed (M-16s), but in most cases no match for experienced North Vietnamese regulars.

The main burden for the military defense of South Vietnam fell on the shoulders of the battle-hardened ARVN. Unfortunately for the regular soldiers of the Southern Republic, they were caught on the horns of the same dilemma that the French were never able to solve. Both armies had found it almost impossible to defend the cities and fight the Communist forces at the same time. French General Henri Navarre had attempted, without any great success, to solve the problem by the use of a highly mobile strike force. President Thieu hoped to overcome this difficulty by maintaining a high degree of troop mobility and counted heavily on the presence of a very large American air armada. The threat posed by the United States air forces stationed in the Far East was certainly a major factor in North Vietnam's decision to remain engaged in small unit warfare throughout 1973.

Near the end of December the Congress approved and sent to the White House three major bills dealing with the sputtering war in South Vietnam. The first of these measures was signed by the President on December 17 and is known as the Foreign Assistance Act of 1973. The Act authorized the expenditure of $504 million for economic assistance to South Vietnam, Cambodia, and Laos. The use of this money, however, was to be governed by a restrictive clause that read:

No assistance shall be furnished under this section to South Vietnam unless the President receives assurance satisfactory to him that no assistance furnished under this part, and no local currencies generated as a result of assistance furnished under this part, will be used for support of police, or prison construction and administration, within South Vietnam.[32]

The new law also prohibited the President from using such monies to finance United States forces in Indochina. A separate paragraph also halted the provision of funds for the purpose of financing "directly or indirectly any military or paramilitary combat operations by foreign forces in Laos, Cambodia, North Vietnam, or Thailand."

On December 20 the Congress approved and sent the foreign aid appropriations bill to the White House. The President signed the measure into law on January 2, 1974. The bill was a considerable disappointment to government officials charged with the responsibility for administering Indochinese affairs. The President had asked for $632 million in Indochina postwar reconstruction moneys, and only $450 million had been appropriated. The initial budget had contained a request of $200 million in emergency funds for Cambodia. The Congress, however, only allocated $150 million for this purpose. They also placed restrictive wording around the expenditure of the Cambodian monies that read: "That the funds appropriated in this paragraph shall be available only upon enactment into law of authorizing legislation."*

During the course of debate on the measure, Fortney H. (Pete) Stark (D., Calif.) had tried to reduce the amount appropriated for Cambodia to $50 million. Otto E. Passman (D., La.), chairman of the foreign operations subcommittee of the House Appropriations Committee, was opposed to the decrease in allocated funds. He based his disagreement on the belief that the Cambodians had a good chance of surviving if only Congress provided the money for bullets. Another supporter of maintaining the Cambodian appropriation at $150 million was Clarence D. Long. The Maryland Democrat reminded his colleagues that in mid-August 1973 the Congress had made a commitment to provide funds to the Cambodians so they could purchase the

[32] Public Law 93-189, December 17, 1973.

* The Congress adjourned without having enacted the legislation necessary to expend the $150 million. Fortunately for Lon Nol's forces, the President had been given drawdown authority to distribute $250 million worth of previously stockpiled war materiel in Southeast Asia.

weapons necessary for their defense. Section 112 of the new law prohibited the use of funds appropriated under this act for police work and prison construction. Even the purchase of computers was forbidden if they were to be used in police matters.[33]

The Congress also sent the Department of Defense appropriations bill to the President on December 20. The measure provided $1.126 billion for military assistance to South Vietnam and Laos.* This figure contained only $19.3 million less than the administration had requested. At one point, however, the Senate had only approved the expenditure of $650 million for these two countries. This significant reduction was based on an amendment that had been offered by William Proxmire (D., Wis.), which had been approved by the Senate Appropriations Committee. House and Senate conferees later restored most of the requested funds. The bill also prohibited the use of Defense Department monies to support "Vietnamese or other free-world forces in actions designed to provide military support and assistance to the government of Cambodia or Laos." Section 741 of the measure contained the usual prohibition against use of these "funds" to finance military activities by United States forces in or over or from off the shores of Indochina.[34]

As the year ended it was obvious to everyone concerned with Indochinese affairs that America was probably not going to use her powerful military forces in Southeast Asia. There were also strong indications that the United States Congress could be persuaded to withhold even more money from the desperate Cambodian and South Vietnamese nations. All that was needed was an increase in the ante.

[33] Public Law 93-240, January 2, 1974.
[34] Public Law 93-238, January 2, 1974.
* The Defense Department appropriation for South Vietnam and Laos for the previous year was $2.735 billion.

VII / The End Of Honor

In 1969 the *Washington Post* published an article by David S. Broder entitled "A Risky New American Sport: The Breaking of the President." In his satirical essay journalist Broder described the process by which the men who had broken Lyndon B. Johnson hoped to break Richard Nixon.

The first step in removing a President, according to Broder, is for the breakers to assume a position of moral superiority by opposing an unpopular war.

The second step involves the development of campus support by recruiting those who might have to fight in the war to demonstrate against it.

The third step includes the discovery that war is unpopular at the polls, which causes the President's party to repudiate him.

Lastly, "Senator Fulbright and the Foreign Relations Committee move in to finish off the job." There is little doubt that Broder's formula, with minor modifications, was used with great skill by the enemies of Richard Nixon, and in August 1974, the President was forced to resign.

A Shift in Strategy

The year 1973 had proven to the politburo leadership that unless conditions changed, the conquest of South Vietnam would end up a harder task than they had assumed. While the North Vietnamese had been able to increase the size of their armed forces inside the Southern Republic, ARVN troopers had successfully blocked the acquisition of any sizable pieces of ground.

This lack of battlefield success led the Communist leaders to conclude that a shift in general strategy was needed. Evidence of the direction their new approach would take appeared when Hanoi diplomats in all parts of the world were called home for consultation in January 1974.

These senior government officials were informed that an increased emphasis was to be accorded the political struggle, as opposed to military operations.[1] The new strategy envisioned the launching of a worldwide propaganda campaign designed to build up the credibility of the Provisional Revolutionary Government in the eyes of other nations. But most of all, the American Congress must be convinced that the South Vietnamese government did not deserve to receive continued financial assistance.

The change in strategic direction posed a rather serious problem for the North Vietnamese, as the American antiwar movement was nearly moribund. There were, however, certain individuals who could be called upon to carry out the politburo's orders in the United States. Among these friends of the Vietcong, Jane Fonda and her husband Tom Hayden were still very much involved in "peace" activities. In fact, their connections extended into the Congress of the United States.

This power to exert influence in the Congress proved to be the key to the reduction in South Vietnamese defense capabilities. Operating through Congressman Ronald Dellums (D., Calif.), who sponsored their activities, Fonda and Hayden were able to obtain a congressional conference room where Hanoi's ideas could be presented.

Once the meeting space was obtained, invitations were issued to congressional aides to attend a series of lectures on "U.S. relations with Southeast Asia." As a result of these activities, for three weeks in the month of February 1974, at least sixty congressional staff assistants attended lectures conducted in a House Judiciary Committee room by Hayden and Fonda.[2]

Following the "seminars," a new political grouping was formed in Washington. This group, composed of thirty-five congressional aides, was known as the Capitol Hill Coordinating Committee. One of its ring leaders was M. J. "Mike" Duberstein, legislative assistant to Ronald Dellums. The committee's sole purpose was to end all congressional aid to the Saigon government.

While the Haydens were conducting their classes on "American Imperialism," the *New York Times* ran an article written by David K. Shipler, then in Saigon. The lengthy essay was entitled "Vast Aid from United States Backs Saigon in Continuing War."[3] In his com-

[1] *China News Analysis,* March 15, 1974.
[2] *Congressional Record,* February 8, 1974.

mentary Shipler stressed what he considered to be American and South Vietnamese violations of the truce agreement. The *Times* reporter described "a vast program of American military aid that continues to set the course of the war," encouraging South Vietnam's violations of the Paris accords.

The obvious bias of the article moved Ambassador Graham Martin to write a stinging rebuttal. In his March 6 cablegram to the Department of State, the ambassador prefaced his remarks by stating:

> 1. As a preliminary to detailed discussion of Shipler *New York Times* article datelined Saigon February 16, it is necessary to record that embassy has long been aware of decisions taken last fall in Hanoi to mount all-out campaign this winter and spring to persuade the Congress to drastically reduce the magnitude of both economic and military aid to the Government of Vietnam.
>
> 2. The Stockholm Conference was to be used as the main coordinating mechanism, and the PRG delegation in Paris was to be the principal channel using the remnants of the American "peace movement" to bring influence to bear on susceptible, but influential, elements of American communications media and, particularly, on susceptible congressional staffers.

He then proceeded to refute Shipler's accusations. The ambassador particularly directed the department's attention to the fact that "the program of military aid does not set the course of the war, the course is set by the continuing Communist buildup." In closing Martin granted permission to release his message for general publication and wrote:

> Embassy believes the Shipler story and this response might well be made available to the Columbia graduate school of journalism as a case study of propaganda under the guise of investigative reporting rather than a responsible journalistic effort. [*Congressional Record*, March 19, 1974]

When Senator Edward M. Kennedy (D., Mass.) read the ambassador's cable, he became incensed over the critical nature of its contents. The senator's anger caused him to direct an interrogatory letter to Henry Kissinger. In his message to the secretary of state Kennedy raised a number of questions regarding "the general character and objectives of American policy toward Indochina." He ended his communication with the statement:

> In conclusion, let me express my personal dismay over the theme in Ambassador Martin's cable of March 6. For him to suggest a tie between

³ *New York Times*, February 25, 1974.

alleged decisions in Hanoi and the views of members of Congress and their staffs about the course of American policy towards South Vietnam and Indochina is the worst kind of innuendo and regrettably ignores the many legitimate questions and concerns of the Congress and the American people over our commitments to the governments of Indochina. . . . [*Congressional Record,* March 19, 1974]

The battle over the right of South Vietnam to survive as a sovereign nation shifted into high gear in Washington during the late spring of 1974. In March the American Security Council released the full report of an independent fact-finding group that had toured Vietnam in January. The investigating committee had been directed by John M. Allison, former assistant secretary of state for Far Eastern Affairs. Other members of the team included: Elbridge Durbrow, former ambassador to South Vietnam (1957–61), Congressman Philip M. Crane (R., Ill.), and Anthony Kubek, research professor at the University of Dallas.

The group had traveled the length and breadth of South Vietnam and conducted interviews with dozens of Vietnamese citizens. There were lengthy meetings with President Thieu, Minister of Information Hoang Duc Nha, and other government officials. The committee also met with members of the South Vietnamese National Assembly, students, shopkeepers, workers, and businessmen.

Ambassador Allison, who had once served in Czechoslovakia, opined:

> People in the cities and in the countryside give no evidence of serious repression or of living in a police state, particularly in comparison to the people of Eastern Europe.

One of the bits of evidence that group members cited as proof that South Vietnam was not a totalitarian society included the fact that the regime had issued weapons to the people. At the time of their visit some 549,000 regional and popular forces were in possession of government-issued M-16 rifles and M-79 grenade launchers. As a result of their investigations the fact-finding committee concluded:

> It would be a mistake of historic proportions should Congress accept now the argument of critics who contend that U.S. participation in the defense of South Vietnam was all wrong and that the U.S. should cut its losses and abandon the South Vietnamese as a hopeless cause.[4]

The 1974 Defense Supplemental Request

On March 18 the House Armed Services Committee convened its hearings on the Pentagon's $6.2 billion request for additional money

---

[4] "Vietnam Report: Not in Vain," *Washington Report,* March 1974.

during 1974. The proposal did not contain any new funds for South Vietnam. It did, however, ask that the ceiling on military aid to Saigon be raised from $1.126 to $1.6 billion, an increase of $474 million. The reason that no new funds were requested was that the Defense Department still had money left over from earlier appropriations.

Admiral Thomas H. Moorer, chairman of the Joint Chiefs of Staff, and William P. Clements, deputy secretary of defense, appeared before the Committee and presented the administration's proposal for additional money. The Pentagon officials claimed that worldwide inflation and the rampaging increases in oil prices were hampering Saigon's economic recovery. They stated their belief that unless Congress raised the ceiling on United States military aid to South Vietnam, a sharp curtailment in the war effort would ensue.

The next day the Senate Armed Services Committee also began its deliberations on the supplemental money request. Senate doves launched one of their bitterest attacks on South Vietnam during these hearings. Edward M. Kennedy (D., Mass.) and James B. Pearson (R., Kansas) attempted to delete the Saigon-aid portion of the supplemental authorization altogether. Alan Cranston (D., Calif.) opposed the raising of the authorization ceiling:

> As for fiscal 1975 and beyond, I urge the Committee to phase out, as rapidly as possible, future military funds for the Thieu government. [*Congressional Report,* March 19, 1974]

When the bill was reported to the House it immediately became enmeshed in a procedural dispute between George Mahon (D., Texas) representing the Committee on Appropriations, and F. Edward Hébert (D., La.) of the Senate Armed Services Committee. Mahon contended that the supplemental provision violated a standing House rule against placing appropriations in a legislative measure. After a lengthy debate, the House voted in favor of Mahon. Hébert, in an attempt to salvage something for South Vietnam, proposed that the ceiling be raised to $1.4 billion. The House defeated the Hébert amendment 177–154 with 101 members not voting.

On May 6 the Senate considered the supplemental appropriations bill. While the Senate Armed Services Committee had rejected the removal of the $1.126 billion ceiling on military aid to South Vietnam, it had approved the spending of an additional $266 million that had been discovered as a result of a bookkeeping adjustment. Edward M. Kennedy (D. Mass.) immediately submitted an amendment to block the expenditure of these monies. George McGovern (D., S.Dak.) moved to support Kennedy's action by introducing a statement from Fred Branfman of the Indochina Resource Center that pictured the

Thieu government as being the aggressor in South Vietnam. Branf-man also expressed his toleration for other points of view when he said:

> For the Administration to suggest that it is in either the American or Cambodian interest for Congress to appropriate more than $600 million in fiscal year 1975 for war in Cambodia is beneath contempt.

The Kennedy amendment was approved by a vote of 43–38. The Senate passed the entire measure later in the day by voice vote.

When House-Senate conferees met to iron out their differences on the bill, the statutory $1.126-billion limitation was allowed to remain. The administration was also prohibited from using the additional $266 million. The President, after many misgivings, signed the measure on June 8, when it became Public Law 93-307. The actions taken by the South Vietnamese army as the result of the congressional cut in funds were later described by G. V. "Sonny" Montgomery (D., Miss.):

> It made the South Vietnamese change their tactics and instead of putting down artillery barrages and bringing in air strikes they have had to use more manpower because we did not give them this supplemental appropriation. The casualty losses for the South Vietnamese have risen twenty percent over the year before. So the South Vietnamese have sacrificed in lives and in wounded. [*Congressional Record,* August 6, 1974]

Foreign Aid for 1975

The President submitted his foreign aid request for fiscal year 1975 (July 1, 1974–June 30, 1975) to the Congress on April 24, 1974. The total aid package came to $5.18 billion. Of this amount, $939.8 million was designated for Indochina reconstruction assistance. In his request for money that would be directed to Indochina, the President reported that the South Vietnamese were making "laudable efforts to solve their own problems," having increased their taxes by forty percent, expanded their exports, and sharply reduced consumption of imported goods.

The foreign aid request was the subject of extended hearings by the House Committee on Foreign Affairs throughout the months of June and July. Henry Kissinger was among the top administration officials who appeared before the Committee. In his testimony regarding South Vietnam the secretary said:

The country has made good use of our assistance. By August 1 we will submit to Congress a 5-year projection which will reflect our expectation of a gradually declining United States role.[5]

On June 5, while engaged in a dialogue with Peter H. B. Frelinghuysen (R., N.J.) concerning Cambodia, Secretary of Defense James Schlesinger was asked: "What would be the result if there should be sharp reduction in the amount of ammunition that could be provided because of insufficient funds?" Schlesinger responded:

The ability of the government to survive would be severely compromised. As you recall, at the time of the cutoff of tactical air support last summer, there was some question whether the government could survive. It pulled itself together, but it is dependent upon its own forces and the munitions that are supplied to these forces. Without such munitions, it is hard to see how it could survive.

The secretary also offered his opinion of the South Vietnamese army in reply to a question posed by Clement J. Zablocki (D., Wis.):

The Armed Forces of South Vietnam are giving an excellent account of themselves when there are flareups of hostilities under the cease-fire agreement.

To many who observed the ARVN of six or seven years ago, the account they are now giving of themselves is splendid. In something on the order of seventy or seventy-five percent of the engagements that occur, ARVN is able to emerge on top.[6]

Representative Bella Abzug appeared before the Committee on June 26 and discussed the situation in Vietnam and Cambodia with particular reference to political prisoners. The New York Democrat was very upset over the jailing of her friend Mrs. Ngo Ba Tanh, who, according to Abzug, had "spent two years in prison merely because of her political neutralism." The real reason for Mrs. Tanh's imprisonment had been explained by Graham Martin at an earlier date. In a letter to Amnesty International on February 12, 1974, the ambassador stated that in October 1973, when he was in Washington, Averell Harrriman had inquired about the welfare of Mme Ngo Ba Than. Martin states that he responded:

I asked him what he thought might have happened to a woman in the United States, who having just concluded a hearing before our mutual friend Arthur Goldberg when he was a Supreme Court Justice, had accosted him as he was about to enter his car, broken the windshield of

[5] Hearings Before the House Committee on Foreign Relations, "Fiscal Year 1975 Foreign Assistance Request," 1974.

[6] Ibid., pp. 54–56.

his car, and then kicked him in his private parts. He said: "My God, she would still be in jail." [*Congressional Record,* April 4, 1974]

The Defense Procurement Act

When the bill that authorized appropriations for defense procurement and weapons development was reported by the House Armed Services Committee on May 10, it contained $1.4 billion for aid to South Vietnam. This figure was $200 million less than the administration had requested. However, if an amendment offered by Otis Pike (D., N.Y.) had been accepted, it would have been cut another $200 million from the amount appropriated. Ten days later the House reduced the amount available for assistance to South Vietnam to $1.126 billion.

Later, in the Senate, Senator Edward M. Kennedy (D., Mass.) submitted an amendment that in effect would have halted the stockpiling of all war materials for use of South Vietnam, South Korea, and Thailand. The Senate approved the Kennedy motion by a voice vote. During the House-Senate conference, however, the conferees removed the Kennedy stockpiling proposal. When the President finally approved the measure of August 5, it stated in part:

> No funds authorized by this or any other Act to or for use by the Department of Defense may be obligated in the fiscal year ending June 30, 1975, for support of South Vietnamese military forces in any amount in excess of the amount of $1,000,000,000.[7]

Nixon Resigns

During the last days in July, the House Judiciary Committee passed three impeachment articles against Richard Nixon. The first article, issued on July 27, charged that the President had engaged in the obstruction of justice in the Watergate case. Two days later the Committee voted to recommend impeachment for abuse of power. On July 30 a final article was approved that charged the President with unconstitutionally defying two subpoenas of the Committee.

These actions caused Nixon to release several tapes that he had previously refused to surrender. The content of the tapes proved to be so damaging that the President's position "eroded" rapidly. Finally, on August 5, Nixon released transcripts of three conversations he had held with H. R. Haldeman on June 23, 1972. These recordings revealed that six days after the break-in, the President had ordered the FBI to halt its investigation of the Watergate affair.

[7] Public Law 93-265, August 5, 1974.

174

After the release of this information, Nixon's support in the Congress simply melted away. The visible loss of a congressional power base led the President to announce over nationwide television on August 8, 1974 that he was resigning the next day. At 11:35 A.M. on August 9, Nixon's letter of resignation was delivered to Secretary of State Kissinger. Twenty-nine minutes later, Gerald Ford was sworn into office by Chief Justice Warren E. Burger.

The Department of Defense Appropriations Act

In its major military appropriations request for fiscal 1975, the Defense Department asked that $1.45 billion in new money and $150 million in already appropriated funds be allocated to South Vietnam. The House Appropriations Committee recommended that this amount be reduced to $922.6 million plus $77.4 million in unused funds.

When the bill reached the floor of the House on August 6, John J. Flynt offered an amendment to reduce the new monies request to $622.6 million. Among his reasons for recommending this significant decrease, the Georgia Democrat said that the United States was not going to keep sending billions of dollars to President Thieu so he could "avoid the political realities of his own country."

Robert L. F. Sikes (D., Fla.) opposed the Flynt amendment and read a letter from Secretary Kissinger that stated in part:

> Cuts already made in our military assistance, combined with the rapid inflation which has eroded the value of that assistance, have brought the South Vietnamese armed forces to a level of austerity which, if reduced further might affect their ability to defend their country against continuing Communist military pressure.

Sikes also warned: "Let us not hand South Vietnam to the Communists on a silver platter. Help the South Vietnamese keep up a brave fight."

Robert N. Giaimo (D., Conn.) rose in support of the Flynt proposal and asked that he be considered a cosponsor of the measure. Silvio O. Conte (R., Mass.) also claimed sponsorship of the Flynt amendment and said: "Peace will only come about when all parties to that conflict recognize there is a no-win military situation there."*

Elford A. Cederberg (R., Mich.) warned that the passage of the Flynt-Giaimo-Conte amendment would be "a signal to North Vietnam that the rest of the world has decided to abandon South Vietnam." He also reminded his colleagues how, during past debates on the American movement out of Vietnam, the champions of with-

---

* Representative Conte did not clarify how the withholding of ammunition from the South Vietnamese army would "send a message" to Hanoi that North Vietnamese forces were engaged in a "no-win" war.

drawal had gained a great deal of support by claiming, "Once we get out, we will give them all the help that they need to sustain themselves."

Democrats Bella Abzug (N.Y.), Joseph P. Addabbo (N.Y.), Robert L. Leggett (Calif.), William Lehman (Fla.), and Parren J. Mitchell (Md.) also spoke in favor of the measure. The Flynt amendment was passed at 9:33 P.M., after a marathon session, by a vote of 233–157 with 44 members not voting. Later in the evening the entire bill was approved by the House with 350 yeas to 43 nays.

When the defense appropriations measure reached the Senate on August 20, Senator Edward M. Kennedy (D., Mass.) made another attempt to halt the stockpiling of war materials for America's Asian allies. The senator's renewed efforts to eliminate these "war reserve stocks" for South Korea, South Vietnam, and Thailand were contained in an amendment he moved to attach to the appropriations bill. Kennedy's proposal, while approved in the Senate, was changed by House-Senate conferees to apply to the transfer of war materials to any country unless such exchanges were authorized by law.

As the Senate continued its debate on the defense appropriations bill, Senator William Proxmire (D., Wis.) submitted an amendment that would have reduced the amount allocated for South Vietnam to $550 million. Senator Dick Clark (D., Iowa) offered his support to the Proxmire revision and stated: "By limiting our military assistance, we do signal ally and adversary alike that it is time to negotiate."

The next day the Senate continued the debate on the Proxmire proposal. During the deliberations on the previous day one of the Wisconsin Democrat's supporters had estimated that the United States had provided the South Vietnamese with eight times more aid than the Russians and Chinese had provided to Hanoi. Senator Barry Goldwater refuted this claim and stated that his opponents were comparing "apples with oranges." The senator made it clear that while American assistance to South Vietnam in 1973 had exceeded Russian and Chinese aid to Hanoi, the ratio was four to three and not eight to one. In addition to clarifying the comparative support levels, the Arizona Republican explained that United States aid to South Vietnam was not limited to military usage. According to Goldwater, American money was also used to build South Vietnamese hospitals, to supply and staff medical facilities, and to purchase many other items that normally would be classified as civilian expenses. The Senate narrowly defeated the Proxmire amendment by a vote of 47–44 and later in the day passed the entire bill. When President Ford signed the appropriations measure, he said:

> The bill has, however, a major drawback. The $700 million funding for South Vietnam is inadequate to provide for all their critical needs, if

South Vietnam's enemies continue to press their attacks. It may, therefore, be necessary to approach the Congress early next year to work out some solutions to meet critical needs which arise.[8]

Looking back on this severe reduction in aid to South Vietnam, President Thieu in an interview on January 30, 1975 said: "After the American Congress last year halved the Ford Administration's $1.4 billion request for military assistance . . . the morale of troops here began to drop."[9]

At the time President Ford signed the defense money bill, North Vietnamese combat strength in South Vietnam had increased to more than 250,000 soldiers supported by 50,000 Vietcong auxiliaries. As if the increase in men was not ominous enough, the offensive capabilities of the NVA expeditionary force had been improved considerably by the addition of several hundred tanks.[10]

In contrast to the rapidly growing North Vietnamese forces, ARVN supplies were being doled out on an austerity basis. Where in the past a soldier going on a patrol had been issued ten grenades, his daily allotment was now down to one. This lack of war materiel had produced a change in the previous fighting mood of the South Vietnamese army. Where the ARVN soldiers had previously moved aggressively against enemy incursions, they now were inclined to assume a passive role.

In spite of the growing passivity of the Saigon troops, the Hanoi leadership seemed to be holding back their invasion army. There is a good probability that the reason for their restraint was that the politburo leaders simply could not believe the Americans had abandoned their ally.

It was not until after the United States elections in the fall of 1974 that North Vietnamese field commanders received the go-ahead in their plans to conquer South Vietnam. As a result of the Watergate scandals, the Democrats had gained forty-three seats in the House. This liberal victory meant that in the 94th Congress there would be 291 Democrats and only 144 Republicans. In the Senate, the Democrats had gained three seats and the lineup was now 61 Democrats to 39 Republicans. This leftward shift of both congressional chambers played a significant role in the North Vietnamese decision to unleash its army.

The order for the NVA to proceed with the conquest of South Vietnam was actually issued by Hanoi during the second week in November. The message was distributed to subordinate units in South

[8] *Weekly Compilation of Presidential Documents,* October 14, 1974.
[9] *New York Times,* January 31, 1975.
[10] Brigadier F. P. Serong, "Vietnam After the Cease-Fire," *Asian Affairs,* September–October, 1974.

Vietnam by the Communist headquarters situated near Saigon; the resolution read, in part:

> Enemy air and artillery capability now limited as a result of reductions in U.S. aid. In short, the enemy is declining militarily and has no chance of regaining the position they held in 1973.
>
> On the other hand, our position is improving. We are now stronger than we were during the Tet offensive in 1968 and the summer of 1972. We now have ample amounts of money, weapons and equipment which makes it possible for us to initiate a sustained attack on a wide front.

Foreign Aid Slashed

The House resumed its deliberations on the President's foreign aid request on December 11, 1974. After the discussions shifted to Indochina, Silvio O. Conte moved to amend the bill to limit assistance to Cambodia to $377 million with a $200 million subceiling on military expenditures. The House approved the Massachusetts Republican's proposal by voice vote and later in the day passed the entire measure. Following a House-Senate conference, which made no significant changes, the bill was sent to the White House.

When President Ford signed the foreign aid legislation, it only contained $449.9 million for South Vietnam and $377 million for Cambodia.* This funding fell some $300 million short of what the administration had requested. The Chief Executive showed his disappointment when he signed the measure on December 30 and commented: "The economic and military assistance levels for Cambodia, particularly, are inadequate to meet minimum basic needs."[11]

The President's warnings were underscored by dangerous rumblings from Vietnam. In mid-December the Communist forces had conducted a series of probing attacks during which they captured four government-held district capitals. As a result of their efforts in Phuoc Long Province, only Phuoc Binh, the provincial capital, remained free from politburo control.

Surrender in Saigon

As the New Year opened, North Vietnamese troops stalked the isolated provincial capital of Phuoc Binh. After the Hanoi regulars had surrounded the town, they seized nearby Ba Ra mountain. The capture of the high ground gave the NVA artillery spotters an almost

---

[11] *Weekly Compilation of Presidential Documents,* January 6, 1975.

* An additional $75 million drawdown of Department of Defense stocks was also authorized for use in Cambodia.

APRIL 12, 1975

CHICK LARSEN

—*Richmond Times-Dispatch*

unlimited field of observation, and soon shells were landing on ARVN troop headquarters. The first ground assaults were launched on January 3, 1975, with attackers advancing behind T-54 tanks. The South Vietnamese defenders, who discovered their American-made rocket launchers would not stop the heavily armored vehicles, were soon defeated and scattered into isolated pockets of resistance. While the Saigon command sent two relief companies of airborne rangers, the 200 men found very few of the defending force still alive and shortly withdrew.

The continued violations of the truce agreement caused the United States to send a strongly-worded note to the Soviet Union, Communist China, and the other guarantors of the Paris accords. The State Department document accused the North Vietnamese of "turning from the path of negotiation to that of war." The note charged that Hanoi, contrary to the agreement, had infiltrated more than 160,000 troops and 400 tanks into the south since the end of January 1973.

Since the American protest was limited to words, the North Vietnamese intensified their military activities. On January 20 the Hanoi command ordered NVA Division 968 to shift the center of its operations from Laos into South Vietnam. Two other divisions also began moving from their positions north of the DMZ into the Southern Republic. The United States military leadership was unable to interpret these troop movements clearly. Following a day-long briefing before a House appropriations subcommittee, Lieutenant General Daniel O. Graham told reporters on January 30 that the movement of the North Vietnamese divisions could be a "feint." On the other hand, both he and Philip C. Habib of the State Department stated to a newsman that Hanoi might be preparing a major offensive.

The increased activity on the Vietnamese battlefields formed the background to a presidential news conference on January 21, 1975. Following his formal presentation, the President and the reporters engaged in the following dialogue:

Q: Mr. President, are there circumstances in which the United States might actively reenter the Vietnam War?

THE PRESIDENT: I cannot foresee any at the moment.

Q: Are you ruling out the possibility of bombing over there or naval action?

THE PRESIDENT: I don't think it is appropriate for me to forecast any specific actions that might be taken. I would simply say that any military actions, if taken, will be only taken following the actions under our constitutional and legal procedures.[12]

[12] *Weekly Compilation of Presidential Documents,* January 27, 1975.

A week after meeting with the newsmen, the President sent a message to the Congress proposing supplemental appropriations for Cambodia and South Vietnam. In his request for funds, among other things, Ford said:

> At a time when the North Vietnamese have been building up their forces and pressing their attacks, United States military aid to the South Vietnamese government has not been sufficient to permit one-to-one replacement of equipment used up or destroyed, as permitted by the Paris Agreement. In fact, with the $700 million appropriation available in the current fiscal year, we have been able to provide no new tanks, airplanes, trucks, artillery pieces, or other major equipment, but only essential consumable items such as ammunition, gasoline, spare parts and medical supplies.[13]

This significant lack of vital military equipment led the President to request a supplemental appropriation of $300 million for assistance to South Vietnam.

The Chief Executive also discussed the open warfare then raging in Cambodia and directed the legislators' attention to the fact that the military pipeline to the Lon Nol government was empty. In order to furnish Cambodia's minimal needs, he requested that the economic and military ceilings on aid to that country be lifted and asked Congress to appropriate an additional $222 million for military aid to the small Buddhist nation.

President Thieu evaluated the $300 million request as "the minimum" his forces needed to defend themselves from North Vietnamese attacks. The Saigon leader gave his response to the American President's actions in a lengthy interview he granted journalists in the Independence Palace on January 30. Thieu also said that every time he visited field commanders they begged for more ammunition. Under the prodding of reporters the South Vietnamese leader continued: "It is not yet time to accuse the United States of betraying this country." However, he added, "most of the people of South Vietnam" were starting to believe that the Americans who had "lured" them into the struggle against the Communists were now running away.[14]

Congressional reaction to the President's request for additional money for Indochina was primarily negative. One liberal organization known as the Members of Congress for Peace Through Law asked the Chief Executive on February 9 for a dialogue on phasing out all United States aid to Cambodia and South Vietnam. The request was in the form of a letter signed by 12 senators and 70 representatives. In their message to the President the congressmen wrote:

[13] *Weekly Compilation of Presidential Documents,* February 3, 1975.
[14] *New York Times,* January 31, 1975.

While continuing high levels of American assistance may perhaps prolong the life of the incumbent South Vietnamese and Cambodian governments, we can see no humanitarian or national interest that justifies the cost of this assistance to our country.[15]

"No humanitarian interest"! "Humanitarian" is defined by one prominent authority as "promoting human welfare." Surely, the signers of the letter would have been promoting the human welfare of the non-Communist Cambodians had they agreed to the President's request. The horrors later perpetrated on the Cambodian people by their Communist conquerors is too well known to need description here. Of course, the Members can always say, "Well, we had no knowledge of what the Khmer Rouge would do."

But can these liberal Congressmen really plead ignorance? Compare, for instance, the membership of the House Committee on Foreign Affairs in the summer of 1974 with the list of signers of the rejection letter. This was the legislative body that heard testimony from Max Friedman, a journalist, regarding Communist activities in Cambodia. Friedman in his presentation to the Committee offered a previously classified United States intelligence document entitled "The Khmer Kahom Program to Create a Communist Society in Southern Cambodia" as evidence of the utter brutality of the Khmer Rouge. There was very little that could be defined as "humanitarian" in the Communist blueprint for the future of Cambodia.[16]

Members of the House Committee who heard Friedman's testimony or had an opportunity to examine the evidence, and who also signed the letter rejecting assistance to the Cambodian people were:*

Jonathan B. Bingham (D., N.Y.)
Charles Diggs (D., Mich.)
Donald M. Fraser (D., Minn.)
Michael Harrington (D., Mass.)
Donald Riegle, Jr. (D., Mich.) *

The struggle over United States aid to South Vietnam at this time became so intense that Tran Van Lam, the president of the South Vietnamese Senate, felt it necessary to lobby personally in Washington for his people. In pursuit of American support Senator Lam and a group of his colleagues attempted to visit several American

[15] Letter from Members of Congress for Peace Through Law to President Gerald Ford, February 6, 1975.

[16] Hearings Before the House Committee on Foreign Affairs, "Fiscal Year 1975 Foreign Assistance Request," 1974.

* See Appendix B for the full list of the Members of Congress for Peace Through Law.

congressmen. The South Vietnamese senators were often left to cool their heels in the anterooms of congressional offices. In one instance, a prominent United States senator stomped out of his office and called to the waiting delegation that he was voting against further aid and did not want to hear their story anyhow.

On February 21 Lam addressed the Washington press corps at a luncheon sponsored jointly by the American Security Council and the Vietnamese-American Council. In his speech the South Vietnamese senator described how the congressional cuts had hurt his country's defense effort. He also addressed the problem of corruption in South Vietnam:

> It is however, essential to establish an order of priorities. Our country was practically born in war and has never had the opportunity to develop to a full extent the practices of democracy, nor has it had sufficient time to train a perfectly qualified and perfectly motivated corps of public servants. The war and its permanent companion, economic difficulty, tend to compound those deficiencies. We are all very much aware of both of those predicaments, and we correct them as best we can.

During his stay in the United States, the aging Vietnamese patriot sent a letter to Vice-President Nelson Rockefeller, who also served as President of the Senate. In his message Lam wrote:

> In the spring of 1973, we signed the Paris Agreement. . . . We were given to understand that should it come to the worst and should the North Vietnamese resort again to the use of force, we would be provided with adequate means to defend ourselves.

He continued:

> The record has shown that since the reduction of military aid to Vietnam by the Congress, Communist attacks have increased in tempo and inflicted on our people more casualties than before.[17]

The increase in Communist activity about which Lam had written took a quantum jump when the North Vietnamese forces hit the Central Highlands on March 5 in a series of coordinated assaults. The sudden attacks were aimed at isolating the main population centers of Pleiku, Kontum, and Ban Me Thuot. Five days later, after a heavy artillery barrage, NVA troops made a lightning thrust into the center of Ban Me Thuot. The South Vietnamese defenders seemed to be caught unawares, and the headquarters of the ARVN 23rd Division was soon surrounded. With the capture of the Highlands city, the entire province of Dar Lac fell into North Vietnamese hands.

While the battle for South Vietnam grew desperate, in Cambodia it

[17] American Security Council, "More Than a Matter of Aid," March 1975.

appeared as if the city of Phnom Penh would fall to the rebels momentarily. The obvious increase in hostilities in Indochina led thirty-seven House Democrats, all but one of them a freshman, to send a letter to President Ford on March 9 indicating they would not vote for his military aid package. A spokesman for the group, Thomas Harkin (D., Iowa), said that he and his colleagues had asked the President to let statesmanship prevail over dollars.*

The next day Senator Claiborne Pell (D., R.I.) submitted a bill in the Senate which would have had the effect of denying any further military aid to Cambodia. Mark Hatfield (R., Ohio) followed Pell's lead and said: "I think most of my colleagues agree with me that we should not authorize any more military assistance to Cambodia." Mike Mansfield (D., Mont.) stated:

> Let us recognize that this area is the concern of the Cambodian people themselves. It is not vital to the security of the United States. Peace will be achieved when the outside powers withhold their war material and related resources and allow the people of Cambodia, regardless of which side they are on—if any—to make their own decisions as to how they should define their destiny, and what they should do to better the future of their country.†

On March 12 Senator George McGovern (D., S. Dak.) entered the testimony that Tom Hayden had previously given to the Senate Committee on Foreign Relations into the *Congressional Record*. According to Hayden, who had met with Ok Sakun, a representative of the Communist-supported Cambodian rebels in Paris on February 28, the revolutionaries were determined to win a complete victory. Hayden stated that Ok Sakun had rejected any negotiations with the Lon Nol government and had said that his organization would

> probably kill Lon Nol, Sirik Matak, Son Ngoc Thanh, Cheng Heng, In Tam, Long Beret and Sosthene Fernandez—the top leaders of the Phnom Penh government.

The congressional opposition to any further military assistance to Cambodia and South Vietnam received a strong impetus when Democratic members of the House of Representatives voted 189–49 against additional aid to these countries. The Democrats, who met in a secret caucus on March 12, voted in favor of an antiwar measure presented by M. Robert Carr (D., Mich.), a freshman representative. The Carr

---

* For a complete list of the signers of this letter see Appendix C.

† The senior senator from Montana did not explain how 43,000 North Vietnamese regulars fit into his plan for Cambodians to solve their own problems. He also failed to discuss how the people of Cambodia were going to make their own decisions when one side had all the guns.

resolution had expressed the sense of the Democratic caucus as being "firmly opposed to the approval of any further military assistance to South Vietnam or to Cambodia in fiscal 1975." There were four other sponsors of the abandonment resolution; they were Bella Abzug (N.Y.), Thomas R. Harkin (Iowa), Toby Moffett (Conn.), and Edward W. Pattison (N.Y.).[18] The following day the Senate Democratic caucus voted 38–5 against further military aid to Cambodia. These lopsided votes in Democratic caucuses sealed the fate of further military aid to America's Southeast Asian allies. There was very little possibility that with the overwhelming majority the Democrats enjoyed in both chambers, any action they so strongly opposed could be successfully sustained.

The news of the congressional defeat reached President Thieu at a particularly bad time. The North Vietnamese forces were threatening to overwhelm government defenses in the Highlands, and Communist troops were on the move throughout South Vietnam. In response to these actions the Saigon leader had called a top-level meeting of South Vietnamese military commanders at Camh Ranh Bay. After several hours of strained discussions, Thieu ordered a general withdrawal from the Central Highlands. The decision to surrender the strategic Highlands was based on the simple fact that there was just not enough military strength to defend all the areas of South Vietnam under attack.*

When Major General Pham Van Phu, commander of ARVN's 2nd Corps, which was stationed in Pleiku, returned to his headquarters, he ordered an immediate withdrawal. The retreat soon turned into a rout as Phu's troops, bogged down by the addition of 200,000 refugees, were ambushed along the route of their march to the coast.

The near disaster in the Highlands led the Saigon command to order a withdrawal from the northernmost province of Quang Tri. As the ARVN soldiers moved south, NVA units attacked the ancient capital of Hue. On March 25 the North Vietnamese succeeded in penetrating the city's defenses and the government forces joined the general retreat to Da Nang. The fall of Quang Tri and Hue had completely isolated the important port of Da Nang. By this time the city was in utter chaos and confusion ruled everywhere.

The South Vietnamese looked in desperation for help from America. Their pleading was in vain, however, for on March 26 the Con-

---

[18] *Congressional Quarterly Weekly Report,* March 15, 1975.

* Edward A. Miller, Jr., legislative assistant to Senator Gary Hart of Colorado, who visited several South Vietnamese generals at the end of March, has written: "Because of aid limits, not much of this kind of defensive warfare was possible. Consequently, the GVN planned a pullback from Pleiku and Kontum" in the Highlands (*Congressional Record,* April 29, 1975).

gress went home for a leisurely Easter recess. The failure of the American Congress to provide some type of assistance to their suffering allies was the subject of a speech that Robert Griffin (R., Mich.) gave on the day of the Easter adjournment:

> By default—and through caucus decisions of the majority party—it has become painfully obvious to all who watch, in the United States and around the world, that Congress is turning its back on allies in Indochina who are struggling to defend themselves.

While the congressmen were en route to their homes, North Vietnamese troops directed the fire of their 130 mm artillery units into Da Nang, and on the next day they entered the city's outer defenses. The government soldiers, who by this time were thoroughly disorganized and virtually leaderless, surrendered in large numbers. At 3:30 P.M. on March 29, Da Nang fell to the advancing Communist forces.

As the men from Hanoi swept towards Saigon, one of the curious beliefs of the American friends of the Vietcong was destroyed forever. This mistaken supposition was that the war in Vietnam was a civil war and that great numbers of South Vietnamese were opposed to the Saigon government. Evidence for the falseness of this assumption was provided by the hundreds of thousands of forlorn Vietnamese who fled their northern conquerors. As a further indication of this enormous misunderstanding, when the Hanoi troops "liberated" the provinces of South Vietnam, the North Vietnamese were unable to find enough southern Communists to run the areas they had conquered. Throughout the "Liberation Zone" it was not unusual to discover a village or town still being administered by its previous non-Communist Saigon appointees. In some cases, however, when residents were not available and the local Communists had proven untrustworthy, military management committees had been forced to take over the operation of the larger cities.[19]

By this time it appeared as if South Vietnam should be written off as a lost cause. This conclusion was the major subject of a long article submitted from Saigon by K. M. Chrysler of *U.S. News and World Report* on March 31. In his commentary on the situation in Vietnam, Chrysler wrote:

> Supplies of virtually everything are pinched. Fire power has dropped. Air support is down. Medical care has deteriorated. Shortages of radio batteries hamper tactical operations.

As to the cause of lack of the implements of war, the reporter stated:

---

[19] *China News Analysis,* December 19, 1975.

There is frustration over the nearly 50 percent cut in military aid this year . . . and the reluctance of the American Congress to appropriate another $300 million in emergency military assistance.

The failure of the Congress to provide its ally with the necessary funds to fight the war did not fail to gain the attention of the Hanoi politburo. On April 1 a party journalist wrote: "The United States Congress no longer granted as much generous aid to the Saigon puppets as it had done previously."[20]

In spite of the North Vietnamese successes, ARVN troops created a temporary defensive arc running from Xuan Loc near the coast to Tay Ninh near the Cambodian border, and then down to the Mekong Delta. Within this shortened perimeter the South Vietnamese soldiers fought a desperate battle for survival. The shortage of equipment soon took its toll as North Vietnamese forces brushed aside the ARVN defenders and moved on to Saigon.

After Congress returned from its Easter recess, Senator Edward M. Kennedy (D., Mass.) convened a meeting of his Judiciary Subcommittee on Refugees and Escapees on April 8. As a member of the Senate and chairman of the subcommittee, Kennedy was able to use his influence to whipsaw the Ford administration. On the one hand, he could successfully lead the fight to cut off appropriations for South Vietnam, which in turn created more refugees. And, on the other hand, he could attack the White House for the existence of large numbers of refugees. Speaking with special reference to the airlifting of Vietnamese babies to the United States, Kennedy said:

> For too many weeks our government has stood paralyzed, as events rapidly overtook whatever small decision our government was making to assist the millions of orphans and refugees and war victims in South Vietnam and Cambodia.[21]

That evening the Academy of Motion Picture Arts and Sciences held its annual awards dinner. During the ceremonies *Hearts and Minds,* a controversial propaganda movie about the Vietnam War, received an Oscar. While accepting his award, producer Bert Schneider, in agreement with director Peter Davis, read a congratulatory telegram from Dinh Ba Thi of North Vietnam. The audience responded to the reading of the message with utter silence. Frank Sinatra, who was serving as master of ceremonies, immediately collab-

---

[20] *The Thieu Regime,* p. 50.

[21] *Congressional Quarterly Weekly Report,* April 12, 1975. The fact that the Massachusetts Democrat had played a major role in paralyzing the government was not mentioned in his report to the subcommittee.

orated with Bob Hope in reading a disclaimer in the name of the Academy.[22]

Earlier in the afternoon George Meany, president of the AFL-CIO, had delivered a speech on American foreign policy at a luncheon of the Maritime Trades Department in Washington, D.C. In his address the labor leader said:

> Let me turn once again to Vietnam. We are now being told by some of our liberal friends on Capitol Hill that South Vietnam is going down the drain—finished because its people no longer have the will to fight.
> This may be—but should we not ask ourselves that, if it is true, could there be a connection between this loss of will on the part of the South Vietnamese and the complete and final refusal by the American Congress to provide them with the material resources needed to defend their country from Communist aggression?[23]

On April 10 in a foreign policy address, President Ford asked the Congress for $722 million in new military aid and $250 million in humanitarian assistance for the collapsing Saigon government. The request did not seem to be directed at a gallant last infusion of money into the South Vietnamese fighting forces, but instead, appeared to be more of a desire to arrange the defeat with a little dignity. The key item of concern to administration officials was the safety of about 5,000 Americans still in Vietnam and several hundred thousand Vietnamese who had cooperated with the United States over the past twenty years.

The President suggested that because of the "gravity" of the situation in Vietnam the Congress respond to the request for funds by April 19. As a result of his appeal, at least eight congressional committees held more than sixteen unproductive meetings during the week of April 14 with a net result of zero.*

Two days after Ford's speech the White House announced the closing of the United States Embassy in Phnom Penh. In a well-planned maneuver known as "Eagle Pull," United States helicopters swooped into the dying city on April 12 and rescued the last Americans and about 1,200 Cambodians. Not all the Cambodian government officials, however, left with the departing airlift.†

As John Gunther Dean, the American ambassador, was about to be

---

[22] *Los Angeles Times,* April 9, 1975.

[23] Text of address by AFL-CIO president George Meany on April 8, 1975, "News from the AFL-CIO, Department of Public Relations."

* The conduct of American foreign relations by congressional committees was beginning to bear some unusual fruit. While diversity was anticipated, a systematic stonewalling of a presidential request came as a surprise to many interested observers.

† Lon Nol had escaped from Cambodia on April 1.

evacuated, he offered General Sirik Matak asylum in the United States. The general responded in writing:

DEAR EXCELLENCY AND FRIEND,

I thank you very sincerely for your letter and for your offer to transport me toward freedom. I cannot, alas, leave in such a cowardly fashion. As for you, and in particular your great country, I never believed for a moment that you would have this sentiment of abandoning a people which has chosen liberty. You have refused us your protection, and we can do nothing about it.

You leave and my wish is that you and your country will find happiness under this sky. But mark it well, that if I shall die here on the spot and in my country that I love, it is too bad, because we are all born and must die one day. [*Congressional Record,* May 1, 1975]

On April 16 Phnom Penh surrendered. As the Communist forces entered the city, they were met by a demoralized populace who feared for their lives. The general anxiety of the inhabitants soon turned to terror as the young guerrilla soldiers forced the residents from their homes at the point of a gun.[24] In a calculated act of destruction that will live in infamy forever, some three million Cambodians were violently driven out of the city of Phnom Penh.

In keeping with their plans of obliterating any remnants of the former society, the Khmer Rouge killer teams began to execute the captured enemy leaders. Among those who payed their "blood debts" were Premier Long Beret; Interior Minister Lon Non, a brother of President Lon Nol; and General Sirik Matak. The former government officials were not the only ones who had been slated for purging, as the rebels also began hunting down the wealthy and members of various religious sects.

The fall of Cambodia cast a cloud of gloom over Saigon, and non-Communist calls for Thieu's resignation were mixed with those of the PRG. After the North Vietnamese victory at Ban Me Thuot, the Communists had made it clear they would not deal with Thieu. This demand served as a strong mechanism for undermining the South Vietnamese leader's authority. It also encouraged the congressional liberals to pressure President Ford for Thieu's removal.

The use of this "carrot-and-stick" approach in the conduct of warfare by the North Vietnamese is almost as old as the Communist party itself. In practicing this stratagem the Communists would usually launch an assault against their opponent of the moment, placing the threatened regime in jeopardy. At the same time they promised peace if the people would overthrow their leaders. The intended victims, desiring to halt the spread of warfare, often removed their support from the authorities. This lack of participation in turn

---

[24] *Freedom at Issue,* January–February 1976.

"Peace at Last"

—*Richmond Times-Dispatch*

weakened the government, and the Communists had gained their ends.*

In the case of South Vietnam the North Vietnamese political maneuver in the spring of 1975 was so successful that Nguyen Van Thieu resigned on April 21.† In his final speech as President of the Republic, the South Vietnamese leader said:

> There was a promise that if the Communists intruded and invaded again, there would be a reaction. But there has been no reaction. . . . What does this amount to? This amounts to a breach of promise, injustice, lack of responsibility and inhumanity toward an ally who has suffered continuously—the shirking of responsibility on the part of a great power.

These charges of faithlessness raised an uproar in the United States, and many congressmen demended that the administration respond to Thieu's accusations. Evidently the President agreed with the necessity to react to the South Vietnamese leader's strong speech, and in a press interview with correspondents of CBS News Ford stated:

> It is my judgment at the moment that the failure of the Congress to appropriate the military aid requested . . . certainly raised doubts in the mind of President Thieu and his military that we would be supplying sufficient military hardware for them to adequately defend their various positions in South Vietnam.
> Now the lack of support certainly had an impact on the decision that President Thieu made to withdraw precipitously. I don't think he would have withdrawn if the support had been there.[25]

After Thieu's resignation the office of president passed to Vice-President Tran Van Huong. The new South Vietnamese leader immediately appealed to the Communists for a cease-fire. The North Vietnamese revealed the true nature of their demand that Thieu resign when they answered Huong's request with a charge that it was a "trick that fooled no one."

The death cries from Saigon shocked congressional liberals with the enormity of their crimes against the South Vietnamese people. There were frantic demands that something be done. Bella Abzug (D., N.Y.) called for the formation of a coalition government. Hubert Humphrey (D., Minn.) and Edward M. Kennedy (D., Mass.) urged that negotiations be resumed. Toby Moffett (D., Conn.) stated his belief

[25] *U.S. News and World Report,* May 5, 1975.

* In validating the standard usage of this technique by the Communists, it is only necessary to search as far back as October 1948, when following the battle of Hsuchow-Peng Pu, the Maoists circulated the slogan "Unless President Chiang goes there can be no peace talks." See, Chiang Kai-shek, *Soviet Russia in China: A Summing Up at Seventy* (New York: Farrar, Strauss and Cudahy, 1957), p. 18.

† On April 26 Thieu was flown to asylum in Taiwan.

that the Congress should call on the United Nations for assistance. Robert Carr (D., Mich.) offered what he considered indisputable evidence from a South Vietnamese "neutralist" that Thieu was maneuvering

to appeal to U.S. conscience and prestige in order to force the U.S. administration to continue dealing with him as the sole existing legal government in South Vietnam. [*Congressional Record,* April 23, 1975]

The continued refusal of the Communists to deal with Huong forced the South Vietnamese National Assembly to adopt a resolution approving the transfer of presidential power to Duong Van Minh. "Big Minh," as he was known affectionately by his many Vietnamese followers, had always been identified with a more neutral position toward the Communists. It was this spirit of compromise that the assembly members grasped for as the North Vietnamese forces closed in on Saigon.

At this point there were still several thousand Americans in Saigon. The obvious danger to these United States citizens caused considerable worry to congressional members. Their concern would have been lessened considerably had they known of the preparations the administration was taking to assure a safe evacuation. From the evidence available it appears that the State Department, in cooperation with the Central Intelligence Agency, obtained permission from the North Vietnamese for the unmolested withdrawal of the Americans and a limited number of Vietnamese from Saigon. The pivotal party in these sensitive arrangements seems to have been the Russian Communists.[26] Whoever was responsible, Ambassador Graham Martin has stated before a House international relations subcommittee that

I was the only person in Saigon who knew the North Vietnamese had undertaken on April 22 that they would not militarily interfere with the evacuation.[27]

In spite of Hanoi's assurances of a safe withdrawal, American armed forces were ordered to accompany the evacuation helicopters into Saigon. The entire undertaking, known as "Operation Frequent Wind," was reported to the Congress in a letter from the President on April 30. In his communication to the House, the Chief Executive wrote:

I wish to report to you that at about 1:00 A.M. EDT, April 29, 1975, U.S. forces entered South Vietnam airspace.
A force of 70 evacuation helicopters and 865 marines evacuated about

[26] Press conference of the Secretary of State, April 29, 1975.
[27] *Newsday,* January 28, 1976.

1,400 U.S. citizens, together with approximately 5,500 third country nationals and South Vietnamese. . . . The last elements of the ground security force departed Saigon at 7:46 P.M. EDT, April 29, 1975. [*Congressional Record*, May 1, 1975]

The day after the Americans and their Vietnamese associates had been removed from Saigon, General Minh surrendered the city and the Republic to the victorious men from Hanoi. As the North Vietnamese troops entered the city, they closed down all domestic communication facilities, and a blanket of silence descended upon South Vietnam. The only voice you could hear was that of United States Senator Hiram Fong (R., Hawaii) who, on hearing of the fall of the Southern Republic, said:

There is no question but what we have betrayed the Cambodians, and we have betrayed the South Vietnamese. There is no question about it. . . . We have not lived up to our commitments.[28]

---

[28] *Congressional Quarterly Weekly Report,* May 3, 1975.

MAY 1, 1975

FREE
S. VIETNAM

CHICK LARSEN

"After 30 Years, the 'Dove' of Peace"
—*Richmond Times-Dispatch*

194

Appendix A

Agreement on Ending the War and Restoring Peace in Vietnam

The Parties participating in the Paris Conference on Vietnam, with a view to ending the war and restoring peace in Vietnam on the basis of respect for the Vietnamese people's fundamental national rights and the South Vietnamese people's right to self-determination, and to contributing to the consolidation of peace in Asia and the world, have agreed on the following provisions and undertake to respect and to implement them:

CHAPTER I

THE VIETNAMESE PEOPLE'S FUNDAMENTAL NATIONAL RIGHTS

Article 1

The United States and all other countries respect the independence, sovereignty, unity, and territorial integrity of Vietnam as recognized by the 1954 Geneva Agreements on Vietnam.

CHAPTER II

CESSATION OF HOSTILITIES—WITHDRAWAL OF TROOPS

Article 2

A cease-fire shall be observed throughout South Vietnam as of 2400 hours GMT, on January 27, 1973. At the same hour, the United

States will stop all its military activities against the territory of the Democratic Republic of Vietnam by ground, air and naval forces, wherever they may be based, and end the mining of the territorial waters, ports, harbors, and waterways of the Democratic Republic of Vietnam. The United States will remove, permanently deactivate or destroy all the mines in the territorial waters, ports, harbors, and waterways of North Vietnam as soon as this Agreement goes into effect. The complete cessation of hostilities mentioned in this Article shall be durable and without limit of time.

Article 3

The parties undertake to maintain the cease-fire and to ensure a lasting and stable peace. As soon as the cease-fire goes into effect:

(a) The United States forces and those of the other foreign countries allied with the United States and the Republic of Vietnam shall remain in-place pending the implementation of the plan of troop withdrawal. The Four-Party Joint Military Commission described in Article 16 shall determine the modalities.

(b) The armed forces of the two South Vietnamese parties shall remain in place. The Two-Party Joint Military Commission described in Article 17 shall determine the areas controlled by each party and the modalities of stationing.

(c) The regular forces of all services and arms and the irregular forces of the parties in South Vietnam shall stop all offensive activities against each other and shall strictly abide by the following stipulations:

- All acts of force on the ground, in the air, and on the sea shall be prohibited;
- All hostile acts, terrorism and reprisals by both sides will be banned.

Article 4

The United States will not continue its military involvement or intervene in the internal affairs of South Vietnam.

Article 5

Within sixty days of the signing of this Agreement, there will be a total withdrawal from South Vietnam of troops, military advisers, and military personnel, including technical military personnel and military personnel associated with the pacification program, armaments, munitions, and war material of the United States and those of the other foreign countries mentioned in Article 3 (a). Advisers from the above-mentioned countries to all paramilitary organizations and the police force will also be withdrawn within the same period of time.

Article 6

The dismantlement of all military bases in South Vietnam of the United States and of the other foreign countries mentioned in Article 3 (a) shall be completed within sixty days of the signing of this Agreement.

Article 7

From the enforcement of the cease-fire to the formation of the government provided for in Articles 9 (b) and 14 of this Agreement, the two South Vietnamese parties shall not accept the introduction of troops, military advisers, and military personnel including technical military personnel, armaments, munitions, and war material into South Vietnam. The two South Vietnamese parties shall be permitted to make periodic replacement of armaments, munitions and war material which have been destroyed, damaged, worn out or used up after the cease-fire, on the basis of piece-for-piece, of the same characteristics and properties, under the supervision of the Joint Military Commission of the two South Vietnamese parties and of the International Commission of Control and Supervision.

CHAPTER III

THE RETURN OF CAPTURED MILITARY PERSONNEL
AND FOREIGN CIVILIANS, AND CAPTURED
AND DETAINED VIETNAMESE CIVILIAN PERSONNEL

Article 8

(a) The return of captured military personnel and foreign civilians of the parties shall be carried out simultaneously with and completed not later than the same day as the troop withdrawal mentioned in Article 5. The parties shall exchange complete lists of the above-mentioned captured military personnel and foreign civilians on the day of the signing of this Agreement.

(b) The parties shall help each other to get information about those military personnel and foreign civilians of the parties missing in action, to determine the location and take care of the graves of the dead

197

so as to facilitate the exhumation and repatriation of the remains, and to take any such other measures as may be required to get information about those still considered missing in action.

(c) The question of the return of Vietnamese civilian personnel captured and detained in South Vietnam will be resolved by the two South Vietnamese parties on the basis of the principles of Article 21 (b) of the Agreement on the Cessation of Hostilities in Vietnam of July 20, 1954. The two South Vietnamese parties will do so in a spirit of national reconciliation and concord, with a view to ending hatred and enmity, in order to ease suffering and to reunite families. The two South Vietnamese parties will do their utmost to resolve this question within ninety days after the cease-fire comes into effect.

CHAPTER IV

THE EXERCISE OF THE SOUTH VIETNAMESE PEOPLE'S
RIGHT TO SELF-DETERMINATION

Article 9

The Government of the United States of America and the Government of the Democratic Republic of Vietnam undertake to respect the following principles for the exercise of the South Vietnamese people's right to self-determination:

(a) The South Vietnamese people's right to self-determination is sacred, inalienable, and shall be respected by all countries.

(b) The South Vietnamese people shall decide themselves the political future of South Vietnam through genuinely free and democratic general elections under international supervision.

(c) Foreign countries shall not impose any political tendency or personality on the South Vietnamese people.

Article 10

The two South Vietnamese parties undertake to respect the cease-fire and maintain peace in South Vietnam, settle all matters of contention through negotiations, and avoid all armed conflict.

Article 11

Immediately after the cease-fire, the two South Vietnamese parties will:

- achieve national reconciliation and concord, end hatred and enmity, prohibit all acts of reprisal and discrimination against individuals or organizations that have collaborated with one side or the other;

- ensure the democratic liberties of the people: personal freedom, freedom of speech, freedom of the press, freedom of meeting, freedom of organization, freedom of political activities, freedom of belief, freedom of movement, freedom of residence, freedom of work, right to property ownership, and right to free enterprise.

Article 12

(a) Immediately after the cease-fire, the two South Vietnamese parties shall hold consultations in a spirit of national reconciliation and concord, mutual respect, and mutual non-elimination to set up a National Council of National Reconciliation and Concord of three equal segments. The Council shall operate on the principle of unanimity. After the National Council of National Reconciliation and Concord has assumed its functions, the two South Vietnamese parties will consult about the formation of councils at lower levels. The two South Vietnamese parties shall sign an agreement on the internal matters of South Vietnam as soon as possible and do their utmost to accomplish this within ninety days after the cease-fire comes into effect, in keeping with the South Vietnamese people's aspirations for peace, independence and democracy.

(b) The National Council of National Reconciliation and Concord shall have the task of promoting the two South Vietnamese parties' implementation of this Agreement, achievement of national reconciliation and concord and ensurance of democratic liberties. The National Council of National Reconciliation and Concord will organize the free and democratic general elections provided for in Article 9 (b) and decide the procedures and modalities of these general elections. The institutions for which the general elections are to be held will be agreed upon through consultations between the two South Vietnamese parties. The National Council of National Reconciliation and Concord will also decide the procedures and modalities of such local elections as the two South Vietnamese parties agree upon.

Article 13

The question of Vietnamese armed forces in South Vietnam shall be settled by the two South Vietnamese parties in a spirit of national reconciliation and concord, equality and mutual respect, without foreign interference, in accordance with the postwar situation. Among the questions to be discussed by the two South Vietnamese parties are steps to reduce their military effectives and to demobilize the troops being reduced. The two South Vietnamese parties will accomplish this as soon as possible.

Article 14

South Vietnam will pursue a foreign policy of peace and independence. It will be prepared to establish relations with all countries irrespective of their political and social systems on the basis of mutual respect for independence and sovereignty and accept economic and technical aid from any country with no political conditions attached. The acceptance of military aid by South Vietnam in the future shall come under the authority of the government set up after the general elections in South Vietnam provided for in Article 9 (b).

CHAPTER V

THE REUNIFICATION OF VIETNAM AND THE RELATIONSHIP BETWEEN NORTH AND SOUTH VIETNAM

Article 15

The reunification of Vietnam shall be carried out step by step through peaceful means on the basis of discussions and agreements between North and South Vietnam, without coercion or annexation by either party, and without foreign interference. The time for reunification will be agreed upon by North and South Vietnam.

Pending reunification:

(a) The military demarcation line between the two zones at the 17th parallel is only provisional and not a political or territorial boundary, as provided for in paragraph 6 of the Final Declaration of the 1954 Geneva Conference.

(b) North and South Vietnam shall respect the Demilitarized Zone on either side of the Provisional Military Demarcation Line.

(c) North and South Vietnam shall promptly start negotiations with a view to reestablishing normal relations in various fields. Among the questions to be negotiated are the modalities of civilian movement across the Provisional Military Demarcation Line.

(d) North and South Vietnam shall not join any military alliance or military bloc and shall not allow foreign powers to maintain military bases, troops, military advisers, and military personnel on their respective territories, as stipulated in the 1954 Geneva Agreements on Vietnam.

CHAPTER VI

THE JOINT MILITARY COMMISSIONS,
THE INTERNATIONAL COMMISSION
OF CONTROL AND SUPERVISION,
THE INTERNATIONAL CONFERENCE

Article 16

(a) The Parties participating in the Paris Conference on Vietnam shall immediately designate representatives to form a Four-Party Joint Military Commission with the task of ensuring joint action by the parties in implementing the following provisions of this Agreement:

- The first paragraph of Article 2, regarding the enforcement of the cease-fire throughout South Vietnam;
- Article 3 (a), regarding the cease-fire by U.S. forces and those of the other foreign countries referred to in that Article;
- Article 3 (c), regarding the cease-fire between all parties in South Vietnam;
- Article 5, regarding the withdrawal from South Vietnam of U.S. troops and those of the other foreign countries mentioned in Article 3 (a);
- Article 6, regarding the dismantlement of military bases in South Vietnam of the United States and those of the other foreign countries mentioned in Article 3 (a);
- Article 8 (a), regarding the return of captured military personnel and foreign civilians of the parties;
- Article 8 (b), regarding the mutual assistance of the parties in getting information about those military personnel and foreign civilians of the parties missing in action.

(b) The Four-Party Joint Military Commission shall operate in accordance with the principle of consultations and unanimity. Disagreements shall be referred to the International Commission of Control and Supervision.

(c) The Four-Party Joint Military Commission shall begin operating immediately after the signing of this Agreement and end its activities in sixty days, after the completion of the withdrawal of U.S. troops and those of the other foreign countries mentioned in Article 3 (a) and the completion of the return of captured military personnel and foreign civilians of the parties.

(d) The four parties shall agree immediately on the organization, the working procedure, means of activity, and expenditures of the Four-Party Joint Military Commission.

Article 17

(a) The two South Vietnamese parties shall immediately designate representatives to form a Two-Party Joint Military Commission with the task of ensuring joint action by the two South Vietnamese parties in implementing the following provisions of this Agreement:

- The first paragraph of Article 2, regarding the enforcement of the cease-fire throughout South Vietnam, when the Four-Party Joint Military Commission has ended its activities;
- Article 3 (b), regarding the cease-fire between the two South Vietnamese parties;
- Article 3 (c), regarding the cease-fire between all parties in South Vietnam, when the Four-Party Joint Military Commission has ended its activities;
- Article 7, regarding the prohibition of the introduction of troops into South Vietnam and all other provisions of this article;
- Article 8 (c), regarding the question of the return of Vietnamese civilian personnel captured and detained in South Vietnam;
- Article 13, regarding the reduction of the military effectives of the two South Vietnamese parties and the demobilization of the troops being reduced.

(b) Disagreements shall be referred to the International Commission of Control and Supervision.

(c) After the signing of this Agreement, the Two-Party Joint Military Commission shall agree immediately on the measures and organization aimed at enforcing the cease-fire and preserving peace in South Vietnam.

Article 18

(a) After the signing of this Agreement, an International Commission of Control and Supervision shall be established immediately.

(b) Until the International Conference provided for in Article 19 makes definitive arrangements, the International Commission of Control and Supervision will report to the four parties on matters concerning the control and supervision of the implementation of the following provisions of this Agreement:

- The first paragraph of Article 2, regarding the enforcement of the cease-fire throughout South Vietnam;
- Article 3 (a), regarding the cease-fire by U.S. forces and those of the other foreign countries referred to in that Article;
- Article 3 (c) regarding the cease-fire between all the parties in South Vietnam;
- Article 5, regarding the withdrawal from South Vietnam of U.S. troops and those of the other foreign countries mentioned in Article 3 (a);
- Article 6, regarding the dismantlement of military bases in South Vietnam of the United States and those of the other foreign countries mentioned in Article 3 (a);
- Article 8 (a), regarding the return of captured military personnel and foreign civilians of the parties.

The International Commission of Control and Supervision shall form control teams for carrying out its tasks. The four parties shall agree immediately on the location and operation of these teams. The parties will facilitate their operation.

(c) Until the International Conference makes definitive arrangements, the International Commission of Control and Supervision will report to the two South Vietnamese parties on matters concerning the control and supervision of the implementation of the following provisions of this Agreement;

- The first paragraph of Article 2, regarding the enforcement of the cease-fire throughout South Vietnam, when the Four-Party Joint Military Commission has ended its activities;
- Article 3 (b), regarding the cease-fire between the two South Vietnamese parties;
- Article 3 (c), regarding the cease-fire between all parties in South Vietnam, when the Four-Party Joint Military Commission has ended its activities;
- Article 7, regarding the prohibition of the introduction of troops into South Vietnam and all other provisions of this Article;
- Article 8 (c), regarding the question of the return of Vietnamese civilian personnel captured and detained in South Vietnam;
- Article 9 (b), regarding the free and democratic general elections in South Vietnam;
- Article 13, regarding the reduction of the military effectives of the two South Vietnamese parties and the demobilization of the troops being reduced.

The International Commission of Control and Supervision shall form control teams for carrying out its tasks. The two South Vietnamese parties shall agree immediately on the location and operation of these teams. The two South Vietnamese parties will facilitate their operation.

(d) The International Commission of Control and Supervision shall be composed of representatives of four countries: Canada, Hungary, Indonesia and Poland. The chairmanship of this Commission will rotate among the members for specific periods to be determined by the Commission.

(e) The International Commission of Control and Supervision shall carry out its tasks in accordance with the principle of respect for the sovereignty of South Vietnam.

(f) The International Commission of Control and Supervision shall operate in accordance with the principle of consultations and unanimity.

(g) The International Commission of Control and Supervision shall begin operating when a cease-fire comes into force in Vietnam. As regards the provisions in Article 18 (b) concerning the four parties, the International Commission of Control and Supervision shall end its activities when the Commission's tasks of control and supervision regarding these provisions have been fulfilled. As regards the provisions in Article 18 (c) concerning the two South Vietnamese parties, the International Commission of Control and Supervision shall end its activities on the request of the government formed after the general elections in South Vietnam provided for in Article 9 (b).

(h) The four parties shall agree immediately on the organization, means of activity, and expenditures of the International Commission of Control and Supervision. The relationship between the International Commission and the International Conference will be agreed upon by the International Commission and the International Conference.

Article 19

The parties agree on the convening of an International Conference within thirty days of the signing of this Agreement to acknowledge the signed agreements; to guarantee the ending of the war, the maintenance of peace in Vietnam, the respect of the Vietnamese people's fundamental national rights, and the South Vietnamese people's right to self-determination; and to contribute to and guarantee peace in Indochina. The United States and the Democratic Republic of Vietnam, on behalf of the parties participating in the Paris Conference on Vietnam, will propose to the following parties that they participate in this International Conference: the People's Republic of China, the Republic of France, the Union of Soviet Socialist Republics, the United Kingdom, the four countries of the International Commission of Control and Supervision, and the Secretary General of the United Nations, together with the parties participating in the Paris Conference on Vietnam.

CHAPTER VII

REGARDING CAMBODIA AND LAOS

Article 20

(a) The parties participating in the Paris Conference on Vietnam shall strictly respect the 1954 Geneva Agreements on Cambodia and the 1962 Geneva Agreements on Laos, which recognized the Cambodian and the Lao peoples' fundamental national rights, i.e., the independence, sovereignty, unity, and territorial integrity of these countries. The parties shall respect the neutrality of Cambodia and Laos. The parties participating in the Paris Conference on Vietnam undertake to refrain from using the territory of Cambodia and the territory of Laos to encroach on the sovereignty and security of one another and of other countries.

(b) Foreign countries shall put an end to all military activities in Cambodia and Laos, totally withdraw from and refrain from reintroducing into these two countries troops, military advisers and military personnel, armaments, munitions and war materiel.

(c) The internal affairs of Cambodia and Laos shall be settled by the people of each of these countries without foreign interference.

(d) The problems existing between the Indochinese countries shall be settled by the Indochinese parties on the basis of respect for each other's independence, sovereignty, and territorial integrity, and non-interference in each other's internal affairs.

CHAPTER VIII

THE RELATIONSHIP BETWEEN
THE UNITED STATES AND
THE DEMOCRATIC REPUBLIC OF VIETNAM

Article 21

The United States anticipates that this Agreement will usher in an era of reconciliation with the Democratic Republic of Vietnam as with all the peoples of Indochina. In pursuance of its traditional policy, the

United States will contribute to healing the wounds of war and to postwar reconstruction of the Democratic Republic of Vietnam and throughout Indochina.

Article 22

The ending of the war, the restoration of peace in Vietnam, and the strict implementation of this Agreement will create conditions for establishing a new, equal and mutually beneficial relationship between the United States and the Democratic Republic of Vietnam on the basis of respect for each other's independence and sovereignty, and noninterference in each other's internal affairs. At the same time this will ensure stable peace in Vietnam and contribute to the preservation of lasting peace in Indochina and Southeast Asia.

CHAPTER IX

OTHER PROVISIONS

Article 23

This Agreement shall enter into force upon signature by plenipotentiary representatives of the parties participating in the Paris Conference on Vietnam. All the parties concerned shall strictly implement this Agreement and its Protocols. Done in Paris this twenty-seventh day of January, One Thousand Nine Hundred and Seventy-Three, in Vietnamese and English. The Vietnamese and English texts are official and equally authentic.

[Separate Numbered Page]

For the Government of the United States of America	For the Government of the Republic of Vietnam
William P. Rogers Secretary of State	Tran Van Lam Minister for Foreign Affairs

[Separate Numbered Page]

For the Government of the Democratic Republic of Vietnam	For the Provisional Revolutionary Government of the Republic of South Vietnam
Nguyen Duy Trinh Minister for Foreign Affairs	Nguyen Thi Binh Minister for Foreign Affairs

The Government of the United States of America, with the concurrence of the Government of the Republic of Vietnam, the Government of the Democratic Republic of Vietnam, with the concurrence of the Provisional Revolutionary Government of the Republic of South Vietnam, with a view to ending the war and restoring peace in Vietnam on the basis of respect for the Vietnamese people's fundamental national rights and the South Vietnamese people's right to self-determination, and to contributing to the consolidation of peace in Asia and the world, have agreed on the following provisions and undertake to respect and to implement them:

[Text of Agreement Chapters I–VIII Same As Above]

CHAPTER IX

OTHER PROVISIONS

Article 23

The Paris Agreement on Ending the War and Restoring Peace in Vietnam shall enter into force upon signature of this document by the Secretary of State of the Government of the United States of America and the Minister for Foreign Affairs of the Government of the Democratic Republic of Vietnam, and upon signature of a document in the same terms by the Secretary of State of the Government of the United States of America, the Minister for Foreign Affairs of the Government of the Republic of Vietnam, the Minister for Foreign Affairs of the Government of the Democratic Republic of Vietnam, and the Minister for Foreign Affairs of the Provisional Revolutionary Government of the Republic of South Vietnam. The Agreement and the protocols to it shall be strictly implemented by all the parties concerned. Done in Paris this twenty-seventh day of January, One Thousand Nine Hundred and Seventy-Three, in Vietnamese and English. The Vietnamese and English texts are official and equally authentic.

For the Government of the United States of America	For the Government of the Democratic Republic of Vietnam
William P. Rogers Secretary of State	Nguyen Duy Trinh Minister for Foreign Affairs

Protocol to the Agreement on Ending the War and Restoring Peace in Vietnam Concerning the Return of Captured Military Personnel and Foreign Civilians and Captured and Detained Vietnamese Civilian Personnel

The parties participating in the Paris Conference on Vietnam, in implementation of Article 8 of the Agreement on Ending the War and Restoring Peace in Vietnam signed on this date providing for the return of captured military personnel and foreign civilians, and captured and detained Vietnamese civilian personnel, have agreed as follows:

THE RETURN OF CAPTURED MILITARY PERSONNEL AND FOREIGN CIVILIANS

Article 1

The parties signatory to the Agreement shall return the captured military personnel of the parties mentioned in Article 8 (a) of the Agreement as follows:

- all captured military personnel of the United States and those of the other foreign countries mentioned in Article 3 (a) of the Agreement shall be returned to United States authorities;
- all captured Vietnamese military personnel, whether belonging to regular or irregular armed forces, shall be returned to the two South Vietnamese parties; they shall be returned to that South Vietnamese party under whose command they served.

Article 2

All captured civilians who are nationals of the United States or of any other foreign countries mentioned in Article 3 (a) of the Agreement shall be returned to United States authorities. All other captured foreign civilians shall be returned to the authorities of their country of nationality by any one of the parties willing and able to do so.

Article 3

The parties shall today exchange complete lists of captured persons mentioned in Articles 1 and 2 of this Protocol.

Article 4

(a) The return of all captured persons mentioned in Articles 1 and 2 of this Protocol shall be completed within sixty days of the signing

208

of the Agreement at a rate no slower than the rate of withdrawal from South Vietnam of United States forces and those of the other foreign countries mentioned in Article 5 of the Agreement.

(b) Persons who are seriously ill, wounded or maimed, old persons and women shall be returned first. The remainder shall be returned either by returning all from one detention place after another or in order of their dates of capture, beginning with those who have been held the longest.

Article 5

The return and reception of the persons mentioned in Articles 1 and 2 of this Protocol shall be carried out at places convenient to the concerned parties. Places of return shall be agreed upon by the Four-Party Joint Military Commission. The parties shall ensure the safety of personnel engaged in the return and reception of those persons.

Article 6

Each party shall return all captured persons mentioned in Articles 1 and 2 of this Protocol without delay and shall facilitate their return and reception. The detaining parties shall not deny or delay their return for any reason, including the fact that captured persons may, on any grounds, have been prosecuted or sentenced.

THE RETURN OF CAPTURED AND
DETAINED VIETNAMESE CIVILIAN PERSONNEL

Article 7

(a) The question of the return of Vietnamese civilian personnel captured and detained in South Vietnam will be resolved by the two South Vietnamese parties on the basis of the principles of Article 21 (b) of the Agreement on the Cessation of Hostilities in Vietnam of July 20, 1954, which reads as follows:

> "The term 'civilian internees' is understood to mean all persons who, having in any way contributed to the political and armed struggle between the two parties, have been arrested for that reason and have been kept in detention by either party during the period of hostilities."

(b) The two South Vietnamese parties will do so in a spirit of national reconciliation and concord with a view to ending hatred and enmity in order to ease suffering and to reunite families. The two South Vietnamese parties will do their utmost to resolve this question within ninety days after the cease-fire comes into effect.

(c) Within fifteen days after the cease-fire comes into effect, the two South Vietnamese parties shall exchange lists of the Vietnamese civilian personnel captured and detained by each party and lists of the places at which they are held.

TREATMENT OF CAPTURED PERSONS DURING DETENTION

Article 8

(a) All captured military personnel of the parties and captured foreign civilians of the parties shall be treated humanely at all times, and in accordance with international practice. They shall be protected against all violence to life and person, in particular against murder in any form, mutilation, torture and cruel treatment, and outrages upon personal dignity. These persons shall not be forced to join the armed forces of the detaining party. They shall be given adequate food, clothing, shelter, and the medical attention required for their state of health. They shall be allowed to exchange post cards and letters with their families and receive parcels.

(b) All Vietnamese civilian personnel captured and detained in South Vietnam shall be treated humanely at all times, and in accordance with international practice. They shall be protected against all violence to life and person, in particular against murder in any form, mutilation, torture and cruel treatment, and outrages against personal dignity. The detaining parties shall not deny or delay their return for any reason, including the fact that captured persons may, on any grounds, have been prosecuted or sentenced. These persons shall not be forced to join the armed forces of the detaining party. They shall be given adequate food, clothing, shelter, and the medical attention required for their state of health. They shall be allowed to exchange post cards and letters with their families and receive parcels.

Article 9

(a) To contribute to improving the living conditions of the captured military personnel of the parties and foreign civilians of the parties, the parties shall, within fifteen days after the cease-fire comes into effect, agree upon the designation of two or more national Red Cross societies to visit all places where captured military personnel and foreign civilians are held.

(b) To contribute to improving the living conditions of the captured and detained Vietnamese civilian personnel, the two South Vietnamese parties shall, within fifteen days after the cease-fire comes into effect, agree upon the designation of two or more national Red Cross societies to visit all places where the captured and detained Vietnamese civilian personnel are held.

WITH REGARD TO DEAD AND MISSING PERSONS

Article 10

(a) The Four-Party Joint Military Commission shall ensure joint action by the parties in implementing Article 8 (b) of the Agreement. When the Four-Party Joint Military Commission has ended its activities, a Four-Party Joint Military team shall be maintained to carry on this task.

(b) With regard to Vietnamese civilian personnel dead or missing in South Vietnam, the two South Vietnamese parties shall help each other to obtain information about missing persons, determine the location and take care of the graves of the dead, in a spirit of national reconciliation and concord, in keeping with the people's aspirations.

OTHER PROVISIONS

Article 11

(a) The Four-Party and Two-Party Joint Military Commissions will have the responsibility of determining immediately the modalities of implementing the provisions of this Protocol consistent with their respective responsibilities under Articles 16 (a) and 17 (a) of the Agreement. In case the Joint Military Commissions, when carrying out their tasks, cannot reach agreement on a matter pertaining to the return of captured personnel they shall refer to the International Commission for its assistance.

(b) The Four-Party Joint Military Commission shall form, in addition to the teams established by the Protocol concerning the cease-fire in South Vietnam and the Joint Military Commissions, a sub-commission on captured persons and, as required, joint military teams on captured persons to assist the Commission in its tasks.

(c) From the time the cease-fire comes into force to the time when the Two-Party Joint Military Commission becomes operational, the two South Vietnamese parties' delegations to the Four-Party Joint

Military Commission shall form a provisional sub-commission and provisional joint military teams to carry out its tasks concerning captured and detained Vietnamese civilian personnel.

(d) The Four-Party Joint Military Commission shall send joint military teams to observe the return of the persons mentioned in Articles 1 and 2 of this Protocol at each place in Vietnam where such persons are being returned, and at the last detention places from which these persons will be taken to the places of return. The Two-Party Joint Military Commission shall send joint military teams to observe the return of Vietnamese civilian personnel captured and detained at each place in South Vietnam where such persons are being returned, and at the last detention places from which these persons will be taken to the places of return.

Article 12

In implementation of Articles 18 (b) and 18 (c) of the Agreement, the International Commission of Control and Supervision shall have the responsibility to control and supervise the observance of Articles 1 through 7 of this Protocol through observation of the return of captured military personnel, foreign civilians and captured and detained Vietnamese civilian personnel at each place in Vietnam where these persons are being returned, and at the last detention places from which these persons will be taken to the places of return, the examination of lists, and the investigation of violations of the provisions of the above-mentioned Articles.

Article 13

Within five days after signature of this Protocol, each party shall publish the text of the Protocol and communicate it to all the captured persons covered by the Protocol and being detained by that party.

Article 14

This Protocol shall come into force upon signature by plenipotentiary representatives of all the parties participating in the Paris Conference on Vietnam. It shall be strictly implemented by all the parties concerned. Done in Paris this twenty-seventh day of January, One Thousand Nine Hundred and Seventy-Three, in Vietnamese and English. The Vietnamese and English texts are official and equally authentic.

For the Government of the United States of America	For the Government of the Republic of Vietnam
William P. Rogers Secretary of State	Tran Van Lam Minister for Foreign Affairs

For the Government of the Democratic Republic of Vietnam	For the Provisional Revolutionary Government of the Republic of South Vietnam
Nguyen Duy Trinh Minister for Foreign Affairs	Nguyen Thi Binh Minister for Foreign Affairs

Protocol to the Agreement on Ending the War and Restoring Peace in Vietnam Concerning the Return of Captured Military Personnel and Foreign Civilians and Captured and Detained Vietnamese Civilian Personnel

The Government of the United States of America, with the concurrence of the Government of the Republic of Vietnam, the Government of the Democratic Republic of Vietnam, with the concurrence of the Provisional Revolutionary Government of the Republic of South Vietnam, in implementation of Article 8 of the Agreement on Ending the War and Restoring Peace in Vietnam signed on this date providing for the return of captured military personnel and foreign civilians, and captured and detained Vietnamese civilian personnel, have agreed as follows:

[Text of Protocol Articles 1–13 same as above]

Article 14

The Protocol to the Paris Agreement on Ending the War and Restoring Peace in Vietnam concerning the Return of Captured Military Personnel and Foreign Civilians and Captured and Detained Vietnamese Civilian Personnel shall enter into force upon signature of this document by the Secretary of State of the Government of the United

States of America and the Minister for Foreign Affairs of the Government of the Democratic Republic of Vietnam, and upon signature of a document in the same terms by the Secretary of State of the Government of the United States of America, the Minister for Foreign Affairs of the Government of the Republic of Vietnam, the Minister for Foreign Affairs of the Government of the Democratic Republic of Vietnam, and the Minister for Foreign Affairs of the Provisional Revolutionary Government of the Republic of South Vietnam. The Protocol shall be strictly implemented by all the parties concerned. Done in Paris this twenty-seventh day of January, One Thousand Nine Hundred and Seventy-Three, in Vietnamese and English. The Vietnamese and English texts are official and equally authentic.

For the Government of the United States of America	For the Government of the Democratic Republic of Vietnam
William P. Rogers Secretary of State	Nguyen Duy Trinh Minister for Foreign Affairs

Protocol to the Agreement on Ending the War and Restoring Peace in Vietnam Concerning the International Commission of Control and Supervision

The parties participating in the Paris Conference on Vietnam, in implementation of Article 18 of the Agreement on Ending the War and Restoring Peace in Vietnam signed on this date providing for the formation of the International Commission of Control and Supervision, have agreed as follows:

Article 1

The implementation of the Agreement is the responsibility of the parties signatory to the Agreement. The functions of the International Commission are to control and supervise the implementation of the provisions mentioned in Article 18 of the Agreement. In carrying out these functions, the International Commission shall:

(a) Follow the implementation of the above-mentioned provisions of the Agreement through communication with the parties and on-the-spot observation at the places where this is required;

(b) Investigate violations of the provisions which fall under the control and supervision of the Commission;

(c) When necessary, cooperate with the Joint Military Commissions in deterring and detecting violations of the above-mentioned provisions.

Article 2

The International Commission shall investigate violations of the provisions described in Article 18 of the Agreement on the request of the Four-Party Joint Military Commission, or of the Two-Party Joint Military Commission, or of any party, or, with respect to Article 9 (b) of the Agreement on general elections, of the National Council of National Reconciliation and Concord, or in any case where the International Commission has other adequate grounds for considering that there has been a violation of those provisions. It is understood that, in carrying out this task, the International Commission shall function with the concerned parties' assistance and cooperation as required.

Article 3

(a) When the International Commission finds that there is a serious violation in the implementation of the Agreement or a threat to peace against which the Commission can find no appropriate measure, the Commission shall report this to the four parties to the Agreement so that they can hold consultations to find a solution.

(b) In accordance with Article 18 (f) of the Agreement, the International Commission's reports shall be made with the unanimous agreement of the representatives of all the four members. In case no unanimity is reached, the Commission shall forward the different views to the four parties in accordance with Article 18 (b) of the Agreement, or to the two South Vietnamese parties in accordance with Article 18 (c) of the Agreement, but these shall not be considered as reports of the Commission.

Article 4

(a) The headquarters of the International Commission shall be at Saigon.

(b) There shall be seven regional teams . . . based at the following places:

Regions	Places
I	Hue
II	Danang
III	Pleiku

IV	Phan Thiet
V	Bien Hoa
VI	My Tho
VII	Can Tho

The International Commission shall designate three teams for the region of Saigon-Gia Dinh.

(c) There shall be twenty-six teams . . . based at the following places in South Vietnam:

Region I

Quang Tri
Phu Bai

Region II

Hoi An
Tam Ky
Chu Lai

Region III

Kontum
Hau Bon
Phu Cat
Tuy An
Ninh Hoa
Ban Me Thuot

Region IV

Da Lat
Bao Loc
Phan Rang

Region V

An Loc
Xuan Loc
Ben Cat
Cu Chi
Tan An

Region VI

Moc Hoa
Giong Trom

Region VII

Tri Ton
Vinh Long
Vi Thanh
Khanh Hung
Quan Long

(d) There shall be twelve teams . . . based at the following places:

Gio Linh (to cover the area south of the
Provisional Military Demarcation Line)

Lao Bao
Ben Het
Duc Co
Chu Lai
Qui Nhon
Nha Trang

Vung Tau
Xa Mat
Bien Hoa Airfield
Hong Ngu
Can Tho

(e) There shall be seven teams, six of which shall be available for assignment to the points of entry which are not listed in paragraph (d) above and which the two South Vietnamese parties choose as points for legitimate entry to South Vietnam for replacement of armaments, munitions, and war material permitted by Article 7 of the Agreement. Any team or teams not needed for the above-mentioned assignment shall be available for other tasks, in keeping with the Commission's responsibility for control and supervision.

(f) There shall be seven teams to control and supervise the return of captured and detained personnel of the parties.

Article 5

(a) To carry out its tasks concerning the return of the captured military personnel and foreign civilians of the parties as stipulated by Article 8 (a) of the Agreement, the International Commission shall, during the time of such return, send one control and supervision team to each place in Vietnam where the captured persons are being returned, and to the last detention places from which these persons will be taken to the places of return.

(b) To carry out its tasks concerning the return of the Vietnamese civilian personnel captured and detained in South Vietnam mentioned in Article 8 (c) of the Agreement, the International Commission shall, during the time of such return, send one control and supervision team to each place in South Vietnam where the above-mentioned captured and detained persons are being returned, and to the last detention places from which these persons shall be taken to the places of return.

Article 6

To carry out its tasks regarding Article 9 (b) of the Agreement on the free and democratic general elections in South Vietnam, the International Commission shall organize additional teams, when necessary. The International Commission shall discuss this question in advance with the National Council of National Reconciliation and Concord. If additional teams are necessary for this purpose, they shall be formed thirty days before the general elections.

Article 7

The International Commission shall continually keep under review its size, and shall reduce the number of its teams, its representatives or other personnel, or both, when those teams, representatives or personnel have accomplished the tasks assigned to them and are not required for other tasks. At the same time, the expenditures of the International Commission shall be reduced correspondingly.

Article 8

Each member of the International Commission shall make available at all times the following numbers of qualified personnel:

(a) One senior representative and twenty-six others for the headquarters staff.

(b) Five for each of the seven regional teams.

(c) Two for each of the other international control teams, except for the teams of Gio Linh and Vung Tau, each of which shall have three.

(d) One hundred sixteen for the purpose of providing support to the Commission Headquarters and its teams.

Article 9

(a) The International Commission, and each of its teams, shall act as a single body comprising representatives of all four members.

(b) Each member has the responsibility to ensure the presence of its representatives at all levels of the International Commission. In case a representative is absent, the member concerned shall immediately designate a replacement.

Article 10

(a) The parties shall afford full cooperation, assistance, and protection to the International Commission.

(b) The parties shall at all times maintain regular and continuous liaison with the International Commission. During the existence of the Four-Party Joint Military Commission, the delegations of the parties to that Commission shall also perform liaison functions with the International Commission. After the Four-Party Joint Military Commission has ended its activities, such liaison shall be maintained through the Two-Party Joint Military Commission, liaison missions, or other adequate means.

(c) The International Commission and the Joint Military Commissions shall closely cooperate with and assist each other in carrying out their respective functions.

(d) Wherever a team is stationed or operating, the concerned party shall designate a liaison officer to the team to cooperate with and assist it in carrying out without hindrance its task of control and supervision. When a team is carrying out an investigation, a liaison officer from each concerned party shall have the opportunity to accompany it, provided the investigation is not thereby delayed.

(e) Each party shall give the International Commission reasonable advance notice of all proposed actions concerning those provisions of the Agreement that are to be controlled and supervised by the International Commission.

(f) The International Commission, including its teams, is allowed such movement for observation as is reasonably required for the proper exercise of its functions as stipulated in the Agreement. In carrying out these functions, the International Commission, including its teams, shall enjoy all necessary assistance and cooperation from the parties concerned.

Article 11

In supervising the holding of the free and democratic general elections described in Articles 9 (b) and 12 (b) of the Agreement in accordance with modalities to be agreed upon between the National Council of National Reconciliation and Concord and the International Commission, the latter shall receive full cooperation and assistance from the National Council.

Article 12

The International Commission and its personnel who have the nationality of a member state shall, while carrying out their tasks, enjoy privileges and immunities equivalent to those accorded diplomatic missions and diplomatic agents

Article 13

The International Commission may use the means of communication and transport necessary to perform its functions. Each South Vietnamese party shall make available for rent to the International Commission appropriate office and accommodation facilities and shall assist it in obtaining such facilities. The International Commission may receive from the parties, on mutually agreeable terms, the necessary means of communication and transport and may purchase from any source necessary equipment and services not obtained from the parties. The International Commission shall possess these means

Article 14

The expenses for the activities of the International Commission shall be borne by the parties and the members of the International Commission in accordance with the provisions of this Article:

(a) Each member country of the International Commission shall pay the salaries and allowances of its personnel.

(b) All other expenses incurred by the International Commission shall be met from a fund to which each of the four parties shall contribute twenty-three percent (23%) and to which each member of the International Commission shall contribute two percent (2%).

(c) Within thirty days of the date of entry into force of this Protocol, each of the four parties shall provide the International Commission with an initial sum equivalent to four million, five hundred thousand (4,500,000) French francs in convertible currency, which sum shall be credited against the amounts due from that party under the first budget.

(d) The International Commission shall prepare its own budgets. After the International Commission approves a budget, it shall transmit it to all parties signatory to the Agreement for their approval. Only after the budgets have been approved by the four parties to the Agreement shall they be obliged to make their contributions. However, in case the parties to the Agreement do not agree on a new budget, the International Commission shall temporarily base its expenditures on the previous budget, except for the extraordinary, one-time expenditures for installation or for the acquisition of equipment, and the parties shall continue to make their contributions on that basis until a new budget is approved.

Article 15

(a) The headquarters shall be operational and in place within 24 hours after the cease-fire.

(b) The regional teams shall be operational and in place, and three teams for supervision and control of the return of the captured and detained personnel shall be operational and ready for dispatch within 48 hours after the cease-fire.

(c) Other teams shall be operational and in place within fifteen to thirty days after the cease-fire.

Article 16

Meetings shall be convened at the call of the Chairman. The International Commission shall adopt other working procedures appropriate for the effective discharge of its functions and consistent with respect for the sovereignty of South Vietnam.

Article 17

The Members of the International Commission may accept the obligations of this Protocol by sending notes of acceptance to the four parties signatory to the Agreement. Should a member of the International Commission decide to withdraw from the International Commission, it may do so by giving three months notice by means of notes to the four parties to the Agreement, in which case those four parties shall consult among themselves for the purpose of agreeing upon a replacement member.

Article 18

This Protocol shall enter into force upon signature by plenipotentiary representatives of all the parties participating in the Paris Conference on Vietnam. It shall be strictly implemented by all the parties concerned. Done in Paris this twenty-seventh day of January, One Thousand Nine Hundred and Seventy-Three, in Vietnamese and English. The Vietnamese and English texts are officially and equally authentic.

[Separate Numbered Page]

For the Government of the
United States of America

For the Government of the
Republic of Vietnam

William P. Rogers
Secretary of State

Tran Van Lam
Minister for Foreign Affairs

[Separate Numbered Page]

For the Government of the
Democratic Republic of
Vietnam

For the Provisional
Revolutionary Government of
the Republic of South Vietnam

Nguyen Duy Trinh
Minister for Foreign Affairs

Nguyen Thi Binh
Minister for Foreign Affairs

*Protocol to the Agreement on Ending the War and Restoring Peace in
Vietnam Concerning the International Commission
of Control and Supervision*

The Government of the United States of America, with the concurrence of the Government of the Republic of Vietnam, the Government of the Democratic Republic of Vietnam, with the concurrence of the Provisional Revolutionary Government of the Republic of South Vietnam, in implementation of Article 18 of the Agreement on Ending the War and Restoring Peace in Vietnam signed on this date providing for the formation of the International Commission of Control and Supervision, have agreed as follows:

[Text of Protocol Articles 1–17 same as above.]

Article 18

The Protocol to the Paris Agreement on Ending the War and Restoring Peace in Vietnam concerning the International Commission of Control and Supervision shall enter into force upon signature of this document by the Secretary of State of the Government of the United States of America and the Minister for Foreign Affairs of the Government of the Democratic Republic of Vietnam, and upon signature of a document in the same terms by the Secretary of State of the Government of the United States of America, the Minister for Foreign Affairs of the Government of the Republic of Vietnam, the Minister for Foreign Affairs of the Government of the Democratic Republic of Vietnam, and the Minister for Foreign Affairs of the Provisional Revolutionary Government of the Republic of South Vietnam. The Protocol shall be strictly implemented by all the parties concerned. Done in Paris this twenty-seventh day of January, One Thousand Nine Hundred and Seventy-Three, in Vietnamese and English. The Vietnamese and English texts are official and equally authentic.

For the Government of the United States of America	For the Government of the Democratic Republic of Vietnam
William P. Rogers Secretary of State	Nguyen Duy Trinh Minister for Foreign Affairs

*Protocol to the Agreement on Ending the War and Restoring Peace in
Vietnam Concerning the Cease-fire in South Vietnam and the Joint
Military Commissions*

The parties participating in the Paris Conference on Vietnam, in implementation of the first paragraph of Article 2, Article 3, Article 5, Article 6, Article 16 and Article 17 of the Agreement on Ending the War and Restoring Peace in Vietnam signed on this date which provide for the cease-fire in South Vietnam and the establishment of a Four-Party Joint Military Commission and a Two-Party Joint Military Commission, have agreed as follows:

CEASE-FIRE IN SOUTH VIETNAM

Article 1

The High Commands of the parties in South Vietnam shall issue prompt and timely orders to all regular and irregular armed forces and the armed police under their command to completely end hostilities throughout South Vietnam, at the exact time stipulated in Article 2 of the Agreement and ensure that these armed forces and armed police comply with these orders and respect the cease-fire.

Article 2

(a) As soon as the cease-fire comes into force and until regulations are issued by the Joint Military Commissions, all ground, river, sea and air combat forces of the parties in South Vietnam shall remain in place; that is, in order to ensure a stable cease-fire, there shall be no major redeployments or movements that would extend each party's area of control or would result in contact between opposing armed forces and clashes which might take place.

(b) All regular and irregular armed forces and the armed police of the parties in South Vietnam shall observe the prohibition of the following acts:

(1) Armed patrols into areas controlled by opposing armed forces and flights by bomber and fighter aircraft of all types, except for unarmed flights for proficiency training and maintenance;

(2) Armed attacks against any person, either military or civilian, by any means whatsoever, including the use of small arms, mortars, artillery, bombing and strafing by airplanes and any other type of weapon or explosive device;

(3) All combat operations on the ground, on rivers, on the sea and in the air;

(4) All hostile acts, terrorism or reprisals; and

(5) All acts endangering lives or public or private property.

Article 3

(a) The above-mentioned prohibitions shall not hamper or restrict:

(1) Civilian supply, freedom of movement, freedom to work, and freedom of the people to engage in trade, and civilian communication and transportation between and among all areas in South Vietnam;

(2) The use by each party in areas under its control of military support elements, such as engineer and transportation units, in repair and construction of public facilities and the transportation and supplying of the population;

(3) Normal military proficiency training conducted by the parties in the areas under their respective control with due regard for public safety.

(b) The Joint Military Commissions shall immediately agree on corridors, routes, and other regulations governing the movement of military transport aircraft, military transport vehicles, and military transport vessels of all types of one party going through areas under the control of other parties.

Article 4

In order to avert conflict and ensure normal conditions for those armed forces which are in direct contact, and pending regulation by the Joint Military Commissions, the commanders of the opposing armed forces at those places of direct contact shall meet as soon as the cease-fire comes into force with a view to reaching an agreement on temporary measures to avert conflict and to ensure supply and medical care for these armed forces.

Article 5

(a) Within fifteen days after the cease-fire comes into effect, each party shall do its utmost to complete the removal or deactivation of all demolition objects, minefields, traps, obstacles or other dangerous objects placed previously, so as not to hamper the population's movement and work, in the first place on waterways, roads and railroads in South Vietnam. Those mines which cannot be removed or deactivated within that time shall be clearly marked and must be removed or deactivated as soon as possible.

(b) Emplacement of mines is prohibited, except as a defensive measure around the edges of military installations in places where they do not hamper the population's movement and work, and movement on waterways, roads and railroads. Mines and other obstacles already in place at the edges of military installations may remain in place if they are in places where they do not hamper the population's movement and work, and movement on waterways, roads and railroads.

Article 6

Civilian police and civilian security personnel of the parties in South Vietnam, who are responsible for the maintenance of law and order, shall strictly respect the prohibitions set forth in Article 2 of this Protocol. As required by their responsibilities, normally they shall be authorized to carry pistols, but when required by unusual circumstances, they shall be allowed to carry other small individual arms.

Article 7

(a) The entry into South Vietnam of replacement armaments, munitions, and war material permitted under Article 7 of the Agreement shall take place under the supervision and control of the Two-Party Joint Military Commission and of the International Commission of Control and Supervision and through such points of entry only as are designated by the two South Vietnamese parties. The two South Vietnamese parties shall agree on these points of entry within fifteen days after the entry into force of the cease-fire. The two South Vietnamese parties may select as many as six points of entry which are not included in the list of places where teams of the International Commission of Control and Supervision are to be based contained in Article 4 (d) of the Protocol concerning the International Commission. At the same time, the two South Vietnamese parties may also select points of entry from the list of places set forth in Article 4 (d) of that Protocol.

(b) Each of the designated points of entry shall be available only for that South Vietnamese party which is in control of that point. The two South Vietnamese parties shall have an equal number of points of entry.

Article 8

(a) In implementation of Article 5 of the Agreement, the United States and the other foreign countries referred to in Article 5 of the Agreement shall take with them all their armaments, munitions, and war material. Transfers of such items which would leave them in South Vietnam shall not be made subsequent to the entry into force of the Agreement except for transfers of communications, transport, and other non-combat material to the Four-Party Joint Military Commission or the International Commission of Control and Supervision.

(b) Within five days after the entry into force of the cease-fire, the United States shall inform the Four-Party Joint Military Commission and the International Commission of Control and Supervision of the general plans for timing of complete troop withdrawals which shall take place in four phases of fifteen days each. It is anticipated that the numbers of troops withdrawn in each phase are not likely to be widely different, although it is not feasible to ensure equal numbers. The approximate numbers to be withdrawn in each phase shall be given to the Four-Party Joint Military Commission and the International Commission of Control and Supervision sufficiently in advance of actual withdrawals so that they can properly carry out their tasks in relation thereto.

Article 9

(a) In implementation of Article 6 of the Agreement, the United States and the other foreign countries referred to in that Article shall dismantle and remove from South Vietnam or destroy all military bases in South Vietnam of the United States and of the other foreign countries referred to in that Article, including weapons, mines, and other military equipment at these bases, for the purpose of making them unusable for military purposes.

(b) The United States shall supply the Four-Party Joint Military Commission and the International Commission of Control and Supervision with necessary information on plans for base dismantlement so that those Commissions can properly carry out their tasks in relation thereto.

THE JOINT MILITARY COMMISSIONS

Article 10

(a) The implementation of the Agreement is the responsibility of the parties signatory to the Agreement. The Four-Party Joint Military Commission has the task of ensuring joint action by the parties in implementing the Agreement by serving as a channel of communication among the parties, by drawing up plans and fixing the modalities to carry out, coordinate, follow and inspect the implementation of the provisions mentioned in Article 16 of the Agreement, and by negotiating and settling all matters concerning the implementation of those provisions.

(b) The concrete tasks of the Four-Party Joint Military Commission are:

(1) To coordinate, follow and inspect the implementation of the above-mentioned provisions of the Agreement by the four parties;

(2) To deter and detect violations, to deal with cases of violation, and to settle conflicts and matters of contention between the parties relating to the above-mentioned provisions;

(3) To dispatch without delay one or more joint teams, as required by specific cases, to any part of South Vietnam, to investigate alleged violations of the Agreement and to assist the parties in finding measures to prevent recurrence of similar cases;

(4) To engage in observation at the places where this is necessary in the exercise of its functions;

(5) To perform such additional tasks as it may, by unanimous decision, determine.

Article 11

(a) There shall be a Central Joint Military Commission located in Saigon. Each party shall designate immediately a military delegation of fifty-nine persons to represent it on the Central Commission. The senior officer designated by each party shall be a general officer, or equivalent.

(b) There shall be seven Regional Joint Military Commissions ... based at the following places:

Regions	Places
I	Hue
II	Danang
III	Pleiku
IV	Phan Thiet
V	Bien Hoa
VI	My Tho
VII	Can Tho

Each party shall designate a military delegation of sixteen persons to represent it on each Regional Commission. The senior officer designated by each party shall be an officer from the rank of Lieutenant Colonel to Colonel, or equivalent.

(c) There shall be a joint military team . . . based at each of the following places in South Vietnam:

Region I

Quang Tri
Phu Bai

Region II

Hoi An
Tam Ky
Chu Lai

Region III

Kontum
Hau Bon
Phu Cat
Tuy An
Ninh Hoa
Ban Me Thuot

Region IV

Da Lat
Bao Loc
Phan Rang

Region V

An Loc
Xuan Loc
Ben Cat
Cu Chi
Tan An

Region VI

Moc Hoa
Giong Trom

Region VII

Tri Ton
Vinh Long
Vi Thanh
Khanh Hung
Quan Long

Each party shall provide four qualified persons for each joint military team. The senior person designated by each party shall be an officer from the rank of Major to Lieutenant Colonel, or equivalent.

(d) The Regional Joint Military Commissions shall assist the Central Joint Military Commission in performing its tasks and shall supervise the operations of the joint military teams. The region of Saigon-Gia Dinh is placed under the responsibility of the Central Commission which shall designate joint military teams to operate in this region.

(e) Each party shall be authorized to provide support and guard personnel for its delegations to the Central Joint Military Commission and Regional Joint Military Commissions, and for its members of the joint military teams. The total number of support and guard personnel for each party shall not exceed five hundred and fifty.

(f) The Central Joint Military Commission may establish such joint sub-commissions, joint staffs and joint military teams as circumstances may require. The Central Commission shall determine the numbers of personnel required for any additional sub-commissions, staffs or teams it establishes, provided that each party shall designate one-fourth of the number of personnel required and that the total number of personnel for the Four-Party Joint Military Commission, to include its staffs, teams, and support personnel, shall not exceed three thousand three hundred.

(g) The delegations of the two South Vietnamese parties may, by agreement, establish provisional sub-commissions and joint military teams to carry out the tasks specifically assigned to them by Article 17 of the Agreement. With respect to Article 7 of the Agreement, the two South Vietnamese parties' delegations to the Four-Party Joint Military Commission shall establish joint military teams at the points of entry into South Vietnam used for replacement of armaments, munitions and war material which are designated in accordance with Article 7 of this Protocol. From the time the cease-fire comes into force to the time when the Two-Party Joint Military Commission becomes operational, the two South Vietnamese parties' delegations to the Four-Party Joint Military Commission shall form a provisional sub-commission and provisional joint military teams to carry out its tasks concerning captured and detained Vietnamese civilian personnel. Where necessary for the above purposes, the two South Vietnamese parties may agree to assign personnel additional to those assigned to the two South Vietnamese delegations to the Four-Party Joint Military Commission.

Article 12

(a) In accordance with Article 17 of the Agreement which stipulates that the two South Vietnamese parties shall immediately designate their respective representatives to form the Two-Party Joint Military Commission, twenty-four hours after the cease-fire comes into force, the two designated South Vietnamese parties' delegations to the Two-Party Joint Military Commission shall meet in Saigon so as to reach an agreement as soon as possible on organization and operation of the Two-Party Joint Military Commission, as well as the measures and organization aimed at enforcing the cease-fire and preserving peace in South Vietnam.

(b) From the time the cease-fire comes into force to the time when the Two-Party Joint Military Commission becomes operational, the two South Vietnamese parties' delegations to the Four-Party Joint Military Commission at all levels shall simultaneously assume the tasks of the Two-Party Joint Military Commission at all levels, in addition to their functions as delegations to the Four-Party Joint Military Commission.

(c) If, at the time the Four-Party Joint Military Commission ceases its operation in accordance with Article 16 of the Agreement, agreement has not been reached on organization of the Two-Party Joint Military Commission, the delegations of the two South Vietnamese parties serving with the Four-Party Joint Military Commission at all levels shall continue temporarily to work together as a provisional two-party joint military commission and to assume the tasks of the Two-Party Joint Military Commission at all levels until the Two-Party Joint Military Commission becomes operational.

Article 13

In application of the principle of unanimity, the Joint Military Commissions shall have no chairmen, and meetings shall be convened at the request of any representative. The Joint Military Commissions shall adopt working procedures appropriate for the effective discharge of their functions and responsibilities.

Article 14

The Joint Military Commissions and the International Commission of Control and Supervision shall closely cooperate with and assist each other in carrying out their respective functions. Each Joint Military Commission shall inform the International Commission about the implementation of those provisions of the Agreement for which that Joint Military Commission has responsibility and which are within the competence of the International Commission. Each Joint Military Commission may request the International Commission to carry out specific observation activities.

Article 15

The Central Four-Party Joint Military Commission shall begin operating twenty-four hours after the cease-fire comes into force. The Regional Four-Party Joint Military Commissions shall begin operating forty-eight hours after the cease-fire comes into force. The Joint military teams based at the places listed in Article 11 (c) of this Protocol shall begin operating no later than fifteen days after the cease-fire comes into force. The delegations of the two South Vietnamese parties shall simultaneously begin to assume the tasks of the Two-Party Joint Military Commission as provided in Article 12 of this Protocol.

Article 16

(a) The parties shall provide full protection and all necessary assistance and cooperation to the Joint Military Commissions at all levels, in the discharge of their tasks.

(b) The Joint Military Commissions and their personnel, while carrying out their tasks, shall enjoy privileges and immunities equivalent to those accorded diplomatic missions and diplomatic agents.

(c) The personnel of the Joint Military Commissions may carry pistols and wear special insignia decided upon by each Central Joint Military Commission. The personnel of each party while guarding Commission installations or equipment may be authorized to carry other individual small arms, as determined by each Central Joint Military Commission.

Article 17

(a) The delegation of each party to the Four-Party Joint Military Commission and the Two-Party Joint Military Commission shall have its own offices, communication, logistics and transportation means, including aircraft when necessary.

(b) Each party, in its areas of control shall provide appropriate office and accommodation facilities to the Four-Party Joint Military Commission and the Two-Party Joint Military Commission at all levels.

(c) The parties shall endeavor to provide to the Four-Party Joint Military Commission and the Two-Party Joint Military Commission, by means of loan, lease, or gift, the common means of operation, including equipment for communication, supply, and transport, including aircraft when necessary. The Joint Military Commissions may purchase from any source necessary facilities, equipment, and services which are not supplied by the parties. The Joint Military Commissions shall possess and use these facilities and this equipment.

Article 18

(d) The facilities and the equipment for common use mentioned above shall be returned to the parties when the Joint Military Commissions have ended their activities.

The common expenses of the Four-Party Joint Military Commission shall be borne equally by the four parties, and the common expenses

of the Two-Party Joint Military Commission in South Vietnam shall
be borne equally by these two parties.

Article 19

This Protocol shall enter into force upon signature by plenipotentiary
representatives of all the parties participating in the Paris Conference on Vietnam. It shall be strictly implemented by all the parties
concerned.

Done in Paris this twenty-seventh day of January, One Thousand
Nine Hundred and Seventy-Three, in Vietnamese and English. The
Vietnamese and English texts are official and equally authentic.

[Separate Numbered Page]

For the Government of the United States of America	For the Government of the Republic of Vietnam
William P. Rogers	Tran Van Lam
William P. Rogers	Tran Van Lam
Secretary of State	Minister for Foreign Affairs

[Separate Numbered Page]

For the Government of the Democratic Republic of Vietnam	For the Provisional Revolutionary Government of The Republic of South Vietnam
Nguyen Duy Trinh	Nguyen Thi Binh
Minister for Foreign Affairs	Minister for Foreign Affairs

*Protocol to the Agreement on Ending the War and Restoring Peace in
Vietnam Concerning the Cease-fire in South Vietnam and the Joint
Military Commissions*

The Government of the United States of America, with the concurrence of the Government of the Republic of Vietnam, the Government
of the Democratic Republic of Vietnam, with the concurrence of the
Provisional Revolutionary Government of the Republic of South Vietnam, in implementation of the first paragraph of Article 2, Article 3,
Article 5, Article 6, Article 16 and Article 17 of the Agreement on

232

Ending the War and Restoring Peace in Vietnam signed on this date which provide for the cease-fire in South Vietnam and the establishment of a Four-Party Joint Military Commission and a Two-Party Joint Military Commission, have agreed as follows:

[Text of Protocol Articles 1-18 same as above]

Article 19

The Protocol to the Paris Agreement on Ending the War and Restoring Peace in Vietnam concerning the cease-fire in South Vietnam and the Joint Military Commissions shall enter into force upon signature of this document by the Secretary of State of the Government of the United States of America and the Minister for Foreign Affairs of the Government of the Democratic Republic of Vietnam, and upon signature of a document in the same terms by the Secretary of State of the Government of the United States of America, the Minister for Foreign Affairs of the Government of the Republic of Vietnam, the Minister for Foreign Affairs of the Democratic Republic of Vietnam, and the Minister for Foreign Affairs of the Provisional Revolutionary Government of the Republic of South Vietnam. The Protocol shall be strictly implemented by all the parties concerned. Done in Paris this twenty-seventh day of January, One Thousand Nine Hundred and Seventy-three, in Vietnamese and English. The Vietnamese and English texts are official and equally authentic.

For the Government of the
United States of America

For the Government of the
Democratic Republic of
Vietnam

William P. Rogers
Secretary of State

Nguyen Duy Trinh
Minister for Foreign Affairs

Protocol to the Agreement on Ending the War and Restoring Peace in Vietnam Concerning the Removal, Permanent Deactivation, or Destruction of Mines in the Territorial Waters, Ports, Harbors, and Waterways of the Democratic Republic of Vietnam

The Government of the United States of America, the Government of the Democratic Republic of Vietnam, in implementation of the second paragraph of Article 2 of the Agreement on Ending the War and Restoring Peace in Vietnam signed on this date, have agreed as follows:

Article 1

The United States shall clear all the mines it has placed in the territorial waters, ports, harbors, and waterways of the Democratic Republic of Vietnam. This mine clearing operation shall be accomplished by rendering the mines harmless through removal, permanent deactivation, or destruction.

Article 2

With a view to ensuring lasting safety for the movement of people and watercraft and the protection of important installations, mines shall, on the request of the Democratic Republic of Vietnam, be removed or destroyed in the indicated areas; and whenever their removal or destruction is impossible, mines shall be permanently deactivated and their emplacement clearly marked.

Article 3

The mine clearing operation shall begin at twenty-four hundred (2400) hours GMT on January 27, 1973. The representatives of the two parties shall consult immediately on relevant factors and agree upon the earliest possible target date for the completion of the work.

Article 4

The mine clearing operation shall be conducted in accordance with priorities and timing agreed upon by the two parties. For this purpose, representatives of the two parties shall meet at an early date to reach agreement on a program and a plan of implementation. To this end:

(a) The United States shall provide its plan for mine clearing operations, including maps of the minefields and information concerning the types, numbers and properties of the mines;

(b) The Democratic Republic of Vietnam shall provide all available maps and hydrographic charts and indicate the mined places and all other potential hazards to the mine clearing operations that the Democratic Republic of Vietnam is aware of;

(c) The two parties shall agree on the timing of implementation of each segment of the plan and provide timely notice to the public at least forty-eight hours in advance of the beginning of mine clearing operations for that segment.

Article 5

The United States shall be responsible for the mine clearance on inland waterways of the Democratic Republic of Vietnam. The Democratic Republic of Vietnam shall, to the full extent of its capabilities, actively participate in the mine clearance with the means of surveying, removal and destruction and technical advice supplied by the United States.

Article 6

With a view to ensuring the safe movement of people and watercraft on waterways and at sea, the United States shall in the mine clearing process supply timely information about the progress of mine clearing in each area, and about the remaining mines to be destroyed. The United States shall issue a communiqué when the operations have been concluded.

Article 7

In conducting mine clearing operations, the U.S. personnel engaged in these operations shall respect the sovereignty of the Democratic Republic of Vietnam and shall engage in no activities inconsistent with the Agreement on Ending the War and Restoring Peace in Vietnam and this Protocol. The U.S. personnel engaged in the mine clearing operations shall be immune from the jurisdiction of the Democratic Republic of Vietnam for the duration of the mine clearing operations. The Democratic Republic of Vietnam shall ensure the safety of the U.S. personnel for the duration of their mine clearing activities on the territory of the Democratic Republic of Vietnam, and shall provide this personnel with all possible assistance and the means needed in the Democratic Republic of Vietnam that have been agreed upon by the two parties.

Article 8

This Protocol to the Paris Agreement on Ending the War and Restoring Peace in Vietnam shall enter into force upon signature by the Secretary of State of the Government of the United States of America and the Minister for Foreign Affairs of the Government of the Democratic Republic of Vietnam. It shall be strictly implemented by the two parties. Done in Paris this twenty-seventh day of January, One Thousand Nine Hundred and Seventy-Three, in Vietnamese and English. The Vietnamese and English texts are official and equally authentic.

For the Government of the
United States of America

For the Government of the
Democratic Republic of
Vietnam

William P. Rogers
Secretary of State

Nguyen Duy Trinh
Minister for Foreign Affairs

FACT SHEET

BASIC ELEMENTS OF VIETNAM AGREEMENT

MILITARY PROVISIONS

Cease-fire
Internationally-supervised cease-fire throughout South and North
Vietnam, effective at 7:00 EST, Saturday, January 27, 1973.

American Forces
Release within 60 days of all American servicemen and civilians
captured and held throughout Indochina, and fullest possible accounting for missing in action.

Return of all United States forces and military personnel from
South Vietnam within 60 days.

Security of South Vietnam
Ban on infiltration of troops and war supplies into South Vietnam.

The right to unlimited military replacement aid for the Republic of
Vietnam

Respect for the Demilitarized Zone.

Reunification only by peaceful means, through negotiations between
North and South Vietnam without coercion or annexation

Reduction and demobilization of Communist and Government
forces in the South.

Ban on use of Laotian or Cambodian base areas to encroach on
sovereignty and security of South Vietnam.

Withdrawal of all foreign troops from Laos and Cambodia

236

Joint United States-Democratic Republic of Vietnam statement that the South Vietnamese people have the right to self-determination.

The Government of the Republic of Vietnam continues in existence, recognized by the United States, its constitutional structure and leadership intact and unchanged.

The right to unlimited economic aid for the Republic of Vietnam

Formation of a non-governmental National Council of National Reconciliation and Concord, operating by unanimity, to organize elections as agreed by the parties and to promote conciliation and implementation of the Agreement.

INDOCHINA

Reaffirmation of the 1954 and 1962 Geneva Agreements on Cambodia and Laos.

Respect for the independence, sovereignty, unity, territorial integrity and neutrality of Cambodia and Laos.

Ban on infiltration of troops and war supplies into Cambodia and Laos.

Ban on use of Laotian and Cambodian base areas to encroach on sovereignty and security of one another and of other countries.

Withdrawal of all foreign troops from Laos and Cambodia.

In accordance with traditional United States policy, U.S. participation in postwar reconstruction efforts throughout Indochina.

With the ending of the war, a new basis for U.S. relations with North Vietnam.

CONTROL AND SUPERVISION

An International Commission of Control and Supervision, with 1160 international supervisory personnel, to control and supervise the elections and various military provisions of the Agreement.

An International Conference within 30 days to guarantee the Agreement and the ending of the war.

Joint Military Commissions of the parties to implement appropriate provisions of the Agreement.

FACT SHEET

INTERNATIONAL COMMISSION OF CONTROL AND SUPERVISION

Members: Canada, Hungary, Indonesia, and Poland

Numbers of Teams:

  1 Headquarters–Saigon
  7 Regional Teams
  3 Teams for Saigon–Gia Dinh region
26 Teams based at localities throughout South Vietnam
12 Teams at border and coastal points
  7 Teams for return of prisoners
  7 Teams for additional points of entry and general use

Number of Personnel: [Each member contributes one-fourth of the total in each case.]

Headquarters	108
Regional Teams	20 each
Gio Linh and Vung Tau teams	12 each
All other teams	8 each
Support personnel	464
Total	1,160

Functions: To supervise and control implementation of those provisions of the Agreement listed in Article 18, through observation and investigation of violations.

Voting: Unanimity, but must investigate at the request of any one of the parties and must report minority and separate views of its members.

Equipment: Any of the parties may supply it with means of communication and transport, and it may purchase other equipment required for the exercise of its functions not provided by the parties to the agreement.

Duration: Until requested to end its activities by the government formed after the general elections provided for in Article 9 (b).

FACT SHEET

FOUR-PARTY JOINT MILITARY COMMISSION

Participants: The four parties to the Agreement.

Numbers of Teams:

  1 Central Joint Military Commission–Saigon
  7 Regional Joint Military Commissions
26 Teams based at localities throughout South Vietnam
    Such other sub-commissions, staffs, and teams as Central Joint
    Military Commission establishes

Number of Personnel: [Each party contributes one-fourth of the total in each case.]

Central Joint Military Commission	236
Each Regional Joint Military Commission	64
Each team	16
Support and Guard personnel (ceiling)	2,200
Total ceiling	3,300

Functions: To coordinate implementation of those provisions of the Agreement listed in Article 16; to deter and detect violations of those provisions; to carry out necessary observations and investigations; and to be a forum to settle differences.

Voting: Unanimity.

Equipment: The parties may supply it with common means of communication and transport. Each delegation shall have its own means of communication and transport.

Duration: 60 days, except for one team which shall continue as long as necessary to account for missing in action and location of graves.

Provisional Two-Party Commission:

Pending the establishment of the Two-Party Joint Military Commission by agreement of the two South Vietnamese parties, the delegations of those two parties to the Four-Party Joint Military Commission shall provisionally carry out the functions of the Two-Party Commission.

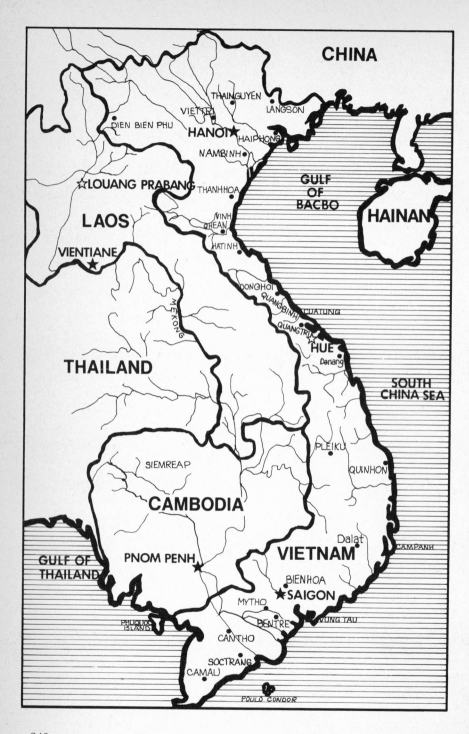

Appendix B

Members of Congress for Peace through Law
SUITE 210, 201 MASSACHUSETTS AVENUE, N.E.
WASHINGTON, D.C. 20002   (202) 544-4250

February 6, 1975

STEERING
COMMITTEE

Joseph S. Clark
Honorary Chairman

John F. Seiberling, M.C.
Chairman

Philip A. Hart, U.S.S.
Vice Chairman

Charles McC. Mathias,
Jr., U.S.S.
Vice Chairman

Gilbert Gude, M.C.
Secretary-Treasurer

U.S. SENATE

Edward W. Brooke
Mark O. Hatfield
Frank E. Moss
Edmund S. Muskie

U.S. HOUSE OF
REPRESENTATIVES

John B. Anderson
Les Aspin
Jonathan B. Bingham
John Dellenback
Bob Eckhardt
Bill Frenzel

The President
The White House
Washington, D.C.

Dear Mr. President:

We, the undersigned Members of Congress for Peace through Law, write to you on a matter of very great concern—the extent and direction of the continuing U.S. involvement in Indochina.

What particularly disturbs us is the clear implication in remarks made by the Secretary of State and the Vice President and by yourself in a recent news conference that this only partly resolved issue—one of the most divisive in the nation's history—is being re-opened for debate. We had thought that the American military withdrawal, the Peace Agreements negotiated by the Administration and the clearly and repeatedly expressed Congressional mandate to gradually eliminate the American role in Indochina had settled the matter. Apparently, that is not the case.

241

H. John Heinz III
Patsy T. Mink

STAFF

Sandford Z. Persons
Executive Director

Murray B. Woldman
Staff Consultant

William H.Kincade
Staff Consultant

Rici Rutkoff
Executive Assistant

We remain resolute in our conviction, supported by the legislation passed in the 93rd Congress, that continuing American military and economic involvement in Indochina will not bring that unhappy region closer to a lasting peace. While continuing high levels of American assistance may perhaps prolong the life of the incumbent South Vietnamese and Cambodian governments, we can see no humanitarian or national interest that justifies the cost of this assistance to our country. Although the phased withdrawal of American support will not in itself bring peace to the region, it is equally clear that its continuation will not do so either.

Another prolonged disagreement over events in Vietnam and our policy there may well lead to acrimonious accusations over who "lost" Indochina, reminiscent of the China debate over two decades ago. The result of that earlier experience was to freeze U.S. options in Asia for a quarter of a century. We must at all costs avoid a repetition of such a struggle which would set the Congress against the Executive.

It is especially unfortunate that the internal debate over Indochina should resume at a time when we are confronted by so many pressing domestic and international problems. These problems do not have easy solutions. They require an extraordinary degree of accord between our two branches of government and among the industrialized and developing nations.

This is not the time for another divisive debate that can only impede the development of the cooperation so necessary in dealing with the complex problems of global inflation, domestic recession, and growing shortages of necessary raw materials. Instead, we need to work together.

We believe the time is now at hand when our government must make a decision, too long postponed at a tragically high cost to both the people of Indochina and to our own citizens as to how we will extricate ourselves from the situation in Southeast Asia once and for all.

We write to ask you and your most senior advisers to accept this expression of our views in a spirit of conciliation. We should get on with the important work ahead of us. Innovative leadership both from you and the Congress will be needed more than ever.

242

Accordingly, we are prepared for a serious, unemotional dialogue on the immediate problem of ending our involvement in Indochina responsibly and honorably. We are not prepared for it to continue indefinitely.

Sincerely,

SENATE

Dick Clark (D., Iowa)
James Abourezk (D., S.Dak.)
Alan Cranston (D., Calif.)
Philip A. Hart (D., Mich.)
Floyd Haskell (D., Colo.)
William D. Hathaway (D., Maine)

Mark O. Hatfield (R., Ore.)
George S. McGovern (D., S.Dak.)
Adlai E. Stevenson III (D., Ill.)
John V. Tunney (D., Calif.)
Harrison Williams, Jr. (D., N.J.)
Hubert H. Humphrey (D., Minn.)

HOUSE OF REPRESENTATIVES

Bella A. Abzug (D., N.Y.)
Joseph P. Addabbo (D., N.Y.)
Thomas L. Ashley (D., Ohio)
Les Aspin (D., Wis.)
Herman Badillo (D., N.Y.)
Jonathan B. Bingham (D., N.Y.)
Michael T. Blouin (D., Iowa)
Edward P. Boland (D., Mass.)
John Brademas (D., Ind.)
George Brown, Jr. (D., Calif.)
Yvonne B. Burke (D., Calif.)
John L. Burton (D., Calif.)
M. Robert Carr (D., Mich.)
Silvio O. Conte (R., Mass.)
John Conyers (D., Mich.)
James C. Corman (D., Calif.)
Ronald V. Dellums (D., Calif.)
Charles Diggs (D., Mich.)
Robert F. Drinan (D., Mass.)
Don Edwards (D., Calif.)
Joshua Eilberg (D., Pa.)
William D. Ford (D., Mich.)
Donald M. Fraser (D., Minn.)
Bill Frenzel (R., Minn.)
William J. Green (D., Pa.)

Gilbert Gude (R., Md.)
James M. Hanley (D., N.Y.)
Thomas Harkin (D., Iowa)
Michael Harrington (D., Mass.)
Elizabeth Holtzman (D., N.Y.)
James J. Howard (D., N.J.)
Andrew Jacobs, Jr. (D., Ind.)
Barbara Jordan (D., Texas)
Robert Kastenmeier (D., Wis.)
Martha Keys (D., Kansas)
Edward I. Koch (D., N.Y.)
Robert L. Leggett (D., Calif.)
Torbert MacDonald (D., Mass.)
Paul N. McCloskey, Jr. (R., Calif.)
Mike McCormack (D., Wash.)
Andrew Maguire (D., N.J.)
Spark M. Matsunaga (D., Hawaii)
Lloyd Meeds (D., Wash.)
Ralph H. Metcalfe (D., Ill.)
Edward Mezvinsky (D., Iowa)
Parren Mitchell (D., Md.)
John J. Moakley (D., Mass.)
William S. Moorhead (D., Pa.)
Charles A. Mosher (R., Ohio)
Gary A. Myers (R., Pa.)

Edward Pattison (D., N.Y.)
Joel Pritchard (R., Wash.)
Charles B. Rangel (D., N.Y.)
Thomas M. Rees (D., Calif.)
Henry S. Reuss (D., Wis.)
Frederick W. Richmond (D., N.Y.)
Donald Riegle, Jr. (D., Mich.)
Peter W. Rodino, Jr. (D., N.J.)
Benjamin Rosenthal (D., N.Y.)
Edward Roybal (D., Calif.)

Fernand St. Germain (D., R.I.)
Patricia Schroeder (D., Colo.)
John Seiberling (D., Ohio)
Fortney Stark, Jr. (D., Calif.)
Gerry Studds (D., Mass.)
James Symington (D., Mo.)
Frank Thompson, Jr. (D., N.J.)
Morris K. Udall (D., Ariz.)
Charles H. Wilson (D., Calif.)
Antonio B. Won Pat (D., Guam)

Appendix C

Congress of the United States
House of Representatives
Washington, D.C. 20515

March 7, 1975

The Honorable Gerald R. Ford
President of the United States
The White House
Washington, D.C.

Dear Mr. President,

In 1964 President Johnson massively expanded United States intervention in Southeast Asia. Now, a decade later, a decade of incredible carnage in Southeast Asia and bitter division here at home, we are being asked to decide once more to send American arms and money to continue this war.

We are writing to you, Mr. President, to let you know of our opposition to this aid request and to ask for your statesmanship in ending this tragedy.

There are those who say that Congress, particularly the new membership, does not understand the consequences of our decisions on further military shipments to Cambodia and South Vietnam. We believe that we do understand.

For many of us, this war has been a constant backdrop, a permanent policy of our government, for most of our adult lives. We watched this war maim and kill our friends, and then maim and kill the trust of American people in their leaders. This war has created within our own government the necessity for deception and distortion. This war has not stood for our historic ideals, nor aided prosperity and happiness at home or in Southeast Asia.

The folly of it all has touched Americans personally and politically. As a new generation of politicians, we think we have been able to look at this disaster differently than many who were in responsibility over the last decade. We do not wish to recount, Mr. President, the familiar arguments—the wasted billions, the 55,000 American dead, the tyrannies maintained by our support, the original U.S. responsibility for war now raging in Cambodia.

You and three other Presidents have tried with utmost sincerity to give to the countries of Southeast Asia the means to fight their internal wars. But history shows clearly that no outside power, however mighty, can regenerate another society or regime that does not have the inner will to maintain itself.

As the distinguished historian, Barbara Tuchman, wrote about the similar efforts of the United States to resurrect the Chiang Kai-shek regime. "In the end China went its own way as if the Americans had never come." In the same sense, Cambodia and South Vietnam will go their own ways; and at this point the American people have stated clearly that they have no interest in postponing this process. It is time for all of us to have the courage to face that reality at last.

Finally, Mr. President, we ask you to approach your decision and ours without recrimination. Our country will never heal the terrible wounds of this war if we try to blame each other for events that no single President or Congress could control. None of us made the Lon Nol or Thieu regimes what they are. None of us can shape the future of Cambodia or South Vietnam.

We face our own war here at home against crippling economic developments, the crisis in energy and other public resources, and other serious problems. We will need to undertake strong action and strong debate under your leadership; it has never been more important that we act with good faith in this endeavor. But we cannot confront and resolve these crises while the United States continues involvement in Southeast Asia.

Sincerely,

Tom Harkin (D., Iowa) Toby Moffett (D., Conn.)
Stephen Solarz (D., N.Y.) Edward M. Pattison (D., N.Y.)
M. Robert Carr (D., Mich.) Paul E. Tsongas (D., Mass.)

Norman Mineta (D., Calif.)
Stephen L. Neal (D., N.C.)
Berkley Bedell (D., Iowa)
Martha Keys (D., Kansas)
Max Baucus (D., Mont.)
Helen Meyner (D., N.J.)
George Miller (D., Calif.)
Henry A. Waxman (D., Calif.)
Christopher J. Dodd (D., Conn.)
Jim Santini (D., Nev.)
Richard Nolan (D., Minn.)
Frederick W. Richmond (D., N.Y.)
Edward P. Beard (D., R.I.)
Philip R. Sharp (D., Ind.)
William M. Brodhead (D., Mich.)
James Weaver (D., Ore.)

John Burton (D., Calif.)
Jim Lloyd (D., Calif.)
Andrew Maguire (D., N.J.)
Timothy Wirth (D., Colo.)
Don Bonker (D., Wash.)
Les AuCoin (D., Ore.)
Thomas J. Downey (D., N.Y.)
Donald W. Riegle, Jr. (D., Mich.)
Robert W. Edgar (D., Pa.)
Gladys Noon Spellman (D., Md.)
Michael T. Blouin (D., Iowa)
Robert J. Cornell (D., Wis.)
Philip H. Hayes (D., Ind.)
James H. Scheuer (D., N.Y.)
Richard L. Ottinger (D., N.Y.)

BIBLIOGRAPHY

Archival Sources

Washington, D.C. National Archives. Department of State General Records.

Collections of Sources and Documents

Congress and the Nation. 3 vols. Washington, D.C. Congressional Quarterly, Inc., 1965 to date.

Congressional Quarterly Almanac. Washington, D.C. Congressional Quarterly, Inc., 1945 to date.

Congressional Quarterly Weekly Report. Washington, D.C. Congressional Quarterly, Inc., 1945 to date.

Public Sources

Foreign Broadcast Information Service. *Daily Report.* Washington, D.C., daily since 1951.

The Pentagon Papers: The Defense Department. *History of United States Decisionmaking on Vietnam.* The Senator Gravel Edition. 5 vols. Boston: Beacon Press, 1971.

United States Congress. *Congressional Record.* Washington, D.C.: Government Printing Office, 1874 to date.

United States Department of the Army. *Vietnam Studies: Command and Control, 1950–1969* by Major General George S. Eckhardt. Office of the Chief of Military History. Washington, D.C.: Government Printing Office, 1974.

United States Department of Commerce. Office of Technical Services. Joint Publications Research Service. *Translations from North Vietnam.* Washington, D.C.: Government Printing Office, 1957 to date.

United States Department of State. *Department of State Bulletin.* Washington, D.C.: Government Printing Office, 1939 to date.

United States Department of State. *Foreign Relations of the United States.* Washington, D.C.: Government Printing Office, 1861 to date.

United States Department of State. *United States Foreign Policy 1971: A Report of the Secretary of State*. Washington, D.C.: Government Printing Office, 1972.

United States Department of State. *United States Foreign Policy 1972: A Report of the Secretary of State*. Washington, D.C.: Government Printing Office, 1973.

United States Senate. Committee on Foreign Relations. *Hearings Before the Committee on Foreign Relations, United States Senate on Causes, Origins and Lessons of the Vietnam War*. 92nd Congress, 2nd Session, May 9–11, 1972. Washington, D.C.: Government Printing Office.

United States Senate. Committee on Foreign Relations. *Vietnam, Cambodia and Laos*. Report by Senator Mike Mansfield, 84th Congress, 1st Session. Washington, D.C.: Government Printing Office, 1955.

United States Senate. Committee on the Judiciary. *The Amerasia Papers: A Clue to the Catastrophe of China*. 2 vols. 91st Congress, 1st Session. Prepared by Anthony Kubek. Washington, D.C.: Government Printing Office, 1970.

Collections of Papers and Writings

Ho Chi Minh. *Ho Chi Minh: Selected Works*. Translated from the Vietnamese. 4 vols. Hanoi: Foreign Languages Publishing House, 1960–1962.

Mao Tse-tung. *Selected Works of Mao Tse-tung*. 4 vols. Peking: Foreign Languages Press, 1967.

Militant Solidarity, Fraternal Assistance: A Collection of Major Soviet Foreign Policy Documents on the Vietnam Problem. Moscow: Progress Publishers, 1970.

Public Papers of the Presidents of the United States. Office of the Federal Register, National Archives and Records Service, General Services Administration. Washington, D.C.: Government Printing Office, 1958 to date.

Rosenman, Samuel I. (ed.) *The Public Papers and Addresses of Franklin D. Roosevelt*. 13 vols. to date. New York: Harper and Brothers, 1960.

Memoirs and Biographies

Dooley, Thomas A. *Deliver Us from Evil: The Story of Viet Nam's Flight to Freedom*. New York: Farrar, Straus and Cudahy, Inc., 1956.

Ho Chi Minh. *The Prison Diary of Ho Chi Minh* with an introduction by Harrison E. Salisbury. New York: Bantam Books, 1971.

Hull, Cordell. *The Memoirs of Cordell Hull*. 2 vols. New York: The Macmillan Company, 1948.

Lansdale, Edward Geary. *In the Midst of Wars: An American's Mission to Southeast Asia*. New York: Harper and Row, 1972.

Roosevelt, Elliott. *As He Saw It*. New York: Duell, Sloan and Pierce, 1946.

Treatises and Monographs

Burchett, Wilfred G. *Vietnam: Inside Story of the Guerrilla War*. New York: International Publishers, 1965.

————. *Vietnam North.* New York: International Publishers, 1966.

Buttinger, Joseph. *Vietnam: A. Dragon Embattled.* 2 vols. New York: Frederick A. Praeger, 1967.

Chen, King C. *Vietnam and China, 1938–1954.* Princeton, N.J.: Princeton University Press, 1969.

Chiang Kai-shek. *Soviet Russia in China: A Summing Up at Seventy.* New York: Farrar, Strauss and Cudahy, 1957.

Clausewitz, Karl von. *On War.* Translated from the German by Professor O. J. Matthijs Jolles of the Institute of Military Studies, The University of Chicago. New York: Random House, 1943.

Conley, Michael C. *The Communist Insurgent Infrastructure in South Vietnam: A Study of Organization and Strategy.* 2 vols. Washington, D.C.: Center for Research of Social Systems, The American University, 1967.

Douglas, William O. *North from Malaya, Adventure on Five Fronts.* Garden City, N.Y.: Doubleday & Company, Inc., 1953.

Eisenhower, Dwight D. *The White House Years: Mandate for Change.* Garden City, N.Y.: Doubleday & Company, Inc., 1963.

Fall, Bernard B. *The Two Viet-Nams: A Political and Military Analysis.* New York: Frederick A. Praeger, 1963.

Gurtov, Melvin. *The First Vietnam Crisis: Chinese Communist Strategy and United States Involvement, 1953–1954.* New York: Columbia University Press, 1967.

Hammer, Ellen J. *The Struggle for Indochina.* Stanford, Calif.: Stanford University Press, 1954.

History of the August Revolution. Hanoi: Foreign Languages Publishing House, 1972.

Hoang Quoc Viet. *A Short History of the Vietnamese Workers and Trade Union Movement.* Hanoi: Foreign Languages Publishing House, 1960.

Hoang Van Chi. *From Colonialism to Communism: A Case History of North Vietnam.* New York: Frederick A. Praeger, 1964.

Honey, P. J. *Communism in North Vietnam.* Cambridge, Mass.: The M.I.T. Press, 1963.

———— (ed.) *North Vietnam Today: Profile of a Communist Satellite.* New York: Frederick A. Praeger, 1962.

Kubek, Anthony. *The Red China Papers.* New Rochelle, N.Y.: Arlington House, 1975.

Lancaster, Donald. *The Emancipation of French Indochina.* New York: Oxford University Press, 1961.

Lane, Thomas A. *America on Trial: The War for Vietnam.* New Rochelle, N.Y.: Arlington House, 1971.

Le Duan. *The Vietnamese Revolution: Fundamental Problems and Essential Tasks.* New York: International Publishers, 1971.

McAlister, John T., Jr. *Viet Nam, The Origins of Revolution.* New York: Alfred A. Knopf, 1969.

Parmet, Herbert S. *Eisenhower and the American Crusades.* New York: The Macmillan Company, 1972.

Penniman, Howard R. *Elections in South Vietnam.* Washington, D.C.: American Enterprise Institute for Public Policy Research and Hoover Institution on War, Revolution and Peace, 1972.

Pike, Douglas. *Viet Cong: The Organization of the National Liberation Front of South Vietnam.* Cambridge, Mass.: The M.I.T. Press, 1966.

Sun Tzu. *The Art of War.* Translated by Samuel B. Griffith with a foreword by B. H. Liddell Hart. London: Oxford University Press, 1963.

Taylor, Maxwell D. *The Uncertain Trumpet.* New York: Harper and Brothers, 1959.

The Thieu Regime Put to the Test 1973–1975. Hanoi: Foreign Languages Publishing House, 1975.

Trager, Frank N. (ed.) *Marxism in Southeast Asia: A Study of Four Countries.* Stanford, Calif.: Stanford University Press, 1959.

Truong Chinh. *Primer for Revolt: The Communist Takeover in Viet-Nam.* Translated from the Vietnamese by the Foreign Languages Publishing House in Hanoi. New York: Frederick A. Praeger, 1963.

Viet-Nam Fatherland Front and the Struggle for National Unity. Hanoi: Foreign Languages Publishing House, 1956.

Vietnam Settlement: Why 1973, Not 1969? Washington, D.C.: American Enterprise Institute for Public Policy Research, 1973.

Vietnam Today. Hanoi: Foreign Languages Publishing House, 1965.

Vo Nguyen Giap. *People's War: People's Army.* Translated from the Vietnamese by the Foreign Languages Publishing House in Hanoi. New York: Frederick A. Praeger, 1962.

———. *To Arm the Revolutionary Masses to Build the People's Army.* Hanoi: Foreign Languages Publishing House, 1975.

———. *The South Vietnam People Will Win.* Hanoi: Foreign Languages Publishing House, 1965.

Newspapers and Periodicals

Asia. Quarterly. New York: 1957 to date.

Asian Affairs: An American Review. Bi-monthly. New York: 1973 to date.

Asian Survey. Monthly. Berkeley, California: 1961 to date.

China News Analysis. Weekly. Hong Kong: 1953 to date.

Current Digest of the Soviet Press. Weekly. New York: 1949 to date.

Foreign Affairs. Quarterly. New York: 1923 to date.

l'Humanité. Daily. Paris: 1904 to date.

Izvestia (News). Daily. Moscow: Presidium of the Supreme Council of the USSR. 1917 to date.

Le Monde. Daily. Paris: 1944 to date.

The New York Times. Daily Newspaper. New York: 1851 to date.

Peking Review. Weekly. Peking: 1958 to date.

Pravda (Truth). Daily. Moscow: Organ of the Central Committee of the Communist Party of the Soviet Union. 1912 to date.

Problems of Communism. Bimonthly. Washington: Government Printing Office. 1951 to date.

Southeast Asian Perspectives. Quarterly. New York: The American Friends of Vietnam, Inc. 1971 to date.

Studies in Comparative Communism. Quarterly. Los Angeles: 1968 to date.
Survey of the China Mainland Press. Several times a week. Hong Kong: U.S. Consulate General. 1950 to date.
The Times Daily. (London) 1785 to date.
Vietnam. Monthly. Hanoi: Tien Bo Printing House. 1970.
Vietnam Bulletin. Weekly. Washington: Embassy of Viet Nam. 1967 to 1975.
Vietnam Courier. Weekly newspaper. Hanoi: 1963 to date.

Index

Davis, Peter, 187
Davis, Rennie, 40, 88, 120
Dean, John Gunther, 188
Dean, John W., III, 138, 153
Dellinger, David, 39, 89, 91
Dellums, Ronald V., 76, 87, 110, 168, 243
Democratic Party Policy Council, 46, 75–76, 77
Derwinski, Edward J., 34
Diggs, Charles C., 110, 182, 243
Dirksen, Everett M., 23
Dobrynin, Anatoly, 109
Dodd, Christopher J., 247
Dole, Robert J., 63, 67, 83, 84
Douthard, William, 87, 88
Dow, John G., 94, 109
Dowd, Douglas, 87
Downey, Thomas J., 247
Drinan, Robert F., S.J., 79, 112–113, 141, 157, 243
Duberstein, Michael J., 168
Duong Van Minh, 96, 192, 193
Durbrow, Elbridge, 170

Eagleton, Thomas F., 45, 80, 149
Easter Offensive (1972), 105–113
Eckhardt, Bob, 40, 241
Edgar, Robert W., 247
Edwards, Don, 59, 110, 143, 243
Eilberg, Joshua, 243
Eisenhower, Dwight D., 15, 60
Ellsberg, Daniel, 93
Evans, Frank, 156

Falk, Richard A., 82
Fauntroy, Walter, 110
Findley, Paul, 112
Flynt, John J., Jr., 157, 175
Fonda, Jane, 119–122, 168
Fong, Hiram, 193
Ford, Gerald R., 152, 156, 157, 161, 175, 176, 178, 180–181, 188, 191, 192–193
Ford, William D., 243
Forest, James, 51
Fraser, Donald A., 59, 182, 243
Frelinghuysen, Peter H.B., 173
Frenzel, Bill, 241, 243
Friedman, Max, 72, 182
Fulbright, J. William, 17, 22, 41, 44, 53, 67, 81, 130, 146, 158, 167

Gardner, John, 77
Gelb, Leslie, 93
Gershen, Martin, 137
Giaimo, Robert N., 152, 155, 157, 175
Gibbons, Sam, 76
Goldwater, Barry M., 35, 118, 176
Goodell, Charles, 39, 44, 59
Goodlett, Carlton (Dr.), 31, 51
Gore, Albert, 52
Graham, Daniel O. (General), 180
Gravel, Mike, 32, 80, 110, 114
Gray, L. Patrick, 138
Green Berets, The, 27
Green, Marshall, 104
Green, William J., 243
Griffin, Robert P., 43, 66, 186
Gromyko, Andrei, 135
Gude, Gilbert, 157, 241, 243
Gulf of Tonkin Resolution, 16, 54, 67
Gullion, Edmund, 29
Guthrie, Arlo, 39

Habib, Philip, 47, 180
Haig, Alexander M. (General), 124, 132, 146
Haldeman, H.R., 174

Hanley, James M., 243
Harkin, Thomas, 184, 185, 242, 246
Harriman, W. Averell, 20, 23, 47, 49, 173
Harrington, Michael J., 79, 110, 143, 182, 243
Harris, Fred, 18, 32, 59, 110
Hart, Philip A., 80, 91, 241, 243
Hartke, Vance, 37, 80, 91, 109
Haskell, Floyd, 243
Hatcher, Richard, 77
Hatfield, Mark O., 59, 68–69, 80, 184, 241, 243
Hathaway, William D., 243
Hawkins, Augustus, 110
Hayden, Tom, 120, 168, 184
Hayes, Philip H., 247
Hays, Wayne L., 33, 66, 154–155
Hearts and Minds, 27, 187
Hébert, F. Edward, 78–79, 171
Heinz, H. John, III, 242
Helstoski, Henry, 110
Hilliard, David, 40, 87
Hoang Xuan Lam (General), 73
Ho Chi Minh, 20, 30, 60
Holtzman, Elizabeth, 113, 157, 243
Howard, James J., 243
Hue massacre, 49
Hughes, Harold E., 45, 59, 80, 82
Humphrey, Hubert H., 76, 82–83, 107, 117, 191, 243
Hunt, John E., 71
Hunter, Edward, 122

Ifshin, David, 89, 120
Indochina Resource Center, 142, 171
Inouye, Daniel K., 80
In Tam, 184
International Commission for Control and Supervision (ICCS), 145, 149
Iossifides, Julius, 147

Jackson, Henry M., 82–83
Jacobs, Andrew, Jr., 34, 59, 76
Javits, Jacob K., 15, 17, 80
Johnson, Lyndon B., 16, 19, 20, 167
Jordan, Barbara, 243

Kaplan, Morton, 133
Kasler, James H. (Colonel), 124
Kastenmeier, Robert W., 32, 110, 243
Kemp, Jack, 154
Kennedy, Edward M., 15, 16n, 18, 32, 35, 80, 91, 169, 171, 174, 176, 187, 191
Kennedy, John F., 16
Kennedy, Joseph P., 15n
Kent State University, 63, 87
Kerry, John, 82, 90
Keys, Martha, 243, 247
King, Coretta Scott, 91
Kissinger, Henry M., 29, 95, 99, 101, 107, 124–126, 132, 134, 146, 148, 151, 169, 172, 175
Koch, Edward, 25, 59, 243
Kosygin, Alexei, 31, 53
Kraft, Joseph, 64n
Kubek, Anthony, 170
Kunstler, William, 58

Laird, Melvin R., 25, 106
"Land to the Tillers" program in South Vietnam, 50, 97
Laos, 41, 51–55, 69, 146, 150, 152, 154, 156, 158, 159, 163, 165, 166, 180
Laos Raid (Operation Lam Son 719), 71–75, 80
Le Duan, 19, 20, 30, 46, 113
Le Duc Tho, 24, 29, 100, 107, 124–125, 127, 132, 148, 151
Leggett, Robert L., 82, 176, 243
Lehman, William, 176